The Plug & Play Book

Stephen J. Bigelow

McGraw-Hill

New York   San Francisco   Washington, D.C.   Auckland   Bogotá
Caracas   Lisbon   London   Madrid   Mexico City   Milan
Montreal   New Delhi   San Juan   Singapore
Sydney   Tokyo   Toronto

McGraw-Hill

A Division of The McGraw·Hill Companies

1 2 3 4 5 6 7 8 9 0   DOC/DOC   9 0 4 3 2 1 0 9

P/N 0-07-134775-5

PART OF

ISBN 0-07-134774-7

*Throughout this book, trademarked names are used. Rather than put a
trademark symbol after every occurrence of a trademarked name, we used the
names in an editorial fashion only, and to the benefit of the trademark owner,
with no intention of infringement of the trademark. Where such designations
appear in this book, they have been printed with initial caps.*

Printed and bound by R. R. Donnelley & Sons Company.

This book is printed on recycled, acid-free paper containing a minimum
of 50% recycled, de-inked fiber.

Contents

Disclaimer and Cautions

It is important that you read and understand the following information. Please read it carefully!

PERSONAL RISK AND LIMITS OF LIABILITY

The repair of personal computers and their peripherals involves some amount of personal risk. Use *extreme* caution when working with AC and high-voltage power sources. Every reasonable effort has been made to identify and reduce areas of personal risk. You are instructed to read this book carefully *before* attempting the procedures discussed. If you are uncomfortable following the procedures that are outlined in this book, do *not* attempt them—refer your service to qualified service personnel.

Neither the author, the publisher, nor anyone directly or indirectly connected with the publication of this book shall make any warranty, either expressed or implied, with regard to this material, including, but not limited to, the implied warranties of quality, merchantability, and fitness for any particular purpose. Further, neither the author, publisher, nor anyone directly or indirectly connected with the publication of this book shall be liable for errors or omissions contained herein, or for incidental or consequential damages, injuries, or financial or material losses resulting from the use, or inability to use, the material contained herein. This material is provided AS-IS, and the reader bears all responsibilities and risks connected with its use.

How-to Quick Reference

CHAPTER 1

System Resources and Plug-and-Play

In the early days of the personal computer, systems were severely limited to the hardware that was sold with them. There were no standards, parts were certainly not interchangeable, and the few upgrades that *were* available had to be obtained directly from the system's manufacturer (at a premium price). But the release of the IBM PC in the early 1980s changed all that. In a risky gamble to create a versatile, low-priced computer, IBM developed an *open bus architecture* (which we know today as the ISA or *Industry Standard Architecture* bus), allowing expansion devices to be added in order to augment the very basic motherboard functions that were available. For the first time, *any* manufacturer could make video cards, drive controllers, I/O cards, modems, network cards, and many other exotic devices, which could easily be installed in any IBM PC or compatible system. In turn, the PC user was freed from the traditionally limited choices of expensive and proprietary hardware. The effect this open bus architecture had on the PC industry was stupefying—in a matter of just a few years, the IBM PC became a staple of the modern office and ushered in a wealth of new expansion devices from creative new companies. Today, you can find descendants of IBM's PC in homes and offices around the world.

Understanding System Resources

But the great advantage of this expandability also carried a great problem. Expansion devices require hardware *resources* (facilities provided by the PC) that are needed in order for the PC to communicate and exchange data with the expansion device. PCs offer only a limited amount of resources for expansion devices to use, and since devices cannot use the same PC resources at the same time, the problem of *hardware resource conflicts* became a serious issue early in the computer revolution as a burgeoning selection of expansion devices competed for available bus slots.

The first key to understanding and eliminating hardware resource conflicts is to understand the importance of each system resource available to you. PCs provide four types of resources: (1) interrupts, (2) DMA channels, (3) I/O space, and (4) memory space. Do not underestimate the importance of these resources—conflicts can occur anywhere and carry dire consequences for a system.

INTERRUPTS

An *interrupt* is probably the most well known and understood type of resource. Interrupts are used to demand attention from the CPU; this allows a device or subsystem to work in the background until a particular event occurs that requires system processing. Such an event may include receiving a character at the serial port, striking a key on the keyboard, or any number of other real-world situations. An interrupt is invoked by asserting a logic level on one of the physical *interrupt request* (IRQ) lines accessible through any of the motherboard's expansion bus slots. AT-compatible PCs provide 16 IRQ lines (denoted IRQ 0 to IRQ 15). These lines run from pins on the expansion bus connector or key ICs on the motherboard to *Programmable Interrupt Controllers* (PICs) on the motherboard. The output signals generated by a PIC trigger the CPU interrupt. Table 1-1 illustrates the IRQ assignments for classic XT and AT-style systems. Table 1-2 illustrates the IRQ assignments for a typical Pentium II 333MHz PC through the *Device Manager* in your Windows *Control Panel* (Figure 1-1). Keep in mind that Tables 1-1 and 1-2 cover *hardware interrupts* only (there are also a proliferation of processor and software-generated interrupts).

NOTE You may access the *Device Manager* under Windows 95 and Windows 98 by clicking *Start, Settings,* and *Control Panel.* Double-click on the *System* icon, then click the *Device Manager* tab. Double-click the computer entry at the top of the device list to view the PC's various resource assignments.

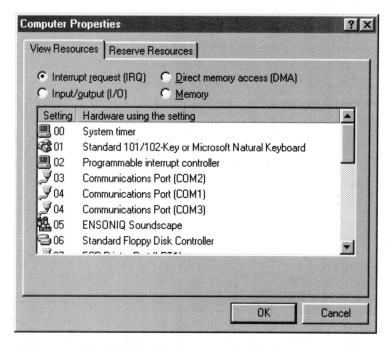

Figure 1-1   Viewing IRQ assignments under Windows 98.

The use of IRQ 2 in an IBM AT-style system deserves a bit of explanation. An AT uses IRQ 2 right on the motherboard, which means the expansion bus pin for IRQ 2 is now empty. Instead of leaving this pin unused, IRQ 9 from the AT extended slot is wired to the pin previously occupied by IRQ 2—in other words, IRQ 9 is being *redirected* to IRQ 2. Any AT expansion device set to use IRQ 2 is actually using IRQ 9. Of course, the interrupt vector table is adjusted to compensate for this sleight of hand.

After an interrupt is triggered, an interrupt handling routine saves the current CPU register states to a small area of memory (called the *stack*), then directs the CPU to the *interrupt vector table,* which is a list of program locations that correspond to each interrupt. When an interrupt occurs, the CPU will jump to the interrupt handler routine at the location specified in the interrupt vector table and execute that routine. In most cases, the interrupt handler is a device driver associated with the device generating the interrupt. For example, an IRQ from a network card will likely call a network device driver to operate the card. For a hard disk controller, an IRQ calls the BIOS ROM code that operates the drive. When the handling rou-

TABLE 1-1 XT and AT Interrupt Assignments*

IBM PC/XT

IRQ	Function
00	**System Timer IC**
01	**Keyboard Controller IC**
02	unused
03	Serial Port 2 (COM2: 2F8h–2FFh and COM4: 2E8h–2EFh)
04	Serial Port 1 (COM1: 3F8h–3FFh and COM3: 3E8h–3EFh)
05	XT Hard Disk Controller Board
06	**Floppy Disk Controller Board**
07	Parallel Port 1 (LPT1: 3BCh [mono] or 378h [color])

IBM PC/AT

IRQ	Function
00	**System Timer IC**
01	**Keyboard Controller IC**
02	**Second IRQ Controller IC**
03	Serial Port 2 (COM2: 2F8h–2FFh and COM4: 2E8h–2EFh)
04	Serial Port 1 (COM1: 3F8h–3FFh and COM3: 3E8h–3EFh)
05	Parallel Port 2 (LPT2: 378h or 278h); often used for Sound Card
06	**Floppy Disk Controller**
07	Parallel Port 1 (LPT1: 3BCh [mono] or 378h [color])
08	**Real-Time Clock (RTC)**
09	unused (*redirected to IRQ 2*)
10	USB (on systems so equipped—can be disabled)
11	Windows sound system (on systems so equipped—can be disabled)
12	Motherboard Mouse Port (PS/2 port)
13	**CPU Math Coprocessor**
14	Primary AT/IDE Hard Disk Controller
15	Secondary AT/IDE Hard Disk Controller (on systems so equipped—can be disabled)

* The bold entries in the table indicate IRQ assignments over which users have no control.

tine is finished, the CPU's original register contents are "popped" from the stack and the CPU picks up from where it left off, without interruption.

It is not vital that you understand precisely how interrupts are initialized and enabled, but you should know the basic terminology. The term *assigned* simply means that a device is configured to use a particular IRQ signal. For example, a typical hard drive controller board is assigned to IRQ 14. Next, interrupts can be selectively enabled or disabled under soft-

TABLE 1-2   Interrupt Assignments for a Typical Pentium II PC*

IRQ	Function
00	**System timer**
01	**Standard 101/102-Key or Microsoft Natural Keyboard**
02	**Programmable interrupt controller**
03	Communications Port (COM2)
04	Communications Port (COM1)
04	Communications Port (COM3)
05	Ensoniq Soundscape (sound card)
06	**Standard Floppy Disk Controller**
07	ECP Printer Port (LPT1)
08	**System CMOS/real-time clock**
09	Ensoniq Soundscape (sound card)
10	Diamond Viper V550 (PCI video card)
10	IRQ Holder for PCI Steering
11	Adaptec AIC-7850 PCI SCSI Controller
11	IRQ Holder for PCI Steering
11	Intel 82371AB/EB PCI to USB Universal Host Controller
11	IRQ Holder for PCI Steering
12	PS/2 Compatible Mouse Port
13	Numeric Data Processor
14	Intel 82371AB/EB PCI Bus Master IDE Controller
14	Primary IDE Controller
15	Intel 82371AB/EB PCI Bus Master IDE Controller
15	Secondary IDE Controller

* The bold entries in the table indicate IRQ assignments over which users have no control.

ware control. An *enabled* interrupt is an interrupt where the PIC has been programmed to pass on an IRQ to the CPU. Just because an interrupt is enabled does not mean that there are any devices assigned to it. Finally, an *active* interrupt is a line where real IRQs are being generated. Note that "active" does not mean assigned or enabled.

Interrupt Sharing Problems

Interrupts are an effective and reliable means of signaling the CPU, but the conventional ISA bus architecture—used in virtually all PCs—does *not* provide a means of determining *which* slot contains the board that called the interrupt. As a result, interrupts traditionally cannot be *shared* by multiple devices; in other words, no two devices can be actively generating interrupt requests on the same IRQ line at the same time. If more than one device is assigned to the same interrupt line, a hardware conflict will occur. In most circumstances, a conflict may prevent the newly installed board (or other previously installed boards) from working. In some cases, a hardware conflict can hang up the entire system.

The *MCA* (MicroChannel Architecture) and *EISA* (Extended ISA) busses overcome this IRQ sharing limitation, but MCA was never widely accepted in the PC industry because the slots are not backwardly compatible with the well-established base of ISA boards. EISA bus slots *are* backwardly compatible with ISA boards, but an ISA board in an EISA slot was still faced with the same IRQ limitations.

However, the *PCI* (Peripheral Component Interconnect) bus—now standard in virtually all Pentium and later PCs—does go a long way toward relieving the problem of IRQ sharing. Though the PCI bus scheme uses the same interrupt circuitry as ISA devices to reach the CPU, a motherboard's PCI chipset and bus design allow up to 32 PCI devices to use the same several IRQs, through a technique called *IRQ Steering*, without causing conflicts. You can see an example of IRQ sharing in the PCI assignments of Table 1-2.

DMA CHANNELS

The CPU is very adept at moving data—it can transfer data between memory locations, I/O locations, or from memory to I/O and back with equal ease. However, PC designers realized that transferring large amounts of data (one word at a time) through the CPU is a hideous waste of CPU time. After all, the CPU really isn't *processing* anything during a data move, just shuttling data from one place to another. If there were a way to off-load such redundant tasks from the CPU, data could theoretically be moved faster than would be possible with CPU intervention. *Direct Memory Access* (DMA) is a technique designed to move large amounts of data from memory to an I/O location, or vice versa, without the direct intervention by the CPU. In theory, the DMA controller IC acts as a stand-alone "data processor," leaving the CPU free to handle other tasks.

A DMA transfer starts with a *DMA Request* (DRQ) signal generated by the requesting device (such as the floppy disk controller board). If the DMA channel has been previously enabled through software drivers or BIOS routines, the request will reach the corresponding DMA controller IC on the motherboard. The DMA controller will then send a *HOLD* request to the CPU, which responds with a *Hold Acknowledge* (HLDA) signal. When the DMA controller receives the HLDA signal, it instructs the bus controller to effectively disconnect the CPU from the expansion bus and allow the DMA controller IC to take control of the bus itself. The DMA controller sends a *DMA Acknowledge* (DACK) signal to the requesting device and the transfer process may begin. Up to 64 KB can be moved during a single DMA transfer. After the transfer is done, the DMA controller will reconnect the CPU and drop its HOLD request—the CPU then continues with whatever it was doing without interruption.

Table 1-3 illustrates the use of DMA channels for both classic XT and current AT systems. There are twice as many DMA channels available in an AT than an XT, but you may wonder why the AT commits fewer channels—the issue is DMA performance. DMA was developed when CPUs ran at 4.77 MHz and is artificially limited to 4-MHz operation. When CPUs began to work at 8 MHz and higher, CPU transfers (redundant as they are) actually became *faster* than a DMA channel. As a result, the AT has many more channels available, but only the floppy drive controller, Enhanced Capabilities Parallel port (ECP port), and other limited-performance devices (such as sound cards) continue to use DMA. In an AT system, DMA channel 4 serves as a cascade line linking DMA controller ICs. Table 1-4 lists the typical DMA assignments found in a Pentium II 333-MHz PC through the Windows *Control Panel* (Figure 1-2).

When a device using DMA is installed in an expansion slot, the channel setting establishes a connection between the device and the DMA controller IC on the motherboard. Often, accompanying software drivers must use a command line switch that points to the corresponding hardware DMA assignment. Also, DMA channels cannot be shared between two or more devices. Although DMA sharing is possible in theory, it is extremely difficult to implement in actual practice. If more than one device attempts to use the same DMA channel at the same time, a hardware resource conflict will result.

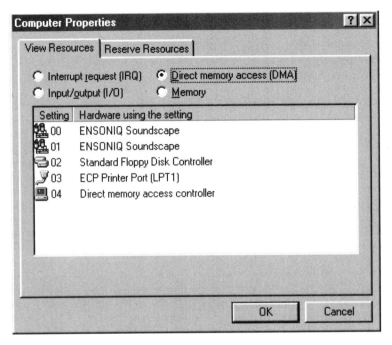

Figure 1-2   Viewing DMA assignments under Windows 98.

TABLE 1-3   XT and AT DMA Assignments

IBM PC/XT	
DMA	**Function**
00	Dynamic RAM refresh
01	unused
02	Floppy disk controller board
03	XT hard disk controller board

IBM PC/AT	
DMA	**Traditional Function**
00	Dynamic RAM refresh
01	unused
02	Floppy disk controller
03	unused
04	reserved (used internally)
05	unused
06	unused
07	unused

TABLE 1-4   DMA Assignments for a Typical Pentium II PC

DMA	Function
00	Ensoniq Soundscape (sound card)
01	Ensoniq Soundscape
02	Standard Floppy Disk Controller
03	ECP Printer Port (LPT1)
04	Direct memory access controller

I/O SPACE

Both XT and AT-style computers provide space for I/O (input/output) ports. An *I/O port* acts very much like a memory address, but it is not for storage; instead, an I/O port provides the means for a PC to communicate directly with a device—allowing the PC to efficiently pass commands and data between the system and various expansion devices. Each device must be assigned to a unique address (or *address range*). Table 1-5 lists the typical I/O port assignments for classic XT and classic AT systems. PS/2 systems use many of the same address assignments, but also add some wrinkles of their own (as shown in Table 1-6). Finally, the I/O scheme for a recent Pentium system (with a 430TX-based motherboard) is listed in Table 1-7 (Figure 1-3).

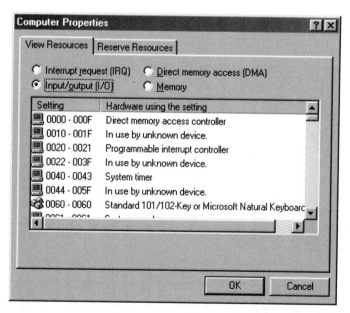

Figure 1-3   Viewing I/O assignments under Windows 98.

TABLE 1-5 Traditional XT/AT I/O Port Addresses

Classic IBM PC/XT Systems

Port	Description	Port	Description
000h–00Fh	8237 DMA IC–channels 0–3	2E4h–2E7h	available
020h–021h	8259 Programmable Interrupt Controller IC	2E8h–2EFh	Serial port 4 (COM4)
040h–043h	8253 System Timer IC	2F8h–2FFh	Serial port 2 (COM2)
060h–063h	8255 Programmable Peripheral Interface IC	300h–31Fh	IBM prototype card
070h, 071h	Real-Time Clock/CMOS, NMI mask	320h–323h	Primary XT HDD controller
080h	POST code port	324h–327h	Secondary XT HDD controller
081h–083h, 087h	DMA Page Registers (0–3)	328h–32Fh	available
0A0h	NMI mask register	330h	available
0C0h–0CFh	reserved	340h	available
0E0h–0EFh	reserved	350h–35Fh	Network card ports (low I/O)
0F0h–0FFh	Math coprocessor	360h–363h	reserved
108h–12Fh	reserved	364h–367h	Network Card Ports (high I/O)
130h–13Fh	available	368h–36Ah	reserved
140h–14Fh	available	36Ch–36Fh	Secondary FDD controller
150h–1EFh	reserved	370h–377h	Parallel Port 1 or 2 (LPT1 or LPT2)
200h–207h	Game ports	378h–37Fh	SDLC 2 (or Bisync 1) ports
208h–20Bh	available	380h–38Ch	Cluster ports (Adapter 0)
20Ch–20Dh	reserved	390h–393h	available
20Eh–21Eh	available	394h–3A9h	SDLC 1 (or Bisync 2) ports
21Fh	reserved	3A0h–3ACh	MDA (monochrome video) port
220h–22Fh	available	3B0h–3BFh	first LPT port of monochrome video board
230h–23Fh	available	3BCh–3BFh	EGA port
240h–247h	available	3C0h–3CFh	CGA port
250h–277h	available	3D0h–3DFh	available
278h–27Fh	Parallel Port 2 or 3 (LPT2 or LPT3)	3E0h–3E7h	Serial Port 3 (COM3)
280h–2AFh	available	3E8h–3EFh	Primary FDD controller
2B0h–2DFh	Alternate EGA ports	3F0h–3F7h	Serial Port 1 (COM1)
2E1h	GPIB port 0 (Adapter 0)	3F8h–3FFh	
2E2h–2E3h	Data Acquisition port 0 (Adapter 0)		

Classic IBM PC/AT Systems

Address	Description	Address	Description
000h–00Fh	DMA Controller IC #1 (channels 0–3)	280h–2AFh	available
020h–03Fh	Programmable Interrupt Controller (PIC) IC #1	2B0h–2DFh	Alternate EGA ports
040h–05Fh	System Timer IC	2E0h–2E7h	GPIB (Adapter 0)
060h	Keyboard/Mouse controller	2E8h–2EFh	Serial Port 4 (COM4)
061h	System Board I/O port	2F8h–2FFh	Serial Port 2 (COM2)
064h	Keyboard/Mouse controller IC	300h–31Fh	available
070h–07Fh	RTC port and NMI mask port	320h–32Fh	available
080h	POST code port	330h	available
081h–08Fh	DMA Page Registers	340h	available
0A0h–0BFh	Programmable Interrupt Controller IC #2	350h–35Fh	available
0C0h–0DEh	DMA Controller IC #2 (channels 4–7)	360h–363h	Network card port (low I/O)
0F0h–0F8h	Math Coprocessor ports	364h–367h	reserved
1F0h–1F8h	Hard Disk Controller Ports	368h–36Ah	Network card port (high I/O)
108h–12Fh	available	36Ch–36Fh	reserved
130h–13Fh	available	370h–377h	Secondary FDD controller
140h–14Fh	available	378h–37Fh	Parallel Printer 1 (LPT1)
150h–15Fh	available	380h–38Ch	SDLC 2 (or Bisync 1) port
170h–177h	Secondary HDD controller	390h–393h	Cluster ports
1F0h–1F7h	Primary HDD controller	394h–3A9h	available
200h–207h	Game port	3A0h–3ACh	SDLC 1 (or Bisync 2) port
208h–20Bh	available	3B0h–3BFh	Monochrome Display Adapter (MDA) port
20Ch–20Dh	reserved	3BCh–3BFh	Parallel Printer 3 (LPT3)
20Eh–21Eh	available	3C0h–3CFh	Enhanced Graphics Adapter (EGA) port
21Fh	reserved	3D0h–3DFh	Color Graphics Adapter (CGA) port
220h–2FFh	available	3E0h–3E7h	available
230h–23Fh	available	3E8h–3EFh	Serial Port 3 (COM3)
240h–247h	available	3F0h–3F7h	Primary FDD controller
250h–277h	available	3F8h–3FFh	Serial Port 1 (COM1)
278h–27Fh	Parallel Printer 2 (LPT2)		

TABLE 1-6 I/O Port Variations for PS/2 Systems

061h–06Fh	System control port B
090h	Central arbitration control port
091h	Card select feedback
092h	System control port A
094h	System board enable/set up register
096h	Adapter enable/set up register
100h–107h	PS/2 programmable option select
3220h–3227h	COM2
3228h–322Fh	COM3
4220h–3227h	COM4
4228h–322Fh	COM5
5220h–3227h	COM6
5228h–322Fh	COM7

NOTE I/O and memory range addresses are given in hexadecimal (or "hex") format—designated with the lowercase "h"; for example, 220h means 220 hexadecimal. If you wish to convert the hexadecimal number to its decimal equivalent, use the table of Appendix C.

As with other system resources, it is vitally important that no two devices use the same I/O port(s) at the same time. If one or more I/O addresses overlap, a hardware resource conflict will result. Commands meant for one device may be erroneously interpreted by another. Keep in mind that whereas many expansion devices can be set at a variety of addresses (such as SCSI adapter cards), some devices cannot (such as COM ports). Devices that are automatically identified and configured by the system BIOS often provide few (if any) configuration options.

MEMORY SPACE

Memory is another vital resource for the PC. Although early devices relied on the assignment of IRQ, DMA channels, and I/O ports, a growing number of modern devices (i.e., SCSI controllers, network cards, video boards, modems, and so on) are demanding memory space for the support of each device's onboard BIOS ROM (also called an *expansion ROM*). No two ROMs can overlap in their address ranges; otherwise, a hardware resource conflict will occur. Table 1-8 lists a memory map for a modern PC using an Intel 430 or 440 type of chipset (or equivalent). You can view the memory

TABLE 1-7 Modern AT I/O Assignments

Based on Basic Pentium System (430TX Chipset)

Address	Assignment	Address	Assignment
0000h–000Fh	PIIX4—DMA 1	0376h	Secondary IDE Channel command port
0020h–0021h	PIIX4—Interrupt Controller 1	0377h	Secondary Floppy Channel command port
002Eh–002Fh	Super I/O Controller configuration registers	0378h–037Fh	LPT1
0040h–0043h	PIIX4—Counter/Timer 1	0388h–038Dh	AdLib (FM synthesizer)
0048h–004Bh	PIIX4—Counter/Timer 2	03B4h–03B5h	Video (VGA)
0060h	Keyboard Controller byte—Reset IRQ	03BAh	Video (VGA)
0061h	PIIX4—NMI, speaker control	03BCh–03BFh	LPT3
0064h	Keyboard Controller, CMD/STAT byte	03C0h–03CAh	Video (VGA)
0070h	(bit 7) PIIX4—Enable NMI	03CCh	Video (VGA)
0070h	(bits 6-0) PIIX4—Real-Time Clock, address	03CEh–03CFh	Video (VGA)
0071h	PIIX4—Real-Time Clock, data	03D4h–03D5h	Video (VGA)
0078h	Reserved—board configuration	03DAh	Video (VGA)
0079h	Reserved—board configuration	03E8h–03EFh	COM3
0081h–008Fh	PIIX4—DMA Page Registers	03F0h–03F5h	Primary Floppy Channel
00A0h–00A1h	PIIX4—Interrupt Controller 2	03F6h	Primary IDE Channel command port
00B2h–00B3h	APM Control	03F7h	Primary Floppy Channel command port
00C0h–00DEh	PIIX4—DMA 2	03F8h–03FFh	COM1
00F0h	Reset Numeric Error	04D0h–04D1h	Edge/level triggered PIC
0170h–0177h	Secondary IDE Controller channel	0530h–0537h	Windows Sound System
01F0h–01F7h	Primary IDE Controller channel	0604h–060Bh	Windows Sound System
0200h–0207h	Audio/Game Port	LPT n + 400h	ECP port, LPT n base address + 400h
0220h–022Fh	Audio (Sound Blaster compatible)	0CF8h–0CFBh	PCI Configuration Address Register
0240h–024Fh	Audio (Sound Blaster compatible)	0CF9h	Turbo and Reset Control Register
0278h–027Fh	LPT2	0CFCh–0CFFh	PCI Configuration Data Register
0290h–0297h	Management extension hardware	0E80h–0E87h	Windows Sound System
02E8h–02EFh	COM4/Video (8514A)	0F40h–0F47h	Windows Sound System
02F8h–02FFh	COM2	0F86h–0F87h	Yamaha OPL3-SA Configuration
0300h–0301h	MPU-401 (MIDI)	FF00h–FF07h	IDE Bus Master Register
0330h–0331h	MPU-401 (MIDI)	FFA0h–FFA7	Primary Bus Master IDE Registers
0332h–0333h	MPU-401 (MIDI)	FFA8h–FFAFh	Secondary Bus Master IDE Registers
0334h–0335h	MPU-401 (MIDI)		

TABLE 1-8 Modern Pentium PC Memory Map*

Address Range (decimal)	Address Range (hex)	Size	Description
1024K–262144K	100000–10000000	255 MB	Extended Memory
960K–1024K	F0000–FFFFF	64 KB	BIOS
944K–960K	EC000–EFFFF	16 KB	Boot Block (available as UMB)
936K–944K	EA000–EBFFF	8 KB	ESCD (PnP/DMI configuration)
932K–936K	E9000–E9FFF	4 KB	Reserved for BIOS
928K–932K	E8000–E8FFF	4 KB	OEM Logo or Scan User Flash
896K–928K	E0000–E7FFF	32 KB	POST BIOS (available as UMB)
800K–896K	C8000–DFFFF	96 KB	Available High DOS memory
640K–800K	A0000–C7FFF	160 KB	Video memory and BIOS
639K–640K	9FC00–9FFFF	1 KB	Extended BIOS data
512K–639K	80000–9FBFF	127 KB	Extended conventional memory
0K–512K	00000–7FFFF	512 KB	Conventional memory

* Based on a typical motherboard using a 430TX/440LX or equivalent chipset.

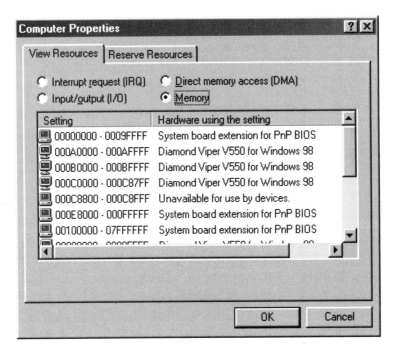

Figure 1-4 Viewing memory assignments under Windows 98.

space assignments for your particular system using the Windows *Device Manager* through your *Control Panel* (Figure 1-4).

INDEX OF TYPICAL RESOURCE ASSIGNMENTS

Now that you've got a handle on the essential resources (and the way they're allocated), it's time to put some of that information to work. Table 1-9 presents a cross section of typical devices and ports found in today's PCs and lists the standard resource assignments most often associated with them. This kind of listing may assist you in spotting potential conflicts before installing new devices. Note that you may encounter *any* combination of resources listed in Table 1-9 for a given device.

Bringing Order to Chaos

The proper configuration of a PC is deceivingly simple: just set each device so that they all use unique hardware resources (and no resources overlap). In practice, however, this proves far more difficult than it sounds—especially when given the proliferation of PC devices that are available today. As a consequence, most PC users are faced with configuration problems at one point or another during their system ownership. This part of the chapter explains the concept of "legacy" devices and introduces the principles of Plug-and-Play technology.

LEGACY DEVICES

Until the early 1990s, expansion devices were configured to use a PC's resources through the use of jumpers. By manually connecting or disconnecting various jumpers on the device, you could configure the interrupt, DMA channel, I/O range, and/or memory range of the device (jumpers also enabled you to enable or disable entire features of the device). The trouble with this approach is that in order to avoid hardware resource conflicts, you'd need to know how *everything* else in the system is configured already—a time-consuming, inexact, and often error-prone practice (especially among novices). In many cases where newly installed devices fail to operate (or caused erratic system behavior), the cause is almost always

TABLE 1-9   Typical Device Assignments

Device		IRQs	DMA Channels	I/O Addresses
AdLib Sound Device				228h
				238h
				239h
				289h
				388h
				389h
Aria Synthesizers				280h–288h
				290h–298h
				2A0h–2A8h
				2B0h–2B8h
Drive Controllers	FDD1	6	2	03F0h–03F5h
	FDD2	6	2	370h–377h
	HDD1	14		01F0h–01F7h
	HDD2	15		0170h–0177h
Gameport Adapters				201–211h
Internal Ports	COM1	4		03F8h–03FFh
	COM2	3		02F8h–02FFh
	COM3	4		03E8h–03EFh
	COM4	3		02E8h–02EFh
	LPT1	7		0378h–037Fh
	LPT2	5		0278h–027Fh
	LPT3	5		3BCh–03BFh
	PS/2 Mouse	12		064h
MPU-401 (MIDI)				300h
(IRQ shared with *Sound Blaster*)				320h
				330h
Network Interface Cards (NICs)		2	1	280h–283h
		3	3	280h–2FFh
		4	5	2A0h–2A3h
		5	7	2A0h–2BFh
		7		300h–303h
		10		300h–31Fh
		11		320h–323h
				320h–33Fh
				340h–343h
				340h–35Fh
				360h–363h
				360h–37Fh

TABLE 1-9   Typical Device Assignments (Cont.)

Device	IRQs	DMA Channels	I/O Addresses
Reserved System Resources	0	0	
	1	2	
		4	
SCSI Host Adapters	10	3	130h–14Fh
	11	5	140h–15Fh
	14		220h–23Fh
	15		330h–34Fh
			340h–35Fh
Sound Blaster	5	1	220h–22Eh
(DMA playback)	7	3	240h–24Eh
	9	5	
	10	7	
	11		
Windows Sound System	5	0	530h
(DMA playback)	7	1	E80h
	9	3	530h–F48h
	10		
	11		

traced to hardware resource conflicts due to configuration oversights by the installer.

If you accidentally configure two or more devices to use the same resources, a hardware resource conflict will result. Correcting a conflict requires you to isolate the offending device(s), identify the available resources, and reconfigure one or more of the offending devices manually—then retest the system. Even for experienced technicians, this continues to be a cumbersome and time-consuming process.

Legacy Devices and the Operating System

Legacy devices are not "intelligent" devices—that is, neither the system BIOS nor the operating system is able to detect the legacy device or the resources that it's using. This poses a special problem for advanced operating systems such as Windows. In order to configure the operating system to use most devices (i.e., a sound card), any .INI entries that define the device's resource assignments *must* match the physical configuration of the device; otherwise, the device will not respond to the operating system, even though the device itself may be adequately configured with no conflicts at all. For example, consider this fragment of the Windows 98 SYSTEM.INI file:

```
[SNDSCAPE.DRV]
Port=330
WavePort=338
IRQ=9
SBIRQ=5
DMA=1
```

You can see that the `Port` and `WavePort` entries indicate I/O addresses, the `IRQ` and `SBIRQ` are interrupts, and the `DMA` entry lists the DMA setting for this particular system's sound card. When Windows starts, it expects the physical configuration of the sound card to match the entries listed. If not, the sound card will not operate. When a legacy card is reconfigured, its corresponding entries in an .INI file must also be updated.

Weaning Off Legacy Devices

Today, we describe any manually configured device (or device with a configuration we cannot change) as a *legacy* device. There are many legacy devices still in service today, such as modems and sound cards, but by late 1997/early 1998, new legacy devices are no longer being developed or manufactured. Instead, the PC industry is embracing Plug-and-Play technology.

THE ROLE OF PLUG-AND-PLAY (PnP)

By the early 1990s, PC designers realized that it was possible to "automate" the processes of device detection and resource allocation each time the system initializes. This way, a device need only be installed and the system would handle its detection and configuration without the assistance or intervention of the installer. Also, the assignment of resources would be "dynamic" so that assignments could change as the PC's configuration changes (i.e., as new devices are added or removed). These concepts have become known as *Plug-and-Play* (PnP), which is now standard in the PC arena. PnP systems require three essential elements in order to function:

1. PnP-compliant *BIOS* (now used in all Pentium-class and later systems)

2. PnP-compliant *devices* (such as video boards, modems, drive controllers, and so on)

3. PnP-compliant *operating systems* (such as Windows 95 or Windows 98)

Plug-and-Play Devices

The Plug-and-Play process begins with the system BIOS and motherboard. Each time the PC is started, the PnP BIOS will first detect any legacy devices and identify the resources being used. Once the non-PnP devices are accounted for, the PnP BIOS will detect each of the PnP devices in the system and assign resources from the pool of remaining IRQs, DMA channels, I/O space, and so on. Yet the PnP BIOS does little more than assign resources—it cannot actively manage the configuration of the system. For that, we need a PnP-compliant operating system such as Windows 98. It is the operating system that completes the assignment of resources, registers each device, and loads the drivers needed to operate them. There are a variety of system device types that are designed to be compatible with Plug-and-Play:

◀ USB devices

◀ IEEE 1394 (a.k.a. "Fire Wire") devices

◀ SCSI devices

◀ PC Card and CardBus devices (for mobile PCs)

◀ VL bus devices

◀ PCI and AGP bus devices

◀ ISA bus devices

◀ EISA bus devices

◀ Most I/O ports (i.e., IDE controllers, COM ports, and LPT ports)

NOTE **USB and AGP support are provided properly only under Windows 98. USB is also supported to some extent by Windows 95 OSR 2.1 and OSR 2.5.**

The Inside Details

When devices are added or removed from a system, the three components of a Plug-and-Play computer will coordinate and perform the following tasks:

◁ *Identify the installed devices.* The PnP system must be able to identify each installed device. This requires the device to have a certain amount of onboard intelligence.

◁ *Determine the device resource requirements.* Based on the device identification, the PnP system must be able to determine the kinds of resources (IRQ, DMA, I/O addresses, or BIOS space) required to support the device.

◁ *Create a complete system configuration, eliminating all resource conflicts.* After all devices have been identified and their resource needs evaluated, the PnP system must then allocate the required resources to each device every time the system initializes (without causing a resource conflict).

◁ *Load the device drivers.* After the operating system starts, it then must load the appropriate device drivers needed to support every device in the system.

◁ *Notify any configuration changes.* Each time a PnP device is added or removed from the PC, the PnP system reports the configuration change. When a device is added, the PnP system attempts to identify it and install the appropriate device drivers. When a device is removed, the PnP system attempts to remove all traces of the device and its drivers.

The PnP system starts with the BIOS at boot time—a certain amount of configuration must first be performed by the system BIOS during system initialization. In order for the system to boot, the PnP BIOS must configure a display device, input device, and initial boot device (i.e., video adapter, keyboard, and floppy/hard drives). Then, the PnP BIOS must pass the information about each of these devices to the operating system (i.e., Windows 95 or Windows 98) for additional configuration of the remaining system devices.

The operating system then continues the configuration process by identifying all devices in the system and gathering their respective resource requirements. Each nonboot device (i.e., modems, video capture devices) must be inactive upon power-up so that the operating system can identify any conflicts between the resource requirements of different devices before configuring them. When different devices require the same resources, the devices must be able to provide information to the operating system about alternative resource requirements. The operating system then uses initial or alternative requirements to assemble a working system configuration. Once any resource conflicts have been resolved, the operating system automatically programs each hardware device with its working configuration and then stores all configuration information in the central database contained in ESCD (Extended System Configuration Data) memory, which is part of the CMOS RAM space. Finally, the operating system loads the device drivers for each device and notifies these drivers of each resource assignment.

If a change occurs to the system configuration during operation (for example, a device is installed or removed), the hardware must be able to notify the operating system of the event so that the operating system can configure the new device. Additionally, applications must be able to respond to configuration changes to take advantage of new devices and to cease calling devices that have been removed. Such dynamic configuration events might include the insertion of a PC card; the addition or removal of a peripheral such as a mouse, CD-ROM drive, printer; or a docking/undocking event for a notebook computer.

NOTE In most cases, configuration changes are made before boot time while the system power is off. Only PCs with a USB port, PC card, and laptop PC designs support "hot" insertion and removal.

When the PnP system works properly, a PnP device can be installed in an available expansion slot on a PnP-supported motherboard (with a PnP BIOS). When Windows 95/98 starts, it recognizes the new PnP device, assigns resources, then attempts to install the proper protected-mode driver (which could be installed from a manufacturer's floppy disk or a Windows 95/98 installation CD). Thereafter, the system "remembers" the new device and reconfigures it each time the system starts. Ideally, if the PnP device is ever removed, Windows 95/98 would automatically clear the device from its "system" and free the resources for other devices.

However, if any one of these three elements is missing (the BIOS, the devices, or the operating system), the system will not be *autoconfigured*. For example, PnP won't work under DOS (though there are DOS PnP drivers that can be used to initialize PnP devices). Older, jumper-configured devices (called *legacy devices*) also won't support PnP, and resources need to be reserved for legacy devices in order to prevent the PnP system from ignoring them entirely. Chapter 3 explains the techniques of PnP management under Windows 95/98 in more detail.

NOTE You can obtain additional technical information about PnP technology from the Microsoft site at *http://www.microsoft.com/win32dev/base/pnp.htm* or from Intel's Plug-and-Play page at *http://www.intel.com/IAL/plugplay/index.htm.*

Detection vs. Enumeration

As you deal with Plug-and-Play, you'll encounter two specific terms: (1) detection and (2) enumeration. Both of these terms are important in the PnP environment. *Detection* is the process Windows 95/98 uses during its search for legacy (non-Plug-and-Play) devices on the computer. Detection is used during Windows Setup and anytime you use the *Add New Hardware* wizard to search for new hardware installed in your computer. Detection does not run each time you start Windows. During the detection process, Windows 95/98 creates a file DETLOG.TXT in the root directory of the boot drive—this file mainly serves as a troubleshooting tool.

By contrast, *Enumeration* is the process Windows 95/98 uses to identify true Plug-and-Play devices in your computer (including those devices on Plug-and-Play busses such as ISAPNP, PCI, and PCMCIA—PC card— devices). Enumeration occurs each time Windows starts and whenever Windows receives notification that a change has occurred in the computer's hardware configuration (such as when you unplug a USB device).

ESCD Basics

The *Extended System Configuration Data* (ESCD) area is an 8-KB block of additional CMOS RAM. The ESCD is used to store critical information about Plug-and-Play, non-Plug-and-Play, ISA, EISA, and PCI devices. It also contains information about the "standard" devices in the system such as COM ports and LPT ports. The system BIOS records changes to the system's configuration as it boots (if you add or remove PnP-compliant devices, you'll probably notice a BIOS message such as *"Updating ESCD"*). The ESCD can help save time in loading the operating system because it need not redetect PnP devices—the OS can simply read the index of PnP information listed in the ESCD.

NOTE If the system's CMOS backup battery fails, the contents of the ESCD (as well as other CMOS RAM setup information) will be lost.

CHECKING FOR PLUG-AND-PLAY

Systems manufactured after 1995 are almost certainly compliant with the Plug-and-Play specifications, but older systems may not be fully compatible (if at all). When working with an unknown PC, you should have some basic guidelines for determining the level of PnP compliance offered by your system. You'll need to make some basic checks of the BIOS, your system devices, and the operating system. Although this kind of evaluation isn't perfect, it *can* suggest possible limitations in your system's configuration.

The BIOS

The BIOS and motherboard are at the hardware heart of Plug-and-Play—without an appropriate motherboard/BIOS, it may difficult (or impossible) for the system to support Plug-and-Play devices. The first means of checking is to watch for the BIOS ID line in the moments just following a system's power-up. In many cases, one of the BIOS ID lines will include a reference to Plug-and-Play such as:

```
Award Plug and Play BIOS Extension v1.0A
```

or some other Plug-and-Play reference such as:

```
Initializing Plug and Play Cards…
```

Another method of testing for Plug-and-Play compliance is to run an "inspection utility" such as PNPBTST.EXE, which is available from the Phoenix Technologies Web site at *www.phoenix.com/techs/freeware.html.* You might also check with the manufacturer of your particular BIOS (i.e., AMI, Award, Microid Research, and so on) for a more specific inspection utility. Table 1-10 provides a list of Web addresses for the most popular BIOS makers. Finally, if you cannot determine the Plug-and-Play compliance of your BIOS, you should contact the tech support line of your BIOS or system manufacturer once you've copied the BIOS ID code displayed during system startup such as:

```
#401A0-0105
12/02/97 - i440LX - <P2L97> - 00
```

TABLE 1-10 Web Index of Popular BIOS Makers

American Megatrends:	*http://www.megatrends.com*
Award BIOS:	*http://www.award.com*
IBM SurePath BIOS page:	*http://www.surepath.ibm.com/*
MicroFirmware:	*http://www.firmware.com/catalog2.htm*
Microid Research (Mr. BIOS):	*http://www.mrbios.com/*
Phoenix Technology:	*http://www.phoenix.com*
SystemSoft:	*http://www.systemsoft.com*
Unicore:	*http://www.unicore.com/*

The Devices

It's a little more difficult to determine whether a device is PnP. Traditionally, a legacy device is one that uses physical jumpers to select hardware resources. By comparison, a PnP device does *not* use jumpers. This is a fair yardstick for internal devices (the *expansion cards*), but is not so good for external devices such as modems, printers, or scanners. To make that kind of determination, you may need to perform a little detective work. The most definitive information comes directly from the device maker in the form of a product manual or Web site—product specifications typically include a mention of whether the device is Plug-and-Play (Figure 1-5).

The Operating System

You'll also need to determine whether the operating system is Plug-and-Play–compliant. DOS and Windows 3.x do *not* support PnP natively—these require a PnP *Configuration Manager* utility loaded in the CONFIG .SYS file at startup in order to provide support for PnP devices in the system (you can find detailed information about DOS and PnP in Chapter 2). Windows 95 and Windows 98 (as well as current versions of OS/2) do offer full PnP support.

NOTE You can download or view the latest PnP documents from the Microsoft Web site at *http://www.microsoft.com/hwdev/respec/pnpspecs.htm*

In order for the PC to recognize and configure a PnP device, each and every device must be able to identify itself and its resource requirements to the system—even motherboard busses and devices must be able to identify themselves. Identification is accomplished through a seven-character code. Each manufacturer is assigned a three-character prefix; the following char-

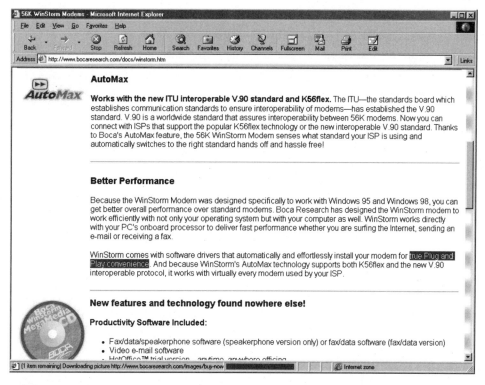

Figure 1-5 Reviewing product specifications for Plug-and-Play compliance.

acter identifies the device type; and the remaining three characters identify the particular device. For example, the PnP code PNP0907 identifies a "Western Digital VGA" device adapter. Microsoft reserves the code "PNP" for itself, but other manufacturers are assigned their own codes (i.e., Creative Labs uses the "CTL" prefix). The advantage of Microsoft's prefixes is that they are generic and you can usually identify a device adequately by utilizing the Microsoft generic equivalent. Appendix B lists the generic PnP identification categories and codes used by Microsoft.

CONTROLLING PLUG-AND-PLAY

Today, Plug-and-Play is largely a fact of life for virtually every PC in service, but you can disable PnP or make performance adjustments at the BIOS level. This is accomplished by tweaking the configuration of your CMOS Setup through the *PCI and/or Plug-and-Play* menu, as shown in Figure 1-6. The most common control is the *PnP OS Installed* switch

```
                        ROM PCI/ISA BIOS (<P2L97>)
                            PNP AND PCI SETUP
                          AWARD SOFTWARE, INC.

 PNP OS Installed    : Yes          DMA  1 Used By ISA : No/ICU
 Slot 1 (RIGHT) IRQ : Auto          DMA  3 Used By ISA : No/ICU
 Slot 2 IRQ         : Auto          DMA  5 Used By ISA : No/ICU
 Slot 3 IRQ         : Auto
 Slot 4/5 (LEFT) IRQ: Auto          ISA MEM Block BASE : No/ICU
 PCI Latency Timer  :  32 PCI Clock
                                    SYMBIOS SCSI BIOS  : Disabled
                                    USB IRQ            : Disabled
 IRQ  3 Used By ISA : No/ICU
 IRQ  4 Used By ISA : No/ICU
 IRQ  5 Used By ISA : No/ICU
 IRQ  7 Used By ISA : No/ICU
 IRQ  9 Used By ISA : No/ICU
 IRQ 10 Used By ISA : No/ICU
 IRQ 11 Used By ISA : No/ICU
 IRQ 12 Used By ISA : No/ICU        ESC : Quit        ↑↓→ : Select Item
 IRQ 14 Used By ISA : No/ICU        F1  : Help        PU/PD/+/- : Modify
 IRQ 15 Used By ISA : No/ICU        F5  : Old Values  (Shift)F2 : Color
                                    F6  : Load BIOS  Defaults
                                    F7  : Load Setup Defaults
```

Figure 1-6   Typical PnP configuration screen in the CMOS Setup [hardcopy only].

(located in the upper-left corner of Figure 1-6). When this setting is *No,* a non-PnP OS is installed (such as DOS) and the BIOS will detect devices and assign resources, as well as prevent the operating system from reassigning those resources. If the setting is *Yes,* a PnP OS is assumed to be installed (such as Windows 98) and the OS is allowed to reassign resources as necessary. Note that this level of control doesn't really disable PnP at the BIOS level—it just controls how the operating system uses PnP.

You'll also notice that you can specify the interrupts that are assigned to your PCI slots using the *Slot 1* through *Slot 4/5* entries. By default, the setting is *Auto,* which allows available IRQs to be assigned automatically. The *PCI Latency Timer* affects the PCI bus timing and controls the performance of the PCI bus, but the *32 PCI Clock* entry ensures top performance for the PCI bus. Below these entries, you can specify the IRQs and DMAs that are assigned to legacy ISA devices. BIOS *needs* this kind of information so that it will reserve those IRQs and prevent them from being assigned to PnP devices. However, this information is not critical when a PnP OS is installed, and the default of *No/ICU* is usually adequate.

You can use the *ISA MEM Block BASE* entry to set the base address and block size of a legacy ISA card that uses a memory segment from C800h to DFFFh. If you have such a card and are not using an ICU to specify the address range, select a base address from the available options. If there is more than one legacy card using that address range, you can select a larger block size (i.e., 8-KB, 16-KB, 32-KB, or 64-KB). When a PnP OS is installed, the default setting of *No/ICU* is fine. Finally, if you're using a USB motherboard with Windows 98, you can enable USB by selecting a USB IRQ.

NOTE When a PnP operating system is installed, you typically do not need to make manual adjustments to the BIOS configuration because the OS will take over PnP assignments from the BIOS anyway.

System Design and Plug-and-Play

In order to properly support Plug-and-Play (as well as the myriad of other PC standards and initiatives that are appearing), Intel and Microsoft have teamed up to develop the "standard" *PC System Design Guide*. This guide first appeared around 1995 and has been updated every year or so with the introduction of new components and technologies. Today, system makers reference the *PC99 System Design Guide*. By ensuring that their systems meet the requirements of the PC99 specification, system makers will guarantee that their computers will be compatible with Plug-and-Play, InstantON, USB, and many other PC standards. Table 1-11 outlines the requirements and recommendations for a PC99-compliant computer based on the *PC99 System Design Guide*.

NOTE You can obtain more information about Microsoft's System Design Guides as well as the complete *PC99 System Design Guide* at *http://www.microsoft.com/hwdev/desguid.htm.*

Getting Started with Configuration Management

Whether you're building a new PC, upgrading an existing system, or troubleshooting a device problem, you'll need to understand the essentials of *configuration management,* which means you should know how to review the hardware that's installed in a PC, determine the resources utilized by each device, detect disabled devices or those with conflicting resources (and correct those conflicts as needed), and check the drivers in use by each device. Effective configuration management is not terribly difficult, but it does require an eye for detail and the proper diagnostic tools. Fortunately,

TABLE 1-11 Basic PC99 Design Specifications*

	Consumer	Office	Mobile	Workstation	Entertainment
CPU speed	300 MHz	300 MHz	233 MHz	400 MHz	300 MHz
Memory	32 MB	64 MB	32 MB	128 MB	64 MB
Meets ACPI 1.0 specification	required	required	recommended	required	required
Meets OnNow and Instantly Available specs	required	required	recommended	required	required
BIOS provides PC99 OnNow support	required	required	required	required	required
BIOS provides PC99 boot support	required	required	recommended	required	required
Expansion slots available for inserting cards	required	required	PC cards	required	required
Audible noise meets PC99 requirements	required	required	required	required	required
Assembly guidelines meet PC99 specs	required	required	required	required	required
Internal modification not available to end users	recommended	recommended	recommended	recommended	recommended
System design offers physical security	recommended	recommended	recommended	recommended	recommended
Devices and drivers meet PC99 specs	required	required	required	required	required
Busses and devices meet PnP specs	**required**	**required**	**required**	**required**	**required**
Unique PnP device ID provided for each system device and add-on device	**required**	**required**	**required**	**required**	**required**
Option ROMs meet PnP requirements	**required**	**required**	**required**	**required**	**required**
"PNP" vendor code used only to define a legacy device's compatible ID	**required**	**required**	**required**	**required**	**required**
Device driver and installation meets PC99 specs	required	required	required	required	required
Minimal user interaction needed to install and configure devices	required	required	required	required	required
Connections use icons, plus keyed or shrouded connectors, with color coding	required	required	recommended	required	required
Hot-plugging capabilities for buses and devices meet PC99 requirements	required	required	required	required	required
System includes Device Bay 1.0-compatible bay	recommended	recommended	recommended	recommended	recommended

Multifunction add-on devices meet PC99 device requirements for each device	required	required	required	required	required
All devices support correct 16-bit decoding for I/O port addresses	required	required	required	required	required
All PC99 input devices support Microsoft DirectInput and work simultaneously	required	required	required	required	required
Each bus meets written specifications and PC99 requirements	required	required	required	required	required
System includes USB with 2 USB ports, minimum	required	required	recommended	required	required
System includes support for IEEE 1394	recommended	recommended	recommended	recommended	3 ports recommended
If present, PCI bus meets PCI 2.1 or later, plus PC99 requirements	required	required	required	required	required
System does *not* include ISA expansion devices or slots	required	required	required	required	required
System includes keyboard connection and keyboard	required	required	required	required	required
System includes pointing-device connection and pointing device	required	required	required	required	required
System includes connection for external parallel devices	required	required	required	required	required
System includes connection for external serial devices	required	required	required	required	required
System includes IR devices compliant with IrDA specifications	recommended	recommended	recommended	recommended	recommended
System includes PC99 CD or DVD drive/controller	required	recommended	recommended	required	DVD-required
System includes audio support that meets PC99 requirements	recommended	recommended	recommended	recommended	required
System includes a modem or other public network communications support	required	recommended	required	required	required
System includes a network adapter	recommended	required	recommended	required	recommended

* Entries in bold are PnP-related specifications.

TABLE 1-11 Basic PC99 Design Specifications (Cont.)*

	Consumer	Office	Mobile	Workstation	Entertainment
System includes smart card support	recommended	recommended	recommended	recommended	recommended
Graphics adapter meets PC99 requirements	required	required	required	required	required
Color monitor is DDC-compliant with unique EDID identifier	required	required	not required	required	required
System meets PC99 DVD-Video and MPEG-2 playback requirements, if system supports DVD-Video	required	required	not required	required	required
Adapter supports television output if system does not include a large-screen monitor	recommended	recommended	recommended	recommended	recommended
System supports PC99 analog video input and capture capabilities	recommended	recommended	recommended	recommended	recommended
System includes analog television tuner	recommended	recommended	recommended	recommended	recommended
System BIOS and option ROMs support Int 13h Extensions	required	required	required	required	required
Host controller for storage device meets PC99 requirements	required	required	required	required	required
Host controllers and hard disk devices support bus mastering	required	required	required	required	required
Hard drive meets PC99 requirements	required	required	required	required	required
Operating system recognizes the boot drive in a multiple-drive system	required	required	required	required	required
Floppy disk capabilities do not use legacy FDC	recommended	recommended	recommended	recommended	recommended
System supports WHIIG	n/a	required	required /w NT	required	n/a
System includes driver support for WMI	n/a	required	required /w NT	required	n/a
Management information service provider enabled by default	n/a	required	required /w NT	required	n/a
Expansion devices can be remotely managed	n/a	required	recommended	required	n/a
SMBIOS 2.2 static table support is provided	n/a	required	recommended	required	n/a

* Entries in bold are PnP-related specifications.

there are some powerful tools available under both Windows 95 and Windows 98 that can help you determine which resources and drivers are being used by the devices in your system as well as the system's overall status.

DEVICE MANAGER

Windows 95 and Windows 98 provide a detailed listing of installed devices using a powerful multipurpose tool called the *Device Manager* (or simply the DM). You access the *Device Manager* by clicking *Start, Settings,* and *Control Panel,* then double-clicking the *System* icon. When the *System Properties* dialog appears (Figure 1-7), click the *Device Manager* tab to open the *Device Manager* dialog. The DM aids configuration management at several important levels:

◁ Lists all of the devices that are installed in the system

◁ Indicates any devices that are conflicting, inoperative, or disabled

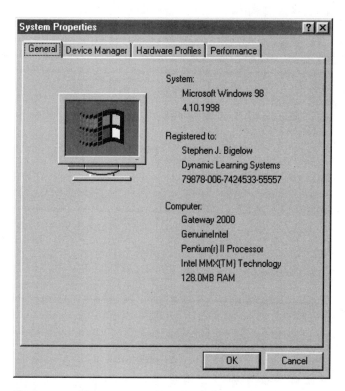

Figure 1-7 The *System Properties* dialog.

◀ Identifies every resource associated with each device

◀ Lists all the drivers used by each device

◀ Allows you to adjust the resources assigned to most devices

◀ Allows you to adjust key settings for certain devices under Windows

Lists all devices. Once you click the *Device Manager* tab, the *Device Manager* dialog opens as in Figure 1-8. The device "tree" shown in the dialog outlines *all* of the devices (both legacy and Plug-and-Play) that are installed in the system. You can scroll up and down the list using the scroll bar at the right. By default, each entry in the device "tree" is listed by classification (i.e., CD-ROM or Display Adapter). To view specific devices for any classification, just double-click on the entry. For example, Figure 1-9 shows what happens when you double-click on the *Disk Drives* entry. To return back to

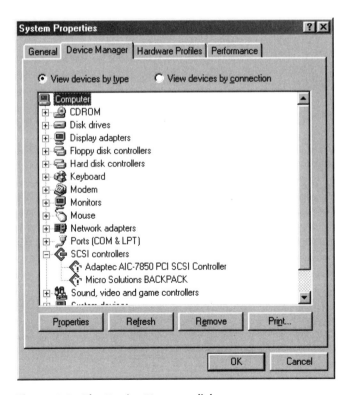

Figure 1-8 The *Device Manager* dialog.

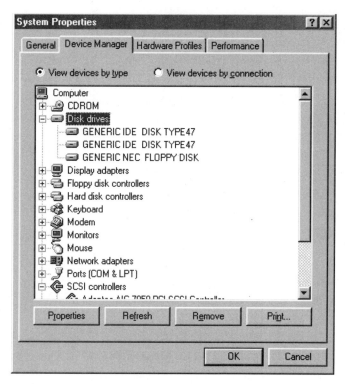

Figure 1-9 Reviewing specific devices in the device "tree."

the classification only, just double-click on that particular entry again.

Indicates discrepant devices. As you look over the device "tree," the DM will mark any devices that are conflicting, inoperative, or disabled. Inoperative or conflicting devices are marked with a yellow exclamation mark (such as the *Adaptec SCSI Controller* in Figure 1-10). Devices that are disabled or electrically damaged are marked with a red "X" (such as the *Diamond Monster 3D II Accelerator* in Figure 1-11). Upon further investigation, you can determine the problem in detail and take steps to reinstall, reconfigure, or replace the troublesome device.

Identifies resources. The DM can display a comprehensive listing of the hardware resources utilized by any given device. To review the resources in use for a device, just highlight the device in the device "tree" and click the *Properties* button (or just double-click the

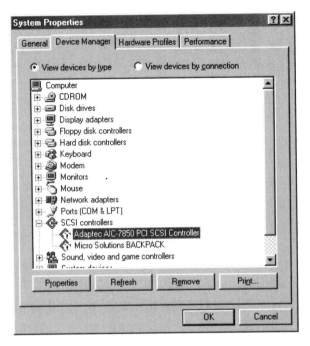

Figure 1-10 Checking conflicting or inoperative devices.

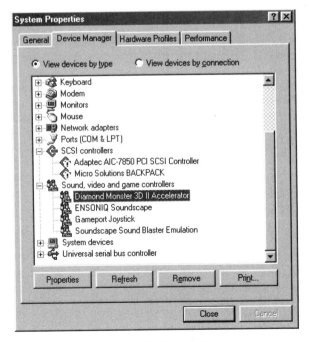

Figure 1-11 Checking disabled devices.

device), then click the *Resources* tab. Figure 1-12 shows the *Properties* dialog for a Diamond Viper V550 video adapter card. By comparing resources between two or more discrepant devices, you can see where device resources may overlap.

Identifies and updates drivers. The DM can also provide a listing of the drivers used by a given device. To review the drivers for a device, simply highlight the device in the device "tree" and click the *Properties* button (or just double-click the device), then click the *Drivers* tab. As Figure 1-13 illustrates, you can either choose to "view" the current drivers or "update" the current drivers if you've downloaded new drivers from the device manufacturer. If you choose to view the drivers in use, you'll see a listing of drivers such as for the *Dial-up Adapter* shown in Figure 1-14.

Adjusts resources. Not only does the DM show the resource settings for various devices, it also allows you to change many of those settings. This allows you to reconfigure Plug-and-Play devices on the fly or even shut them down entirely. When you're viewing device resources (Figure 1-12), uncheck the *Use automatic settings* check

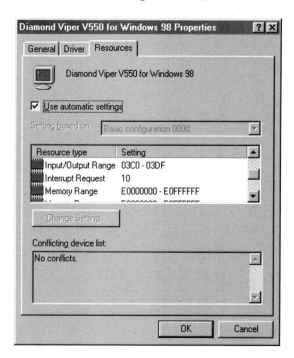

Figure 1-12 Viewing specific resources for a device.

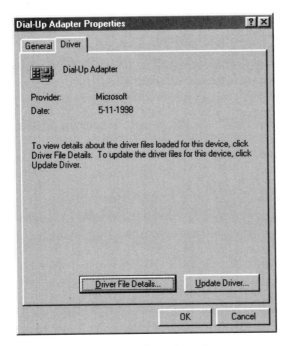

Figure 1-13 Selecting the *Driver* tab.

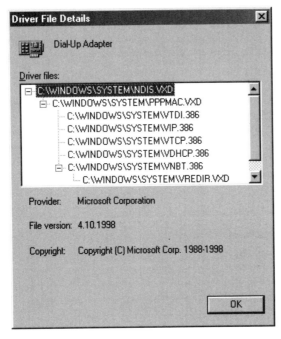

Figure 1-14 Viewing specific drivers for a device.

box, highlight the resource type to change, then click the *Change Resources* button. An editing dialog box will appear (depending on what resource you wish to edit) as in Figure 1-15. You can then enter the new resource(s), save your changes, and reboot the system.

NOTE If you're adjusting the settings of a legacy device, you'll need to power down the PC and reconfigure the legacy device to match the new settings that you've entered. For Plug-and-Play devices, new settings are initialized once the PC is rebooted.

NOTE After rebooting, be sure to recheck the *Device Manager* to verify that your resource changes have not accidentally caused another accidental conflict.

Adjusts settings. Many devices (especially drives) can be adjusted through the DM if there is provision for a *Settings* tab. Once you select the device from the device "tree," just click the *Settings* tab to open the *Settings* dialog (Figure 1-16). Depending on the particular device that you select, you may be able to adjust settings like *Auto insert notification* or *Drive letter.* If you change the settings for a

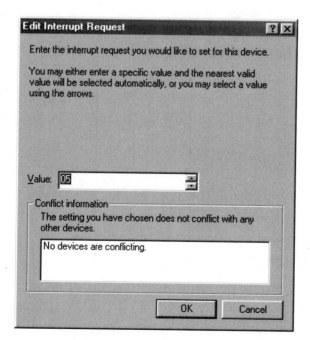

Figure 1-15 Manually editing resource assignments.

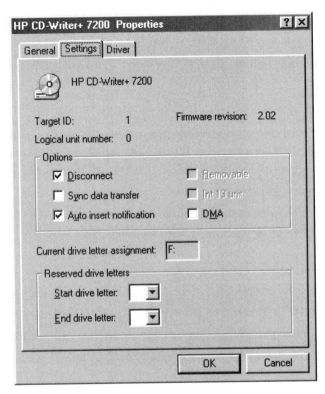

Figure 1-16 Controlling device settings.

device, you'll probably need to reboot the PC for those changes to take effect.

SYSTEM INFORMATION

There are many occasions when it's necessary to have a summary of system configuration data at your fingertips. Under Windows 95, this typically requires you to print a summary of devices from the *Device Manager* (see the *Print* button in the lower-right corner of Figure 1-8). The *Device Manager* then prints a lengthy report to your system printer and you can sort through that report to find the information that you need. Unfortunately, if there's no printer handy, you cannot generate a summary. With the introduction of Windows 98, however, you can use the *System Information* tool to access detailed system setup information. You start *System Information* by clicking *Start, Programs, Accessories, System Tools,* and *System Information.* When *System Information* first starts, you'll see a *System Infor-*

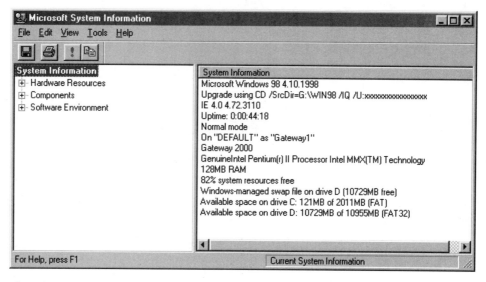

Figure 1-17   *System Information* summary dialog under Windows 98.

mation summary similar to Figure 1-17. Below the *System Information* summary, you can obtain details about the *Hardware Resources, Components,* or *Software Environment* by double-clicking on the corresponding entry in the left window.

Hardware Resources

Once you expand the *Hardware Resources* section, you'll see that you can obtain specific details about key aspects of your system's hardware such as *Conflicts/Sharing* (ideal for detecting hardware conflicts quickly), *DMA, Forced Hardware, I/O, IRQs,* and *Memory.* Clicking any of these entries will provide you with specific details. For example, Figure 1-18 illustrates a typical report generated when selecting *I/O.* You can then use the data generated by *System Information* to troubleshoot conflicts or find out how the system resources are being allocated.

Components

The *Components* section of *System Information* is used to reveal detailed data about each major class of devices installed in the PC. You'll be able to "see" inside the PC as never before. You can retrieve data about your *Multimedia* system (including audio codecs, video codecs, and the system's CD-ROMs), the *Display* adapter, *Infrared* devices, *Input* devices, *Miscella-*

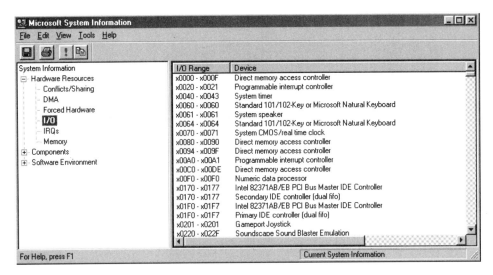

Figure 1-18 Viewing typical information under *Hardware Resources.*

neous devices (such as printers and tape drives), the *Modem, Network* configurations such as dial-up networking (including Winsock settings for accessing the Internet), the system's I/O *Ports,* drives and other *Storage* devices, *Printing* devices, *USB* devices, and *System* (a.k.a. motherboard) devices. Figure 1-19 illustrates a typical *Components* report for the *USB* system.

You'll also notice that the *Components* section includes two other sections: (1) *Problem Devices* and (2) *History.* These are particularly useful selections when troubleshooting a system. The *Problem Devices* entry will quickly identify any components that are disabled or not functioning properly. The *History* entry provides you with a complete log of the changes that have been effected to the system devices over time, so you can identify what's been added, removed, or changed.

Software Environment

The *Software Environment* section of *System Information* is particularly useful for identifying the software drivers and applications running on a PC or isolating old or outdated files. After expanding the *Software Environment* entry, you can select a detailed report of *Drivers* (including Kernel drivers, MS-DOS drivers, and User-Mode drivers), you can find the *16-bit Modules Loaded* and *32-bit Modules Loaded* on the system, identify the

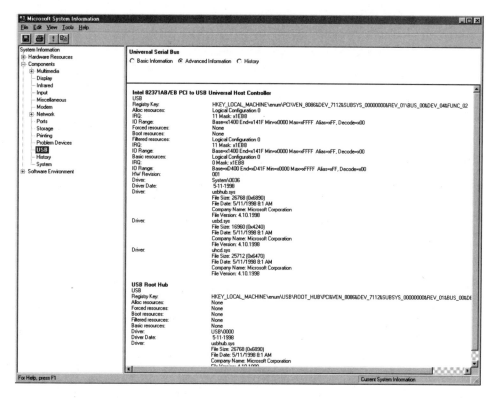

Figure 1-19 Typical *Components* report for the *USB* system.

Running Tasks at the moment, check the *Startup Programs* loaded at boot time, determine any software-generated *System Hooks,* and find a complete database of *OLE Registration* (including .INF and Registry entries). Figure 1-20 shows a typical report of *32-bit Modules Loaded* in the system.

NOTE The version numbers and date entries listed for each module make it very convenient to identify old files that may need updating.

System Information Tools

In addition to a wealth of detailed information, *System Information* also provides several powerful tools that can help you review and evaluate that information. When you click the *Tools* entry on the *System Information* menu bar, you'll be able to access the following features:

> *Windows Report Tool.* Here's a handy tool when you need to check in with the PC manufacturer's technical support, but aren't quite sure

Microsoft System Information

File   Edit   View   Tools   Help

System Information
- ⊞ Hardware Resources
- ⊞ Components
- ⊟ Software Environment
  - ⊟ Drivers
    - Kernel Drivers
    - MS-DOS Drivers
    - User-Mode Drivers
  - **16-bit Modules Loaded**
  - **32-bit Modules Loaded**
  - Running Tasks
  - Startup Programs
  - System Hooks
  - ⊟ OLE Registration
    - INI File
    - Registry

Name	Version	Manufacturer	Description	Path	Date
USER32.DLL	4.10.1998	Microsoft Corporation	Win32 USER32 core component	C:\WINDOWS\SYSTEM\USER32...	4/29/98 4:03:
GDI32.DLL	4.10.1998	Microsoft Corporation	Win32 GDI core component	C:\WINDOWS\SYSTEM\GDI32.DLL	4/29/98 4:24:
ADVAPI32.DLL	4.80.1675	Microsoft Corporation	Win32 ADVAPI32 core component	C:\WINDOWS\SYSTEM\ADVAPI3...	4/29/98 4:03:
KERNEL32.DLL	4.10.1998	Microsoft Corporation	Win32 Kernel core component	C:\WINDOWS\SYSTEM\KERNEL...	4/29/98 4:25:
MPR.DLL	4.10.1998	Microsoft Corporation	WIN32 Network Interface DLL	C:\WINDOWS\SYSTEM\MPR.DLL	4/29/98 4:03:
MSNP32.DLL	4.10.1998	Microsoft Corporation	Network provider for Microsoft netw...	C:\WINDOWS\SYSTEM\MSNP32...	4/29/98 4:03:
MSNET32.DLL	4.10.1998	Microsoft Corporation	Microsoft 32-bit Network API Library	C:\WINDOWS\SYSTEM\MSNET3...	4/29/98 4:03:
NWNP32.DLL	4.00.950	Microsoft Corporation	Network provider for Novell NetWare	C:\WINDOWS\SYSTEM\NWNP32...	6/30/95 4:56:
NWNET32.DLL	4.00.950	Microsoft Corporation	32-bit NW API library	C:\WINDOWS\SYSTEM\NWNET...	6/30/95 4:56:
RNANP.DLL	4.10.1998	Microsoft Corporation	Dial-Up Networking Notifier	C:\WINDOWS\SYSTEM\RNANP...	4/29/98 4:04:
MPREXE.EXE	4.10.1998	Microsoft Corporation	WIN32 Network Interface Service P...	C:\WINDOWS\SYSTEM\MPREXE.	4/23/98 2:19:
MPRSERV.DLL	4.10.1998	Microsoft Corporation	Multinet Router	C:\WINDOWS\SYSTEM\MPRSER...	4/29/98 4:03:
MSPWL32.DLL	4.10.1998	Microsoft Corporation	Password list management library	C:\WINDOWS\SYSTEM\MSPWL3...	4/29/98 4:03:
S2LUCP1.CPL	1.3.0.17	Symantec Corporation	LiveUpdate Manager	C:\WINDOWS\SYSTEM\S2LUC...	8/13/97 10:4E
VERSION.DLL	4.10.1998	Microsoft Corporation	Win32 VERSION core component	C:\WINDOWS\SYSTEM\VERSIO...	4/29/98 4:05:
MAIN.CPL	4.10.1998	Microsoft Corporation	Control Panel DLL	C:\WINDOWS\SYSTEM\MAIN.CPL	4/29/98 4:05:
VERSCPL.CPL	6.10.001	Corel Corporation	CoreVersions (TM)	C:\WINDOWS\SYSTEM\VERSCP...	11/8/96 9:59:
FINDFAST.CPL	7.00.1827	Microsoft Corporation	Microsoft Find Fast Control Panel	C:\WINDOWS\SYSTEM\FINDFAS...	6/26/95 12:2(
COMDLG32.DLL	4.72.3110.2	Microsoft Corporation	Common Dialogs DLL	C:\WINDOWS\SYSTEM\COMDLG...	4/29/98 4:03:
CFGMGR32.DLL	4.10.1998	Microsoft Corporation	Configuration Manager Win32 Interf...	C:\WINDOWS\SYSTEM\CFGMGR...	4/29/98 4:24:
NTDLL.DLL	4.10.1998	Microsoft Corporation	Win32 NTDLL core component	C:\WINDOWS\SYSTEM\NTDLL.D...	4/29/98 4:03:
OLEAUT32.DLL	2.20.4122	Microsoft Corporation	Microsoft OLE 2.20 for Windows N...	C:\WINDOWS\SYSTEM\OLEAUT...	4/29/98 4:03:
URLMON.DLL	4.72.3110.6	Microsoft Corporation	OLE32 Extensions for Win32	C:\WINDOWS\SYSTEM\URLMO...	4/29/98 4:05:
WEBCHECK.DLL	4.72.3110.6	Microsoft Corporation	Web Site Monitor	C:\WINDOWS\SYSTEM\WEBCH...	4/29/98 4:05:
LINKINFO.DLL	4.10.1998	Microsoft Corporation	Windows Volume Tracking	C:\WINDOWS\SYSTEM\LINKINF...	4/29/98 4:05:
MSSHRUI.DLL	4.70.1181	Microsoft Corporation	Shell extensions for sharing	C:\WINDOWS\SYSTEM\MSSHR...	8/29/96 12:1:
SVRAPI.DLL	4.10.1998	Microsoft Corporation	32-bit common Server API library	C:\WINDOWS\SYSTEM\SVRAPI...	4/29/98 4:03:
MSWEBAPI.DLL	4.70.1181	Microsoft Corporation	Web Api	C:\WINDOWS\SYSTEM\MSWEB...	8/29/96 12:11
INFOADMN.DLL	4.70.1181	Microsoft Corporation	Internet Info Server Admin Client AP...	C:\WINDOWS\SYSTEM\INFOAD...	8/28/96 11:4E
RPCRT4.DLL	4.71.1718	Microsoft Corporation	Remote Procedure Call DLL	C:\WINDOWS\SYSTEM\RPCRT4...	4/29/98 4:03:
OLE32.DLL	4.71.1719	Microsoft Corporation	Microsoft OLE for Windows and Wi...	C:\WINDOWS\SYSTEM\OLE32.D...	4/29/98 4:03:
SHDOCVW.DLL	4.72.3110.3	Microsoft Corporation	Shell Doc Object and Control Library	C:\WINDOWS\SYSTEM\SHDOCV...	4/29/98 4:04:
SHELL32.DLL	4.72.3110.6	Microsoft Corporation	Windows Shell Common Dll	C:\WINDOWS\SYSTEM\SHELL32...	4/29/98 4:03:
EXPLORER.EXE	4.72.3110.1	Microsoft Corporation	Windows Explorer	C:\WINDOWS\EXPLORER.EXE	3/18/98 10:04
COMCTL32.DLL	4.72.3110.1	Microsoft Corporation	Custom Controls Library	C:\WINDOWS\SYSTEM\COMCTL...	4/29/98 4:03:
SHLWAPI.DLL	4.72.3110.0	Microsoft Corporation	Shell Light-weight Utility Library	C:\WINDOWS\SYSTEM\SHLWAP...	3/11/98 4:05:
SYSTRAY.EXE	4.10.1998	Microsoft Corporation	System Tray Applet	C:\WINDOWS\SYSTEM\SYSTRA...	4/29/98 3:03:
BATMETER.DLL	5.00.0319.0	Microsoft Corporation	Battery Meter Helper DLL	C:\WINDOWS\SYSTEM\BATMET...	4/29/98 4:03:
POWRPROF.DLL	5.00.0422.0	Microsoft Corporation	Power Profile Helper DLL	C:\WINDOWS\SYSTEM\POWRP...	5/4/98 7:00:3
SETUPAPI.DLL	5.00.1671.1	Microsoft Corporation	Windows NT Setup API	C:\WINDOWS\SYSTEM\SETUPA...	4/29/98 4:04:
WINSPOOLDRV	4.10.1998	Microsoft Corporation	Win32 WINSPOOL core component	C:\WINDOWS\SYSTEM\WINSPO...	4/29/98 4:03:
LZ32.DLL	4.10.1998	Microsoft Corporation	Win32 LZ32 core component	C:\WINDOWS\SYSTEM\LZ32.DLL	4/29/98 4:03:
WINNM.DLL	4.10.1998	Microsoft Corporation	System APIs for Multimedia	C:\WINDOWS\SYSTEM\WINNM...	4/29/98 4:03:
DBMGR.DLL	4.03.1998	Microsoft Corporation	Game Device Profiler Database Ma...	C:\MSINPUT\GAMING DEVICES\...	1/10/97 1:31:
GBLANG32.DLL	1.50	Microsoft Corporation	Game Device Profile Language DLL	C:\WINDOWS\SYSTEM\GBLANG...	10/24/96 7:4€
DIRECTCD.EXE	2.0a (120)	Adaptec	DirectCD Application	C:\PROGRAM FILES\CD-WRITER\...	11/26/97 5:5'
MFC42.DLL	4.21.7325	Microsoft Corporation	MFCDLL Shared Library - Retail Ver...	C:\WINDOWS\SYSTEM\MFC42.D...	11/22/97 12:4
MSVCRT.DLL	5.00.7128	Microsoft Corporation	Microsoft (R) C Runtime Library	C:\WINDOWS\SYSTEM\MSVCRT...	5/9/97 11:03:
UDFRW.LIB.DLL	2.0a (120)	Adaptec	DirectCD Rewritable Library	C:\PROGRAM FILES\CD-WRITER\...	11/26/97 5:5'
CDUDF.LIB.DLL	2.0a (120)	Adaptec	DirectCD Library	C:\PROGRAM FILES\CD-WRITER\...	11/26/97 5:5'

Current System Information

For Help, press F1

Figure 1-20 Typical *Software Environment* report for 32-bit Modules Loaded.

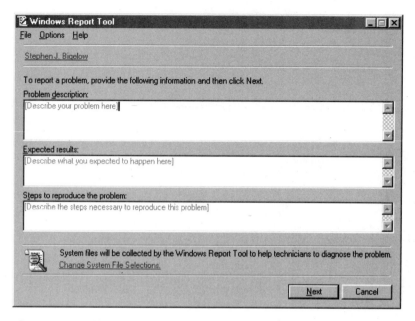

Figure 1-21   The Windows 98 *Report Tool.*

just what information you need to have on hand. The Windows *Report Tool* (Figure 1-21) allows you to describe the problem in detail (along with your expected results and method of duplicating the problem), then includes the necessary system information based on the *context* of your problem description. Once technical support folks receive your Windows Report, they can look at your relevant system information and work with you to resolve the problem.

System File Checker. The *System File Checker* (Figure 1-22) can be used to verify the integrity of your operating system files, restore them if necessary (i.e., if they are corrupted), and extract compressed files—such as drivers—from your installation disks. This is a handy tool for keeping operating system and driver files up to date. You can also have the *System File Checker* back up the existing files before restoring the original files or customize search criteria based on folder and file extensions.

Registry Checker. The Registry is one of the essential foundations of proper Windows 98 operation. If there's a problem with the Registry files, the system may not function properly—it may not even boot. Your system always keeps a backup copy of the Registry files

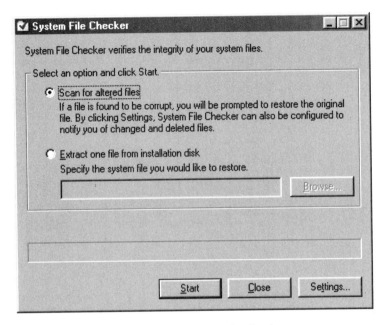

Figure 1-22 The Windows 98 *System File Checker.*

(including user account information, protocol bindings, software program settings, and user preferences) and you can use that backup copy if your current Registry ever encounters a problem. Each time you restart your computer, the *Registry Checker* automatically scans your Registry. If a problem is detected, *Registry Checker* automatically replaces the Registry with the backup copy.

Automatic Skip Driver Agent. Some software installations (especially new device driver installations) can prevent Windows from running properly and sometimes prevent Windows from running at all. Isolating and disabling such troublesome software has traditionally been a difficult hit-and-miss proposition that required tedious device removals, cumbersome searches of .INI files, or risky editing of the Registry. Windows 98 introduces the *Automatic Skip Driver Agent* (ASD), which identifies failures that cause Windows 98 to stop responding and marks those troublesome files so they are bypassed on subsequent startups. All devices that have failed to start are listed by ASD. You can use ASD to enable any device previously disabled by ASD and Windows 98 will attempt to use the device on the next startup attempt. If the device continues to fail, your computer will stop responding. But when you restart your computer again, ASD will prevent that operation from running, allowing the PC to start.

Dr. Watson. There's a tremendous amount of software written for Windows platforms—but not all of it works properly (or works together). In many cases, software combinations can cause the system to misbehave or crash. *Dr. Watson* (Figure 1-23) is a diagnostic tool that takes a "snapshot" of your system whenever a software-related fault occurs—it intercepts software faults, identifies the software that caused the problem, and provides a detailed description of the cause. *Dr. Watson* for Windows 98 can usually diagnose the problem and suggest a course of action. When you select *Dr. Watson* from the *Tools* menu, it loads into the *System Tray,* but it does not run. To activate *Dr. Watson,* click its icon in the *System Tray* and select *Dr. Watson* from the pop-up menu. This will take the "snapshot" of your system and generate the detailed diagnosis, as in Figure 1-23. You can also exit *Dr. Watson* from that pop-up menu.

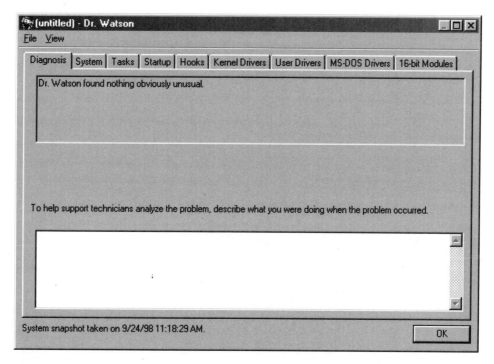

Figure 1-23 The Windows 98 *Dr. Watson* report.

NOTE *Dr. Watson* is not loaded by default. To launch *Dr. Watson* automatically each time the PC starts, create a shortcut in your Startup group to \WINDOWS\DRWATSON.EXE.

> *System Configuration Utility.* When problems arise with a Windows configuration, you typically need to make adjustments to .INI files using editors such as Notepad or SYSEDIT. Not only is this process tedious, but it often introduced errors if you typed incorrectly. The Windows 98 *System Configuration Utility* (MSCONFIG.EXE) automates that tedious, time-consuming, error-prone troubleshooting by allowing you to modify the system configuration through the use of categorized check boxes—reducing the risk of the typing errors of ordinary editors. The *System Configuration Utility* (Figure 1-24) also can create a backup copy of your system files before you begin troubleshooting.

NOTE Always back up your current system configuration files with MSCONFIG before troubleshooting begins, to ensure that any changes made with the *System Configuration Utility* are reversible. Click the *General* tab, click *Create Backup,* and then click *OK.*

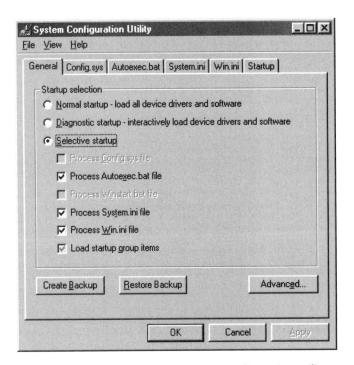

Figure 1-24 The Windows 98 *System Configuration Utility.*

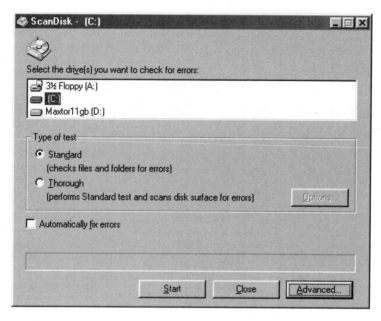

Figure 1-25 The Windows 98 *ScanDisk* dialog.

ScanDisk. File errors on a disk can cause serious problems with Windows or its applications. ScanDisk (Figure 1-25) checks your hard disk for logical and physical errors. ScanDisk can then repair the damaged areas. The version of ScanDisk used with Windows 98 supports both FAT16 and FAT32 partitions.

NOTE When using FAT32, be sure to use the version of ScanDisk that accompanies Windows 98. Disk tools that are not designed for FAT32 partitions can damage the disk and result in serious data loss.

Version Conflict Manager. During the installation of new software (including Windows 98), it's possible that older versions of software may be detected and replaced with newer versions—this is perfectly normal. The older versions are backed up and saved on your hard disk. If you have conflicts with your system files or software files after you install an application, the Windows 98 *Version Conflict Manager* (Figure 1-26) is used to restore a backed-up file. The *Version Conflict Manager* lists all your backup files, the dates they were backed up, and the version numbers of both backup and

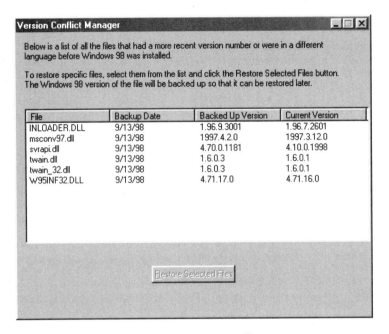

Figure 1-26 The Windows 98 *Version Conflict Manager.*

current files. When you restore a backed-up file, the current version is then backed up (so both versions remain available). This offers technicians a powerful tool for adjusting driver versions to fix compatibility problems that often crop up as newly updated files mix with older ones.

Plug-and-Play Under
DOS and Windows 3.1x

As you learned in the first section, a Plug-and-Play computer system requires *three* essential elements: (1) a Plug-and-Play BIOS (and motherboard), (2) a Plug-and-Play operating system, and (3) one or more Plug-and-Play devices. However, DOS and Windows 3.1x represent a special problem for today's computers because they are *not* Plug-and-Play–compliant operating systems. The result is that neither DOS nor Windows 3.1x recognizes the presence of PnP hardware devices, thus failing to assign the resources necessary to use them. For example, if you're using a PnP sound card under DOS, you will probably not get any sound during game play. Whereas most of today's PCs have forgone the use of DOS and Windows 3.1x in favor of Windows 95 and Windows 98, a vast number of computer users continue to operate their favorite games and utilities under DOS—but have trouble enabling the installed PnP devices. If you have (or work on) such "classic" systems, there is a workaround that *can* support Plug-and-Play functionality through DOS and Windows 3.1x (as well as the native DOS mode of Windows 95/98).

Enabling PnP in the Real-Mode

Although Windows 95 and Windows 98 are designed to be a platform for PnP devices, DOS and Windows 3.1x cannot automatically identify and configure PnP devices without additional software drivers. This makes it difficult to use many PnP devices under DOS, but with the proliferation of DOS games and other applications still in service, PnP support is unquestionably a necessity. In other cases, older hardware platforms may lack the support to fully implement a PnP system (such as older BIOS). This part of the chapter examines the techniques used to implement PnP support under DOS and Windows 3.x.

If you do not have access to a PnP operating system (i.e., you're using DOS or Windows 3.1x), you will need to install a PnP *configuration manager* (or *configuration driver*) in CONFIG.SYS, which will perform resource allocation and configuration for a PnP device. A PnP configuration manager determines the resource settings of all your system devices and legacy cards, configures PnP cards, and provides relevant configuration information to other drivers or applications that access your PnP cards. By contrast, a PnP *configuration utility* allows you to view, enter, or change the resource settings of the PnP and legacy cards in your system—the new or changed settings are then used by the PnP configuration driver to configure new PnP cards. For example, the PnP driver for an Ensoniq Soundscape board is DWCFGMG.SYS entered into a CONFIG.SYS command line. The corresponding PnP utility for that Ensoniq board is SSINIT.EXE, which is entered into an AUTOEXEC.BAT command line.

THE PnP CONFIGURATION MANAGER

A PnP configuration manager must be loaded in the CONFIG.SYS file. For Creative Labs PnP devices, the Creative PnP Configuration Manager (CTCM) would load the driver CTCM.EXE in a command line such as:

```
device=c:\ctcmdir\ctcm.exe
```

where `c:\ctcmdir` is the directory where you have installed CTCM. This CTCM statement must be placed before *all* the statements that load other low-level device drivers (such as CTSB16.SYS and SBIDE.SYS) so that your Creative PnP cards will be configured *before* these device drivers try to use them. For an Ensoniq Soundscape sound board, the PnP configuration driver would be installed such as:

```
device=c:\plugplay\drivers\dos\dwcfgmg.sys
```

In most cases, an automated installation routine (from a floppy diskette accompanying the new device) will copy the PnP files to your hard drive and make any necessary changes to your CONFIG.SYS file before rebooting. But if you have to install the software manually, make sure to place the driver command line(s) for each PnP device *after* the PnP configuration manager.

THE PnP CONFIGURATION UTILITY

A PnP configuration utility is loaded in the AUTOEXEC.BAT file—it is this utility that actually configures and initializes the PnP device. For Creative Labs PnP devices, the Creative PnP Configuration Utility (CTCU) is entered in the AUTOEXEC.BAT command line(s) such as:

```
set CTCM=C:\ctcmdir
C:\ctcmdir\CTCU /S /W=C:\windows
```

where `C:\ctcmdir` and `C:\windows` are the directories where your CTCM, CTCU, and Windows 3.x files are installed, respectively. For an Ensoniq Soundscape sound board, a typical entry would appear similar to:

```
set sndscape=c:\sndscape
lh c:\sndscape\ssinit /I
```

Once again, most PnP products will come with an automated installation routine on diskette. But when you are troubleshooting a defective installation or performing a manual installation, the format shown previously can help you avoid problems.

BLASTER VARIABLES AND PnP

When configuring a PnP sound board, you will usually have to deal with a BLASTER variable in the AUTOEXEC.BAT file. For legacy sound cards, the BLASTER variable includes fixed settings for address, interrupt, and DMA information such as:

```
set BLASTER=A220 I5 D1 T1
```

With a PnP installation, however, the BLASTER variable is redefined to "X-out" the interrupt and DMA entries as illustrated below:

```
set BLASTER=A220 IXX DX T1
```

The actual values for interrupt and DMA will be entered when the PnP configuration utility runs.

POTENTIAL PROBLEMS WITH GENERIC PnP CONFIGURATION SOFTWARE

There are a number of "generic" PnP driver/utility sets designed to support a wide range of PnP devices under DOS or Windows 3.1x. One of the most popular is the *Intel Configuration Manager* (ICM) and *ISA Configuration Utility* (ICU)—both developed by Intel Corporation. In fact, this software may already be installed on your PC (or bundled with PnP cards). Although the idea of generic PnP software is an appealing one, such generic software is not necessarily compatible with *all* types of PnP boards on all possible PC platforms. When the software and hardware are incompatible, you will typically see one of the following error messages:

◁ Failed NVS write

◁ Failure to detect PnP BIOS machine

◁ Failure to assign new configuration to PnP card

◁ ICM may not be able to configure your PnP card properly

As a general rule, when you have only one or two PnP devices in the system, you should use the manufacturer-specific software that accompanies a PnP device rather than "generic" PnP software.

NOTE ISA configuration utilities (ICUs) are designed for ISA-based systems only. Do NOT install an ICU on an EISA-based system—use the EISA Configuration Utility (ECU) instead.

POTENTIAL PROBLEMS WITH MANUFACTURER'S PnP SOFTWARE

Although manufacturer-specific PnP software will generally provide excellent service, there are some potential limitations to keep in mind. When you use a non-PnP operating system such as DOS or Windows 3.1x (and you do not have a PnP BIOS), your PnP card works like a software-configurable card. In such a situation, the PnP driver needs to know which resources have been reserved by all the legacy cards, PnP cards, and system devices in your system *before* it can allocate conflict-free resources to your new PnP card. Normally, the PnP driver can "see" all the resource settings, but you may need to use the PnP utility to enter the resource settings of all the legacy cards in your PC.

You may still encounter hardware conflicts if the resource settings specified through a PnP utility are incomplete or wrong. If this happens, use the configuration utility to select a different group of resources for the PnP card that caused the conflict. You may need to try a few combinations until you find one that works. This can be tedious, but it is easier than the traditional method of changing DIP switches or jumpers.

HANDLING PnP CONFIGURATION ISSUES

Real-mode PnP configuration managers and utilities allow you to use PnP devices in the DOS or Windows 3.1x environment. In many cases, this real-mode support for PnP works adequately, but there are several issues that can arise that you should know how to deal with:

Choosing between the PnP BIOS, PnP software, or PnP OS. There are a number of PC setups that allow you to configure a PnP device based on the PnP BIOS, the PnP driver/utility software, or the PnP operating system. When you are faced with such a choice, it is often better to use the PnP software or operating system *rather* than the BIOS. Set the BIOS so that it will *not* configure PnP devices. The reason is that a BIOS does not have any way of knowing how legacy devices are configured, so allowing the BIOS to configure a "mixed" system (with legacy and PnP devices) introduces an excellent chance for hardware conflicts.

NOTE For "pure" system configurations (containing all PnP devices) you can choose to let the PnP BIOS configure PnP devices.

Upgrading a PnP system to Windows 95/98. You may have a system with PnP devices that is running with PnP configuration driver and utility software under DOS or Windows 3.1x. When Windows 95/98 is installed, it should recognize the PnP device(s) during the hardware detection phase of the installation, then install the proper software for dealing with the device(s) under Windows 95 or 98. At the same time, Windows 95/98 should "remark-out" (a.k.a. REM-out) the real-mode driver and utility software entries under CON-FIG.SYS and AUTOEXEC.BAT. Disabling these real-mode drivers can cause a problem when returning to the DOS mode later, but you can reenable the software by removing the REM statements and rebooting.

Replacing generic PnP software with manufacturer-specific software.
If there is already generic software used to initialize and run your
PnP device(s), that software should be disabled *before* installing
manufacturer-specific software. You can do this by placing the
REM statement before the generic software's command lines in
CONFIG.SYS and AUTOEXEC.BAT—then rebooting. It is not
necessary to remove generic PnP software files from the system.

The system hangs or reboots whenever the driver software loads. The
upper memory area (UMA) of your PnP BIOS machine is probably
mapped by EMM386 using the HIGHSCAN option (and thus can
get corrupted easily). When memory corruption occurs, CTCM (or
other DOS PnP software) will not work properly. Your system may
then hang or reboot whenever you load CTCM. To resolve this
problem, remove the HIGHSCAN option in the EMM386 statement in the CONFIG.SYS file. For example, change the statement:

```
device=c:\dir\emm386.exe highscan
```

to

```
device=c:\dir\emm386.exe
```

where `c:\dir` is the directory in which your EMM386 utility is
installed.

Installing Plug-and-Play Support

When you install a PnP device under an operating system such as Windows
95, the device will be detected, the resources assigned automatically, and
the device will operate once the necessary drivers are installed. Under DOS,
Windows 3.1x, and the MS-DOS mode of Windows 95/98, you will need
to install and configure a Plug-and-Play configuration manager and configuration utility. For the purposes of this chapter, we consider the installation
and setup process for Creative Labs PnP software: the Creative PnP Configuration Manager (CTCM) and Creative PnP Configuration Utility
(CTCU).

NOTE Always review any README file contained on the installation diskette before
attempting to install PnP software.

BASIC INSTALLATION

The PnP manager and utility software will come on a diskette with an automatic installation routine. Simply insert the diskette in the floppy drive and type:

```
C:\> a:install        <Enter>
```

If you use a floppy drive other than A:, substitute that drive letter instead; then follow the instructions displayed on the screen to complete the installation process. When the installation is complete, you should have the CTCM added to the CONFIG.SYS file such as:

```
device=c:\ctcm\ctcm.exe
```

Of course, you may select another directory rather than c:\ctcm during the installation.

If the automatic installation fails for any reason, you can also add this command line to CONFIG.SYS manually. Check the CONFIG.SYS file and verify that the ctcm command line is placed *before* all other low-level device drivers that must use the PnP device such as CTSB16.SYS (the actual sound card driver) or SBIDE.SYS (the sound card's IDE interface driver). This ensures the PnP card will be successfully configured *before* other device drivers attempt to use that PnP card.

After the installation, you will also add the following CTCU lines added to your AUTOEXEC.BAT file:

```
SET CTCM=c:\ctcm
c:\ctcm\ctcu /s /w=c:\windows
```

The term c:\ctcm is the directory where the CTCM and CTCU utilities are installed, and c:\windows is the directory where Windows 3.1x is installed. If these directories are different, you may need to manually adjust the command lines in your particular AUTOEXEC.BAT file.

Once the installation is complete, CTCM and CTCU will run each time you boot the system. CTCM will check for and configure any Creative Labs PnP cards. CTCU will run silently in the background to update any parameters needed by the Creative Labs and Windows drivers. The CTCU will also update the BLASTER environment variable if a Creative Labs sound card is detected in the system.

NOTE When configuring PnP cards in the Windows 95/98 DOS mode, only CTCM is required because CTCM can obtain both legacy (non-PnP) and PnP settings from Windows 95/98.

NOTE The Creative Labs PnP software is designed specifically for Creative Labs cards. You may also have other PnP software installed on the system such as the Intel Configuration Manager (ICM) and ISA Configuration Utility (ICU).

RUNNING CTCM MANUALLY

Normally, you should not have to reconfigure your PnP card(s) after the system boots, but you can do that by running the CTCM from your DOS prompt (be sure to exit to the DOS mode if you're in Windows 3.1x or Windows 95/98). Simply change to the directory containing CTCM (i.e., c:\ctcm), type CTCM and press <Enter>. The CTCM will run and configure your PnP card(s), then update the BLASTER environment variable.

RUNNING CTCU MANUALLY

In most cases, the CTCU runs silently in the background to track resources used by legacy devices and to allocate remaining resources to PnP devices, so you generally do not have to run the CTCU manually. However, there are several circumstances where you should work directly with CTCU:

◁ The PnP device does not work because the assigned resources are not appropriate. For example, a PnP device is set to use high DMA, but your system doesn't support high DMA.

◁ You add a legacy card and need to reserve resources for which the legacy card has been configured.

◁ You change the configuration of a legacy card and need to change the reserved resources.

◁ You remove a legacy card from the system and need to free the resources previously reserved for that card.

NOTE CTCU does not use the resource list used by Intel's ICM. If you have ICM installed, do not use CTCU to change or disable device settings—use the ICU instead.

To start the CTCU interface, exit Windows 3.1x, 95, or 98 to the DOS mode, then change to the directory containing CTCU (i.e., c:\ctcm). Type CTCU and press <Enter>. The CTCU main menu will appear (Figure 2-1). From the main menu, you can control PnP cards, legacy cards, system devices, and PCI devices.

Figure 2-1   The CTCU main menu.

NOTE   **You can use the mouse or keyboard to navigate in CTCU.**

PnP CARDS

Selecting the *PnP Cards* menu opens the *Plug-and-Play* dialog (Figure 2-2), which you can use to view the resource settings of the PnP cards in your system (and change the settings of Creative Labs PnP cards). You may select a card from this list to display a list of logical devices on that particular card. To review the resources for a PnP device, select a card and click the *Resources* button, which opens a *Resources* dialog (Figure 2-3). The settings shown may include input/output (I/O) ranges, interrupts (IRQs), Direct Memory Access (DMA) channels, and 32-bit memory ranges (depending on the PnP card you have and its selected configuration). To change a resource configuration, click the down arrow next to the *Configuration* box and then select a suitable configuration that offers all the settings that your card needs. To disable a logical device, click the *Disable* checkbox. A mark will appear in the box and CTCM will not configure that device the next time it runs.

Reconfiguring Resources

To view or change a resource setting, select the setting and click the *Reconfigure* button in the *Resources* dialog. Depending on the setting you have chosen, you can alter the I/O range, IRQ, DMA channel, or memory range.

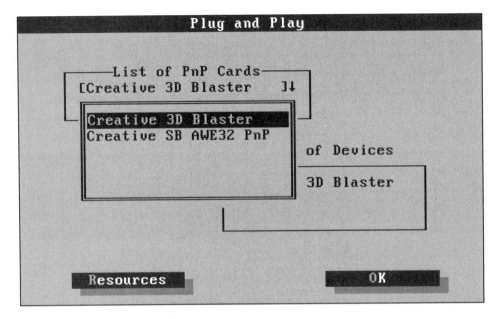

Figure 2-2 The CTCU *PnP* dialog.

The *I/O Range* dialog (Figure 2-4) displays the current I/O resource setting and offers a list of possible alternatives. To change this setting, select a suitable setting from the list and click the *OK* button. The *Interrupt* dialog (Figure 2-5) displays the current interrupt resource setting and shows list of other available settings. To change the interrupt, select another interrupt

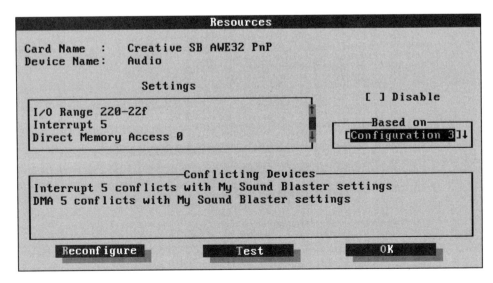

Figure 2-3 The CTCU *Resources* dialog.

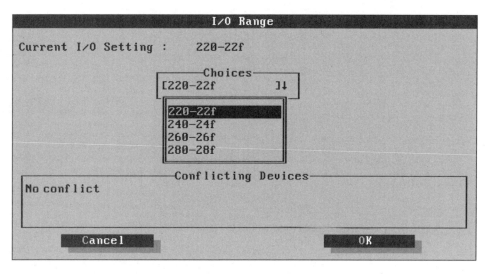

Figure 2-4 The CTCU *I/O Range* dialog.

from the list and click the *OK* button. The *Direct Memory Access* dialog (Figure 2-6) displays the current DMA resource setting and a list of possible alternatives. To change the DMA setting, select another DMA channel from the list and click the *OK* button. The *Memory Range* dialog (Figure 2-7) displays the current 32-bit memory range(s) used by the device and shows a list of other possible settings. To change a memory range, select another range from the list and click the *OK* button.

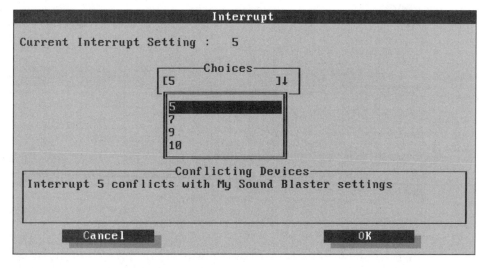

Figure 2-5 The CTCU *Interrupt* dialog.

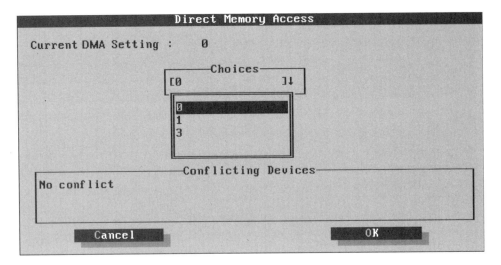

Figure 2-6 The CTCU *DMA* dialog.

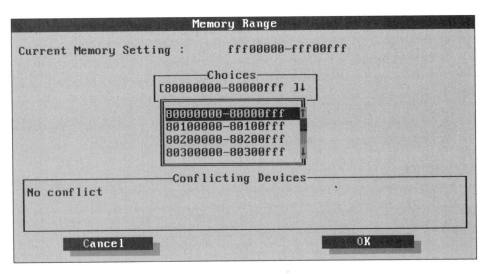

Figure 2-7 The CTCU *Memory Range* dialog.

NOTE Each of these resource dialogs has a *Conflicting Devices* message box, which will indicate any hardware conflicts that may result from the settings you have just selected for your card.

Testing New Resources

Once you have reconfigured and saved the resource settings of your card, click the *Test* button in the *Resources* dialog. CTCU will test the setting

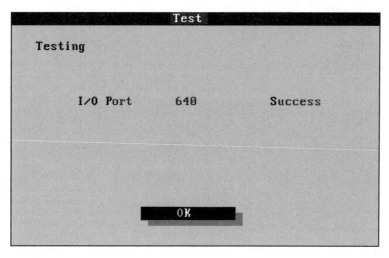

Figure 2-8 The CTCU *Test option* dialog.

allocated to your device and inform you of the outcome (Figure 2-8). If you find that the test fails, reconfigure and test the device again.

LEGACY CARDS

Since there is no way for legacy devices to report the resources they are using, it is necessary to "reserve" the resources used by all the legacy devices in your system, which prevents those resources from being assigned to PnP cards. When you select the *Legacy Cards* from the CTCU menu, the *Legacy* dialog opens (Figure 2-9) and allows you to view and change the resource reservations for any legacy devices. You should also use this menu to free reserved resources when removing a legacy device from the system. The *Legacy* dialog provides five controls: *View All, View, Add, Remove,* and *Change.*

The *View All* dialog (Figure 2-10) provides a convenient summary of all the resources that have been reserved in the system. These resources are grouped by type and displayed in four boxes: (1) Input/Output range (I/O), (2) Interrupt Request line (IRQ), (3) Direct Memory Access channel (DMA), and (4) 32-bit memory range (Mem). If you select the *View* button, the *View* dialog (Figure 2-11) opens to display the resources reserved for the selected legacy device. Clicking the *Add* button opens the *Add* dialog (Figure 2-12), where you can enter details for a new (or existing) legacy

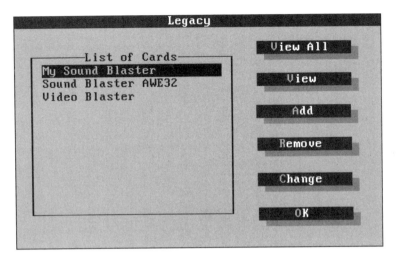

Figure 2-9 The CTCU *Legacy* dialog.

device in the system. When adding a device, you *must* enter the card's name in the *Card Name* field. To remove a selected card's settings, select the *Remove* button. After the settings are deleted, you can then shut down the PC and physically remove the card from the system. To reinstall that same card later, you'll need to *Add* the card again (or check the *Card Removed* box in the *Change* dialog). Finally, you can adjust the resources reserved for a legacy card by opening the *Change* dialog (Figure 2-13).

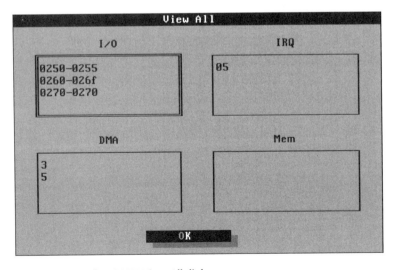

Figure 2-10 The CTCU *View All* dialog.

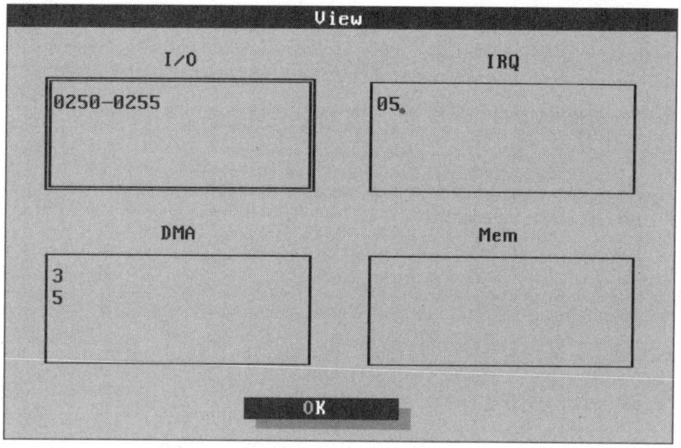

Figure 2-11 The CTCU *View* dialog.

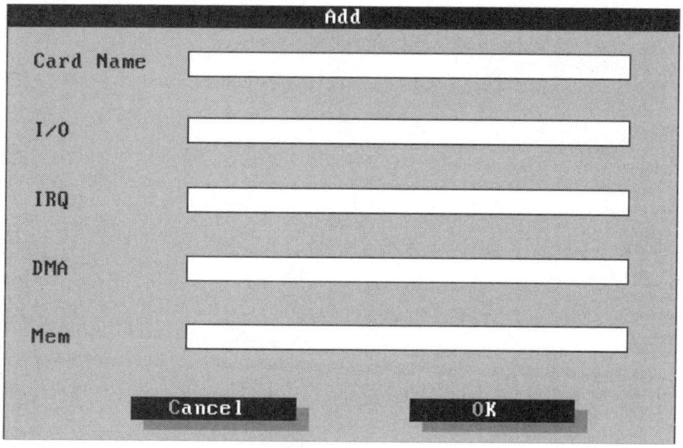

Figure 2-12 The CTCU *Add* dialog.

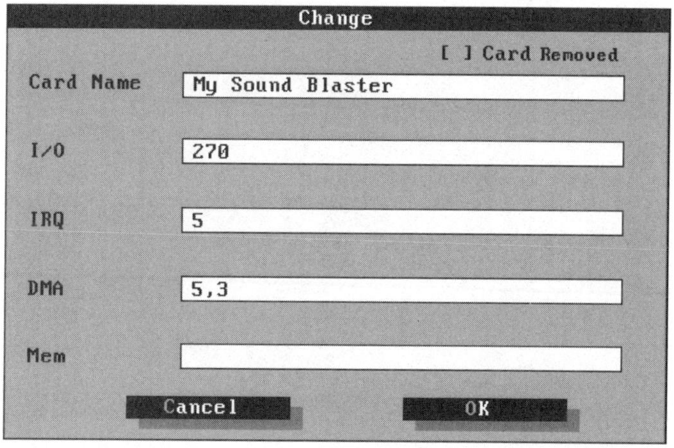

Figure 2-13 The CTCU *Change* dialog.

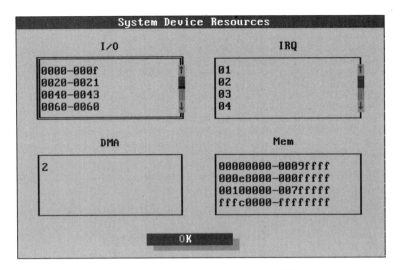

Figure 2-14 The CTCU *System Device Resources* dialog.

SYSTEM DEVICES

When planning resource assignments, it's often helpful to know the resources assigned to system devices. You can use the *System Devices* menu to open the *System Devices* dialog (Figure 2-14). This dialog appears similar to the *View All* dialog under *Legacy Cards,* but each of the four resource areas lists resources used by the system rather than by expansion cards. You cannot change the resources reserved for system devices.

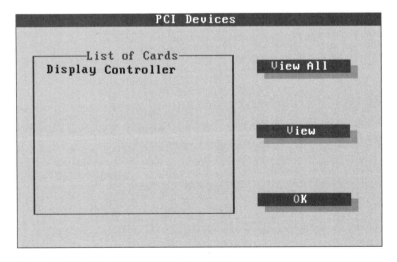

Figure 2-15 The CTCU *PCI Devices* dialog.

PCI DEVICES

You may also need to review the resource settings assigned to your system's PCI cards. The *PCI Devices* menu will open the *PCI Devices* dialog (Figure 2-15), which allows you to view—but not change—the PCI device resources. Using the *PCI Devices* dialog, you can either view all the resources used by all PCI devices in the system (the *View All* button) or view the resources for a specific PCI device only (the *View* button).

Tips for Installing PnP Configuration Software

Almost all PnP configuration software is installed automatically using an installation routine on a floppy disk included with your new PnP device. In most cases, the automated installation routine works properly, but there are some situations where trouble can arise:

Careful for multipath startup files. If your system uses a multipath CONFIG.SYS file, the installation routine might corrupt the CONFIG.SYS file by duplicating certain sections of the file, then introducing errors to those sections. Always check the CONFIG .SYS file for errors before rebooting the system. If there is a problem, restore the original CONFIG.SYS file, then manually add the proper configuration manager command line to the beginning of the file such as:

```
device=c:\plugplay\drivers\dos\dwcfgmg.sys
```

Careful for the boot drive. Most automated PnP installers assume that your C: drive is the system's boot drive (and that your CONFIG .SYS file is located in the root of the C: drive). If your boot drive is not C:, you'll need to manually move the ESCD file (i.e., ESCD.RF) to the proper root directory of your boot drive, then add the proper configuration manager command line to the CONFIG.SYS file on that boot drive. For example, utilities such as the Stacker disk compression program can change the boot drive from C: to another drive—such as H:.

Use the same PnP directory when upgrading. If you have already installed one version (DOS or Windows 3.1x) of the PnP software, be sure to install any other version in the *same* directory as the first version. If you use a different directory, the system configuration information displayed when you invoke the Windows ICU might look different from that displayed when you invoke the DOS ICU.

TIPS FOR DOS INSTALLATIONS

Keep in mind the following for DOS installations:

Run from the native DOS mode. Do not attempt to install PnP software from an MS-DOS window. Instead, install after booting directly to DOS.

Check for free memory. When installing PnP software for DOS, be sure that you have enough free conventional memory (usually 488 KB or more). It may be necessary to "boot clean" from a blank bootable floppy in order to free enough memory.

Try disabling the expanded memory manager. The PnP installation routine is often incompatible with expanded memory managers (i.e., EMM386). It may be necessary to "boot clean" from a blank bootable floppy in order to avoid potential memory manager problems.

Check for original file permissions. When reinstalling or upgrading PnP software, make sure that the file permissions have not been changed to "read-only"; otherwise, the installation routine may fail.

TIPS FOR WINDOWS 3.1x INSTALLATIONS

For Windows 3.1x installations:

Disable any screen savers. Problems have been known to occur when Windows screen savers become active during ICU setup. Just to make sure that you don't encounter problems due to the screen saver, disable the screen saver before installation (you can reenable the screen saver again later).

Disable your antivirus program. ICU installation under Windows will almost certainly encounter problems while running Vsafe under

DOS 6.0. Try disabling the features that check and protect executable files (you can reenable those features later) or temporarily shut down the antivirus program.

Do not delete previous versions of the Windows ICU. Problems are known to occur if a previously installed ICU version was deleted. The Windows installer will not place the proper device driver entries into the /windows/system.ini file if there is already an entry in the WIN.INI file such as:

```
[ConfigMgr]
Installed=yes
```

Delete this entry from the WIN.INI file and run the Windows installation again.

Typical PnP Software Issues

Although most versions of the configuration manager and utility are thoroughly tested, they are certainly not perfect, and it is common for problems to arise—especially with older 386 and 486 systems, which offered varying levels of Plug-and-Play support. The following list denotes many of the known issues encountered with configuration managers and ICUs. This part of the chapter should help you spot potential problem areas in the configuration manager and ICU.

Configuration shifts after moving PCI card resources. When configuration manager or ICU software moves the resources assigned to a PCI card, the software allocates memory resources "as needed" (according to the run-time memory requirements of the PCI card). If the resources that are moved are *smaller* than the PCI card's memory requirements at boot time, the BIOS will try to reallocate the PCI card resources the next time the system boots, thus potentially causing a configuration different from that assigned by the PnP software.

Count the PCI bus slots. Configuration manager and ICU software typically does not support more than one PCI bus slot. If you're using more than one PCI device in the system at any given time, you may have troubles using configuration software to assign resources.

Turn off ROM shadowing. PnP software cannot always deal very well with shadowing, so there may be incompatible devices attempting to shadow their ROM in the same memory region. You should have *all* expansion devices use the same mode (shadowed or not shadowed)—as a rule, "not shadowed" is the preferred mode. You can control ROM shadowing through the system's CMOS Setup.

8-bit ISA cards can be trouble. Configuration manager and ICU software cannot differentiate between 8-bit ISA (i.e., XT slot) and 16-bit (i.e., AT slot) devices, and this allows both types of devices to use conflicting memory space in the same 128-KB memory block. This results in hardware conflicts, such that devices will refuse to work. Remove any 8-bit devices in the system and replace them with 16-bit devices.

GENERAL CONFIGURATION MANAGER SOFTWARE ISSUES

Use later versions of EMM386. When a PnP configuration manager executes a 32-bit I/O read to a Plug-and-Play BIOS, the system may often hang up or reset. This occurs when using older versions of PnP configuration software, as well as older versions of EMM386 (prior to version 4.49). If you cannot obtain later PnP configuration software from your device vendor, you can download a later version of EMM386.EXE from Microsoft (*www.microsoft.com*), or update your DOS version outright (which will have a later version of HIMEM and EMM386).

Disable the use of MEMMAKER under DOS. The MEMMAKER utility provided with DOS 6.21 and 6.22 is known to cause system reboots when PnP software is installed. If MEMMAKER's "aggressive" memory scanning option is selected, the HIGHSCAN parameter is added to the EMM386 command line in CONFIG.SYS. This option often causes EMM386 to map memory into space used by the system BIOS (i.e., F000:0000h to F000:FFFFh). In most cases, the reboots occur when the configuration management software begins its initialization (though this may vary from system to system depending on the particular system BIOS). To avoid this problem, do not select "aggressive" memory scanning with MEMMAKER or disable the use of MEMMAKER entirely.

Check where BIOS stores the ESCD. Some Plug-and-Play systems map the ESCD contents into the E000:0000h memory block. However, EMM386 does not recognize ESCD information, and usually maps memory right over the ESCD area—this corrupts the ESCD storage on your system. Contact the BIOS maker and determine the memory range where BIOS stores the ESCD, then use the "exclude" switch in your EMM386 command line to exclude that memory range from EMM386.

Check for Plug-and-Play extensions. If there are no Intel Plug-and-Play BIOS extensions, PnP boot devices are *not* reconfigured by the configuration manager software.

Check for incompatible software. Certain drivers and TSRs may conflict with the operation of your configuration manager software. Unusual system behavior or odd system delays are two typical symptoms of this problem. If you suspect a software conflict, try adding the /STATIC or ?NOVCPI switches to your DWCFGMG .SYS driver command line in CONFIG.SYS (your own PnP driver may use similar switches).

There may be problems with an ACFG BIOS. When using the /FILE switch with your configuration manager software under an ACFG BIOS, you must provide motherboard information in the ESCD.RF file; otherwise, the configuration manager cannot run. Fortunately, you really only need to use the /FILE switch when testing EISA systems.

GENERAL ICU SOFTWARE ISSUES

There may be trouble with the ICU.NDX file. When saving a system image file (i.e., "Save Image File" or "Save Image File As . . ."), the ICU.NDX index file is not updated. Unlisted cards may be listed as *Unknown Card* rather than the name you assigned to it, but the assigned resources should be saved properly. You can avoid this kind of problem by choosing the *Save* item on the *File* menu *before* you save the image file. In addition, if you copy the image file to another system, you must also copy the ICU.NDX index file.

You may encounter errors when modifying a card's function. When modifying the function of a Plug-and-Play card, you may see a conflict message that indicates the card is conflicting with itself. This normally occurs when you prepare to lock the card's resources. Try to reconfigure the card functions in a different order.

Reassigning resources to a new device may cause problems with PCI cards. When you assign resources to a new card (which were previously in use by another card), the ICU will reconfigure the PnP ISA cards first, *then* the PCI cards. However, PCI cards are restricted to specific interrupts. In some cases, this reconfiguration will fail because the configuration manager software assigns PnP ISA cards to the interrupts being used by the PCI cards—then the ICU cannot configure the PCI cards. Use the ICU to reassign the PCI cards to different interrupts, then try to configure the new device.

PnP cards may cause errors with boot functions. If a boot function on a PnP card causes a conflict error on a system *without* a PnP BIOS, you'll see one of two messages. First, you may see the message:

```
"This card will be configured when the system is rebooted"
```

This may not be true. If this message appears, there *is* a configuration that works. But since systems without a Plug-and-Play BIOS lack the ability to configure boot functions of PnP cards, the system cannot find the valid working configuration for you. Find a valid configuration and configure the PnP card manually using jumpers or a software configuration utility provided by the card maker. You might also see the error:

```
"A conflict has been detected with <conflicting_card>. The con-
flicting resource is <resource_and_value>"
```

The error might not inform you of the exact conflict keeping the card from being configured. You may need to troubleshoot and resolve the conflict manually.

Do not assign IRQ 2. The ISA architecture redirects IRQ 2 through IRQ 9. This means you *cannot* use IRQ 2—you must use IRQ 9 instead (even if IRQ 2 is listed as an available resource). The ICU will usually indicate this selection as *IRQ 9(2)*.

Avoid reserved I/O ports. The ISA architecture reserves a standard suite of resources, but the ICU sometimes mistakenly allows I/O ports 279h and A79h to be assigned. Avoid the use of ports 279h and A79h.

Resource Conflicts Under DOS

Dealing with PnP under DOS often means allocating resources for legacy devices, then assigning PnP resources for PCI cards and other devices. In many cases, this also means you'll need to troubleshoot resource conflicts between legacy cards or PCI devices vying for the same resources. Fortunately, resource conflicts are almost *always* the result of a PC upgrade gone awry. Thus, a technician can be alerted to the possibility of a system conflict by applying the *Last Upgrade* rule. The rule consists of three parts:

1. A piece of *hardware* and/or *software* has been added to the system *very* recently.

2. The trouble occurred *after* a piece of hardware and/or software was added to the system.

3. The system was working fine *before* the hardware and/or software was added.

If all three of these commonsense factors are *true,* chances are very good that you are faced with a hardware or software conflict. Unlike most other types of PC problems that tend to be specific to the faulty subassembly, conflicts usually manifest themselves as much more general and perplexing problems. The following symptoms are typical of serious hardware or software conflicts:

◁ The system locks up during initialization.

◁ The system locks up during a particular application.

◁ The system locks up when a particular device (i.e., a TWAIN scanner) is used.

◁ The system locks up randomly or without warning regardless of the application.

◁ The system may not crash, but the device that was added may not function (even though it seems properly configured). Devices that were in the system previously may still work correctly.

◁ The system may not crash, but a device or application that was working previously no longer seems to function. The newly added device (and accompanying software) may or may not work properly.

What makes these problems so generic is that the severity and frequency of a fault, as well as the point at which the fault occurs, depend on such factors as the particular *devices* that are conflicting, the *resource(s)* that are conflicting among the devices (i.e., IRQs, DMAs, or I/O addresses), and the *function* being performed by the PC when the conflict manifests itself. Since every PC is equipped and configured a bit differently, it is virtually impossible to predict a conflict's symptoms more precisely.

CONFIRMING AND RESOLVING CONFLICTS

Recognizing the possibility of a conflict is one thing, proving and correcting it is another issue entirely. However, there are some very effective tactics at your disposal. The first rule of conflict resolution is *Last In First Out* (or LIFO). The LIFO principle basically says that *the fastest means of overcoming a conflict problem is to remove the hardware or software that resulted in the conflict.* In other words, if you install board X and board Y ceases to function, board X is probably conflicting with the system, so removing board X should restore board Y to normal operation. The same concept holds true for software: If you add a new application to your system, then find that an existing application fails to work properly, the new application is likely at fault. Unfortunately, removing the offending element is not enough; you still have to install the new device or software in such a way that it will no longer conflict in the system.

NOTE DOS PnP tools such as the Creative PnP Configuration Utility (CTCU) typically provide a *Conflicting Devices* section of their resource configuration dialogs, which can sometimes help you to identify potential resource conflicts under DOS (see Figures 2-4 to 2-7).

DEALING WITH SOFTWARE CONFLICTS

There are two types of software that can cause conflicts in a typical PC: TSRs and device drivers. *TSRs* (sometimes called *pop-up utilities*) load into memory, usually during initialization, and wait for a system event (i.e., a modem ring or a keyboard "hot key" combination). There are no DOS or system rules that define how such utilities should be written. As a result, many tend to conflict with application programs (and even DOS itself). If you suspect that such a pop-up utility is causing the problem, find its reference in the AUTOEXEC.BAT file and disable it by placing the command REM in front of its command line such as:

```
REM c:\utils\newmenu.exe /A:360 /D:3
```

The REM command turns the line into a "REMark," which can easily be removed later if you choose to restore the line. Remember to reboot the computer so that your changes will take effect.

Device drivers present another potential problem. Most hardware upgrades require the addition of one or more device drivers. Such drivers are called from the CONFIG.SYS file during system initialization (or loaded with Windows) and use a series of command line parameters to specify the system resources that are being used. This is often necessary to ensure that the driver operates its associated hardware properly. If the command line options used for the device driver do not match the hardware settings (or overlap the settings of another device driver) system problems can result. If you suspect that a device driver is causing the problem, find its reference in the CONFIG.SYS file and disable it by placing the command REM in front of its command line such as:

```
REM device=c:\drivers\newdrive.sys /A:360 /I:5
```

The REM command turns the line into a "REMark," which can easily be removed later if you choose to restore the line. Remember that disabling the device driver in this fashion will prevent the associated hardware from working, but if the problem clears, you can work with the driver settings until the problem is resolved. Remember to reboot the computer so that your changes will take effect.

Finally, consider the possibility that the offending software has a bug. Try contacting the software manufacturer—there may be a fix or undocumented feature that you are unaware of. There may also be a patch or update that will solve the problem.

DEALING WITH HARDWARE CONFLICTS

A PC user recently added a CD-ROM and adapter board to his system. The installation went flawlessly using the defaults—a 10-minute job. Several days later when attempting to back up the system, the user noticed that the parallel port tape backup did not respond (although the printer that had been connected to the parallel port was working fine). The user tried booting the system from a "clean" bootable floppy disk (no CONFIG.SYS or AUTOEXEC.BAT files to eliminate the device drivers), but the problem remained. After a bit of consideration, the user powered down the system, removed the CD-ROM adapter board and booted the system from a "clean" bootable floppy disk. Sure enough, the parallel port tape backup started working again.

Stories such as this remind technicians that hardware conflicts are not always the monstrous, system-smashing mistakes that they are made out to be. In many cases, conflicts have subtle, noncatastrophic consequences. Since the CD-ROM was the last device to be added, it was the first to be removed. It took about 5 minutes to realize and remove the problem. However, *removing* the problem is only part of conflict troubleshooting—reinstalling the device *without* a conflict is the real challenge.

Ideally, the way to correct a conflict would be to alter the conflicting setting—that's dynamite in theory, but another thing in practice. the trick is that you need to know what resources are in use and which ones are free. Unfortunately, there are only two ways to find out. On the one hand, you can track down the user manual for every board in the system, then inspect each board individually to find its settings, then work accordingly. This will work (assuming you have the documentation) but it is cumbersome and time-consuming. As an alternative, you can use a resource testing tool such as the *Discovery Card* (by ForeFront Group). The *Discovery Card* plugs into a 16-bit ISA slot and uses a series of LEDs to display each IRQ and DMA channel in use. Any LED not illuminated is an available resource. It is then simply a matter of setting your expansion hardware to an IRQ and DMA channel that is not illuminated. Remember that you may have to alter the command line switches of any device drivers to reflect changes in resource assignments.

CHAPTER 3

Plug-and-Play Under Windows 95/98

Windows 95 and 98 have transformed the landscape of Plug-and-Play. The PnP software incompatibilities and resource conflict problems that were so common under DOS and Windows 3.1x are a thing of the past. Under Windows 95 and 98, PnP devices can now be detected automatically, and drivers not already present in the Windows system can easily be added from installation disks accompanying each new device. Windows 95 and 98 also provide powerful tools such as the *Device Manager,* which can be used to investigate the status of each system device, reassign resources, and check for common device problems. This chapter highlights actual step-by-step installations and explains how to manage PnP devices under Windows 95 and 98.

NOTE The steps illustrated in this chapter may vary a bit depending on the version of Windows being used and the particular device being installed (i.e., a display adapter, drive controller, modem, and so on).

Installing Legacy Devices

Legacy devices are the traditional "jumpered" devices that need to be configured manually. Under DOS, legacy devices run just fine and require no special support, but they can cause a problem under PnP operating systems such as Windows 98. Remember that a PnP system relies on the ability to *automatically* identify and assign resources to each and every device in the system. Since "legacy" devices are not designed to communicate their configuration to the operating system, there is no way for Windows 95/98 to detect the device—much less assign resources for it. This means Windows 95/98 could accidentally assign to a PnP device resources that are already in use by a legacy device. Windows 95/98 circumvents this problem by requiring you to "register" legacy devices using the *Add New Hardware* wizard under the *Control Panel*. Once a legacy device is installed and the system is rebooted, use the *Add New Hardware* wizard to "tell" Windows about the new device, and install the proper drivers for it.

AUTOMATIC LEGACY INSTALLATION

Remember that legacy devices are configured manually and cannot report their configuration to Windows 95/98 automatically. When installing new legacy hardware in the system, you must run the *Add New Hardware* wizard to register the device with Windows 98 and add the appropriate driver:

1. Click the *Start* button, highlight *Settings,* then click *Control Panel.*
2. In the *Control Panel,* double-click the *Add New Hardware* icon (Figure 3-1).
3. In the *Add New Hardware* wizard, click *Next* twice to allow for the detection of new PnP devices. When the dialog asks: "*Do you want Windows to search for your new hardware?*", select the *Yes* radio button (Figure 3-2) and click *Next* again.
4. Allow Windows 95/98 to detect the new device, then follow the instructions to install the driver(s).

MANUAL LEGACY INSTALLATION

There are many cases where the *Add New Hardware* wizard cannot detect the new legacy device. When this occurs, you'll need to rerun the *Add New Hardware* wizard, but rather than allow the wizard to check for new legacy devices manually, you'll need to enter the new device manually as shown below.

1. Click the *Start* button, highlight *Settings,* then click *Control Panel.*
2. In the *Control Panel,* double-click the *Add New Hardware* icon (Figure 3-1).

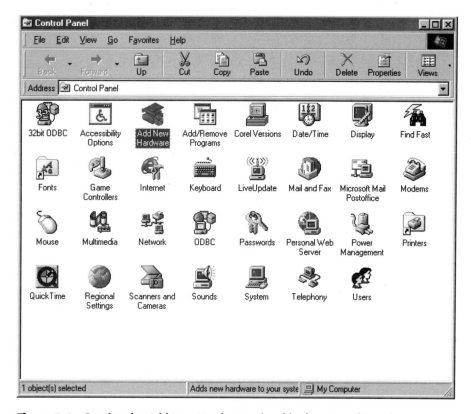

Figure 3-1   Starting the *Add New Hardware* wizard in the *Control Panel.*

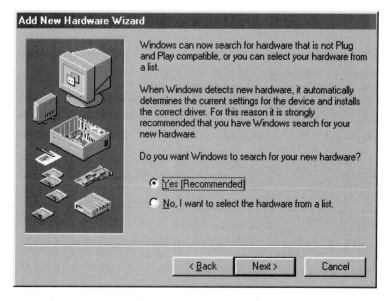

Figure 3-2   Autodetecting new legacy devices.

3. In the *Add New Hardware* wizard, click *Next* twice to allow for the detection of new PnP devices. When the dialog asks: "*Do you want Windows to search for your new hardware?*", select the "*No, I want to select the hardware from a list*" radio button (Figure 3-2) and click *Next* again.

4. You'll see a listing of device types (Figure 3-3). Highlight the type (or "class") of legacy device that you're installing (i.e., "*Sound, video, and game controllers*") and click *Next*.

5. The next dialog provides a listing of manufacturers and models (Figure 3-4). Highlight the name of the manufacturer—a corresponding list of models will appear. If you're installing that particular model, simply highlight the model and click *Next*. If you're installing a device that's *not* listed, or you're installing the drivers from an installation diskette or CD, click the *Have Disk* button.

6. The *Install from Disk* dialog appears (Figure 3-5), which allows you to select the drive and subdirectory containing the .INF file necessary to install the new device's drivers. Once you've specified the correct drive and subdirectory, click *OK* to copy the drivers to the system.

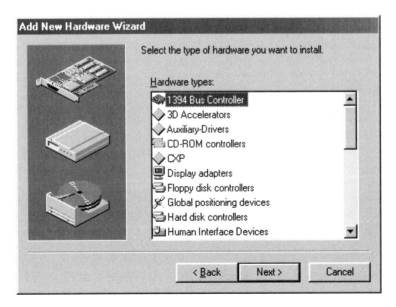

Figure 3-3 Selecting the legacy hardware type.

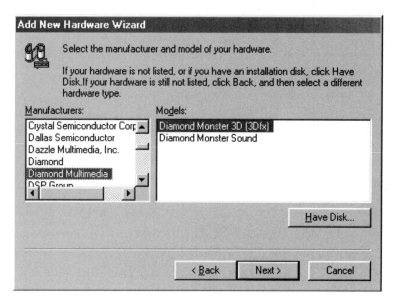

Figure 3-4   Selecting the manufacturer and model.

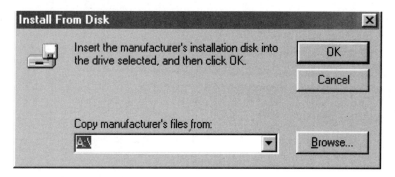

Figure 3-5   Installing new drivers from disk.

7. After the files are copied, you will probably need to restart Windows for the new drivers to take effect and enable your new device.

Installing PnP Devices

One of the great advantages of Plug-and-Play is the ability of a PC to automatically detect the installation of a new device, assign resources to the device, and install drivers to operate the device under Windows. In most cases, PnP devices are detected and installed with a minimum of fuss, but there are some important variations to the process that you should be familiar with.

Plug-and-Play devices may take many different forms: ISA cards, PCI cards, AGP cards, external modems, external drives, printers, and many other diverse devices may all be categorized as "PnP"—but all should follow the basic principles outlined in this section.

FULLY AUTOMATIC INSTALLATION

The easiest installation process is *fully automatic*. This takes place when a new PnP device is detected, and the drivers necessary to support the device are already available in the Windows environment. Many basic USB devices (such as a USB hub or mouse) are detected and installed without ever needing to copy drivers or reboot the system. However, fully automatic installations are rare because most new devices require the addition of device drivers that are included with the retail package. Even many USB devices (such as USB scanners) will require driver installations after the initial device detection.

SEMIAUTOMATIC INSTALLATION

By far, the most common installation process is *semiautomatic*. Windows detects the presence of a newly installed device, but you must specify the location of drivers (from diskette or CD) in order to copy drivers to the PC and complete the installation process. For this example, let's consider a typical PnP modem such as a US Robotics Sportster.

1. After Windows reboots, it detects your modem and provides a message that new hardware was found (as in Figure 3-6).

2. Windows then compiles a driver database. The *Add New Hardware* wizard appears and allows you to select the desired source for the driver; click *OK*:

   - *"Windows default driver"* (grayed out in this example)
   - *"Driver from disk provided by hardware manufacturer"*
   - *"Do not install a driver (Windows will not prompt you again)"*
   - *"Select from a list of alternate drivers"*

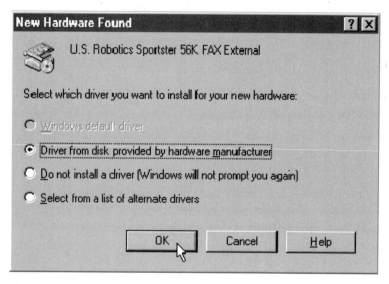

Figure 3-6 Detecting a new PnP device.

3. In most cases, you'd select the option "*Driver from disk provided by hardware manufacturer.*" The *Install from Disk* dialog will appear (Figure 3-5), where you can specify the drive and path to the device's .INF file and drivers. Click *OK* to copy the drivers and reboot the PC.

NOTE Depending on what kind of device you're installing, you may also need to make changes to other icons in the *Control Panel.* For example, when installing a new modem, you'd need to update the *Modem* icon. For a new display adapter, you'd want to update the settings in your *Display* icon, and so on. Refer to the specific installation instructions that accompany your particular device for postinstallation setup.

Alternate Installation

The installation process may appear a bit different under Windows 98. After installing a new device under Windows 98, it identifies your new device and displays the message that new hardware was found. Windows then compiles a driver database. The *Add New Hardware* wizard appears and displays a message such as "*This wizard searches for new drivers for . . .*". When you receive this message, follow the steps below:

1. Click *Next*. The wizard then asks: "*What do you want to do?*"

2. Select "*Display list of all the drivers . . .*" and click *Next*.

3. Select "*Show Compatible Hardware*" and click *Have Disk*.

4. Insert the device's installation disk or CD, then type the drive and path to the drivers. Click *OK*.

5. Click *OK* again, then click *Next*. The system will probably reboot after the driver files are copied.

NOTE If the installation process determines that files currently on the system are newer than the files to be copied, you'll be prompted to choose the file version you want. In virtually all cases, you should choose to keep the newer files.

MANUAL INSTALLATION

In a few rare cases, the Windows 95/98 system will fail to detect a new PnP device. This is *not* normal and is almost always the result of a system problem that prevents Windows from detecting the new device. You'll find that there are four typical problem areas: (1) hardware conflicts, (2) software conflicts, (3) installation problems, or (4) defective hardware. If a PnP device isn't properly detected, simply follow the checklist below:

Check for hardware conflicts. Although the PC is supposed to allocate hardware resources dynamically, it's possible that your system either is out of resources or cannot locate available resources that are within the usable range of the new device. If this happens, you may need to "massage" the installation by manually reconfiguring the resources for another device to make room for the new device or freeing resources by removing an unneeded device.

Check for software conflicts. Some PnP devices will not be detected if you had previously installed similar devices that have left traces of their drivers in the Windows Registry or .INI files. For example, the *Intel Create & Share Camera Pack* (i.e., Intel's PCI capture/modem card) will not be detected if you've previously had an *Intel Smart Video Recorder* or other BT848-based device (such as a TV card) in the system. This happens because the BT848 drivers and .INI file are already on the system and were not deleted when the old device was removed. You'll need to track down the old software and delete those references before the new device is detected.

Check the device installation and configuration. It's possible that the new device isn't configured or installed properly. For example, when installing a new drive controller, you must make sure that you've correctly enabled the desired drive controller port; otherwise, it will not be detected. Also inspect the device to confirm that it's securely installed in a bus slot or attached properly to an external port (i.e., an external modem must be cabled to one of the PC's serial ports).

Replace the defective device. If the new device still refuses to respond, it may be defective. Try to replace the device with another one, or try the device on another PC.

Running an Autodetection

If you find that there is no problem with the new device or its installation, you may be able to autodetect the device using the *Add New Hardware* wizard. Under Windows 98, the *Add New Hardware* wizard will execute a check for new PnP devices before it searches for legacy devices.

1. Click the *Start* button, highlight *Settings,* then click *Control Panel.*
2. In the *Control Panel,* double-click the *Add New Hardware* icon (Figure 3-1).
3. In the *Add New Hardware* wizard, click *Next* once to see the PnP *autodetection* dialog (Figure 3-7), which says: "*Windows will now search for any new Plug-and-Play devices on your system.*"
4. Click *Next* to run the autodetection cycle.
5. If a new PnP device is detected, you'll be able to identify the device and install the drivers for it.
6. After the new device is installed, you'll probably need to reboot the system.

Manual Installation with Specific Setup Utilities

Some devices provide a custom installer routine rather than relying on the *Add New Hardware* wizard to copy files. This is often the case when the

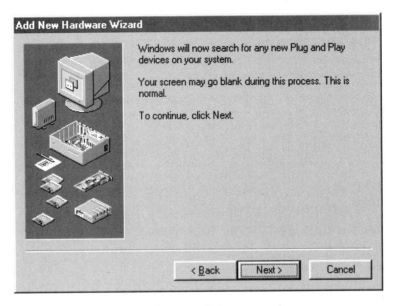

Figure 3-7 The PnP *autodetection* dialog.

device includes application software in addition to drivers. If your new device provides an installation program, your best bet is to use the manufacturer's installer.

1. After the new device is installed and recognized by Windows 95/98, place the driver CD in the CD-ROM drive.

2. If the CD-ROM drive is set to autorun, the installer routine will probably start automatically and you can install the drivers (and any other applet software) as necessary (such as the *Diamond Viper V550 Setup* menu in Figure 3-8).

3. If the CD-ROM is not set to autorun, you should double-click the *My Computer* icon from your desktop, then double-click the *CD-ROM* drive's icon.

4. Double-click the *Setup* or *Install* icon on the CD to start the installer routine.

5. Once the installer starts, you'll usually be able to take a moment to review any necessary README files before starting the actual installation by clicking *Next*.

6. The installer takes over and leads you step by step through the rest of the installation—checking for the installed devices. After the cor-

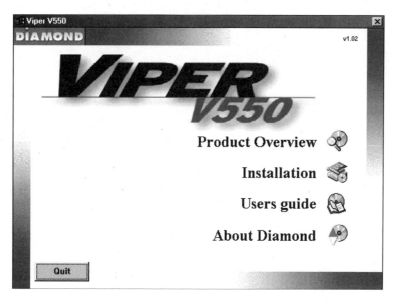

Figure 3-8 A typical *autoinstaller setup* menu.

rect devices have been detected, click *Next* to select the directory where the driver and program files are to be stored.

7. Click the *Finish* button to copy the necessary files and complete the installation. Reboot the PC when prompted.

Updating and Managing PnP Devices

Plug-and-Play technology provides technicians and end users with powerful automated configuration tools that take much of the trial-and-error guesswork out of today's hardware installations and upgrades. Still, PnP platforms are far from perfect, and *managing* the mix ·of PnP and legacy devices in today's systems takes a bit of care. This part of the chapter provides some techniques for updating and managing PnP and legacy devices under Windows 95/98.

UPDATING DEVICE DRIVERS

All devices installed under Windows 95/98 (both PnP and legacy) are heavily dependent on protected-mode device drivers. Over time, drivers often need to be updated in order to resolve bugs located in existing drivers, streamline the performance of the particular device, or overcome incompatibilities with other devices or drivers. An important part of *device management* under Windows involves *driver updates*. In a few cases, new drivers are provided on a *maintenance diskette* sent by the manufacturer to all registered users—but this is rare because of the expense involved in duplicating and mailing diskettes. Today, new drivers are downloaded from the manufacturer's tech support Web site and then installed. But in either case, *all* drivers must be installed properly—usually through the *Add New Hardware* wizard. The following steps outline the process for installing a new driver under Windows 95:

1. In the *Control Panel,* double-click the *Add New Hardware* icon.

2. Click *Next,* click *No,* and then click *Next* (do not let the wizard autodetect devices).

3. Click the *type* of hardware for which you are installing the driver and then click *Next.*

4. Click *Have Disk.*

5. Type the path for the driver you are installing and click *OK,* or click *Browse* and locate the driver manually. You must type the path for or locate the OEMSETUP.INF file from the manufacturer.

6. In the dialog box listing the .INF file, click *OK.* Click *OK* to continue.

7. Click the correct driver and then click *OK.*

8. Click *Finish.*

This same essential process will work with Windows 98, but for driver updates Windows 98 provides a slightly more convenient tool, called the *Update Device Driver* wizard, which you can invoke by using the *Device Manager:*

1. In the *Control Panel,* double-click the *System* icon, then click the *Device Manager* tab.

2. Double-click a device to be updated or highlight the device (such as the *Adaptec AIC-7850 PCI SCSI Controller* in Figure 3-9) and click the *Properties* button.

Figure 3-9 Selecting a device to update.

3. This opens the *Properties* dialog for that device. Click on the *Driver* tab to access the device driver information (Figure 3-10).

4. If you want to examine the current state of your drivers, click the *Driver File Details* button. This presents you with a summary of driver information in the *Driver File Details* dialog (Figure 3-11).

5. Otherwise, click the *Update Driver* button on the *Driver* tab. This will start the *Update Device Driver Wizard* (Figure 3-12). Click *Next*. You can then select whether to search for a new driver or display all the drivers in a specific location (Figure 3-13).

6. Now specify the locations where Windows will search for new drivers. As you see in Figure 3-14, you can search a floppy disk, CD-ROM, a Microsoft Windows Update (Web download), or specify some other location (i.e., an Iomega Zip drive).

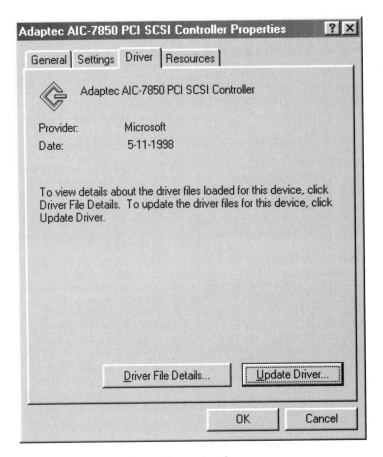

Figure 3-10 Using the *Update Driver* feature.

7. If updated drivers are found in the location you specify, you'll be able to choose the best driver from a list and install it. However, if there are no other drivers to choose from (or you're already using the best available driver), you'll see a message such as the one shown in Figure 3-15.

8. To view or choose an alternate driver, click the "*Install one of the other drivers*" radio button, then click the *View List* button. A *Select Other Driver* dialog will appear (Figure 3-16). Highlight the desired file and click *OK*, or click *Cancel* to abort.

9. When a new driver is selected, click the *Finish* button to install the driver, then reboot the system if necessary.

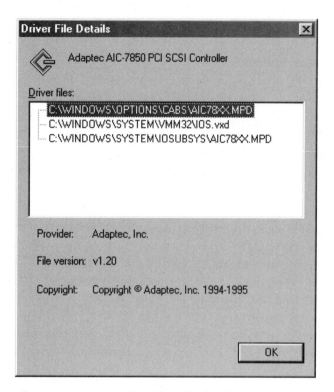

Figure 3-11   Reviewing driver file details.

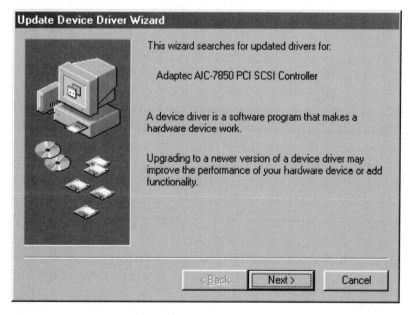

Figure 3-12   Starting the *Update Device Driver Wizard*.

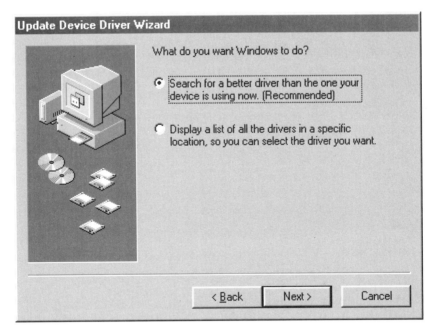

Figure 3-13 Selecting a source for new drivers.

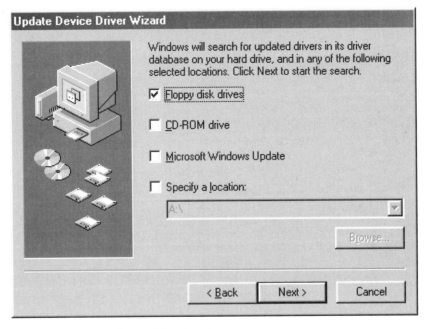

Figure 3-14 Specifying a driver location.

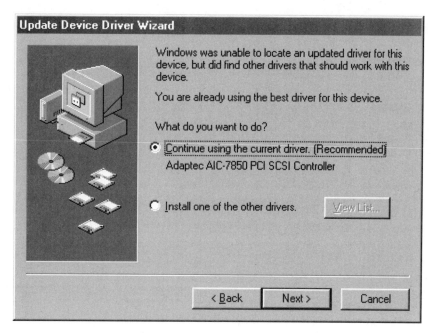

Figure 3-15   Choosing the best new driver.

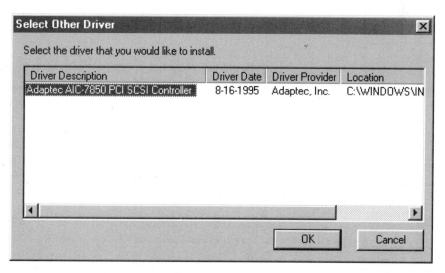

Figure 3-16   Selecting another available driver.

UPDATING MODEMS/DRIVERS MANUALLY

With the popularity of online resources such as AOL and the Internet, most current PCs are equipped with a modem. Although modem installation is very similar to other device installations, modems may offer some peculiar wrinkles that often demand a slightly different installation approach (they are also not always detected with 100 percent reliability). The following steps outline a manual modem installation/upgrade under Windows 95/98:

1. In the *Control Panel,* double-click the *Modems* icon. This goes straight to the *Modems Properties* dialog box.

2. If this is to be the first modem installed in the computer, the *Install New Modem* wizard starts automatically. If not, click *Add* (Figure 3-17).

3. The *Install New Modem* wizard will start (Figure 3-18). If you want Windows to autodetect your modem, click *Next;* if not, click

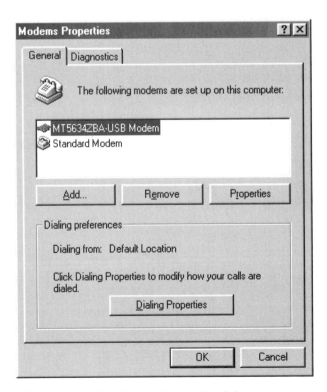

Figure 3-17 The *Modems Properties* dialog.

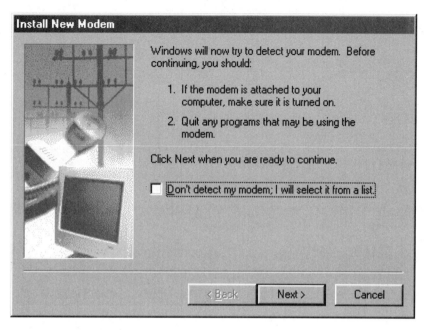

Figure 3-18   Starting the *Install New Modem* wizard.

the *"Don't detect my modem . . ."* check box to select it and then click *Next*.

4. If you chose to have Windows detect your modem, Windows queries the serial ports on your computer looking for a modem. If Windows detects an incorrect modem, click *Change* and select the appropriate manufacturer and model. Click *Next* and then continue with Step 7.

5. If you chose to select your modem manually, click the appropriate manufacturer and model (Figure 3-19) and then click *Next*. If your modem drivers are on diskette or CD-ROM, click the *Have Disk* button to install those drivers.

6. Click the appropriate communications port and then click *Next*.

7. Click *Finish* to install the selected modem drivers and reboot the system if necessary.

UPDATING VIDEO ADAPTERS/DRIVERS MANUALLY

Over the last few years, there has been a tremendous surge in the power and performance of video adapters. New chipsets, new bus slots (i.e.,

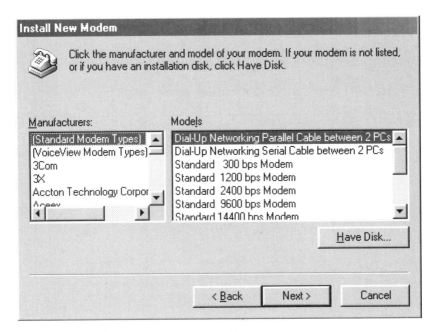

Figure 3-19 Selecting a modem manually.

AGP), and standard APIs such as Microsoft's DirectX have dramatically improved the quality and speed of everyday PC video systems—especially in video playback and 3D rendering applications. Unfortunately, video adapters are highly dependent on video drivers, so it's often necessary to update video drivers as old drivers are streamlined and bugs are fixed. Whether you're upgrading an existing video card or just upgrading to a current driver, you'll need to know how to add the driver as painlessly as possible. Fortunately, you can update your video drivers directly through the *Display* icon. Follow the process below for Windows 95:

1. In the *Control Panel,* double-click the *Display* icon. This goes straight to the *Display Properties* dialog box.

2. Click the *Settings* tab to review the display characteristics (Figure 3-20), then click the *Change Display Type* button.

3. The *Change Display Type* dialog (Figure 3-21) will allow you to alter either your video adapter or your monitor selection. If you'd like to update your monitor, click the *Change* button under *Monitor Type;* otherwise, click the *Change* button under *Adapter Type.*

4. The *Select Device* dialog appears (Figure 3-22) and lists all the compatible devices that are currently available. If you have a new driver (either on disk or downloaded from the Internet), click the *Have Disk* button, then select the correct path to the new driver in the *Install from Disk* dialog.

5. After the new drivers are loaded, you may need to reboot the system.

The driver update process is extremely similar under Windows 98, but you'll be using the *Update Device Driver* wizard to complete the update as shown below:

1. In the *Control Panel,* double-click the *Display* icon. This goes straight to the *Display Properties* dialog box.

2. Click the *Settings* tab to review the display characteristics (Figure 3-23), then click the *Advanced* button.

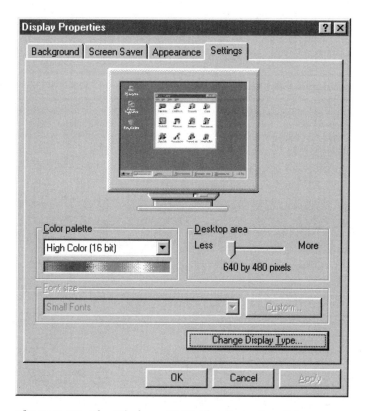

Figure 3-20   The Windows 95 *Display Properties* dialog.

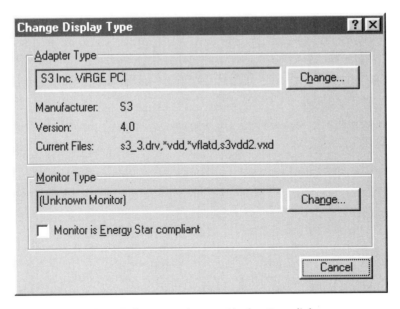

Figure 3-21   The Windows 95 *Change Display Type* dialog.

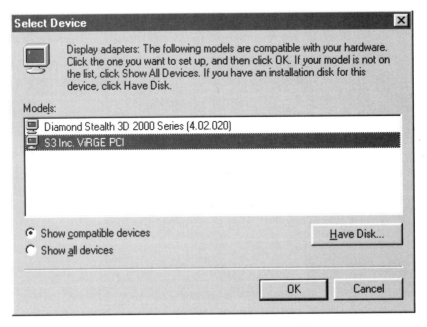

Figure 3-22   Selecting a new video adapter under Windows 95.

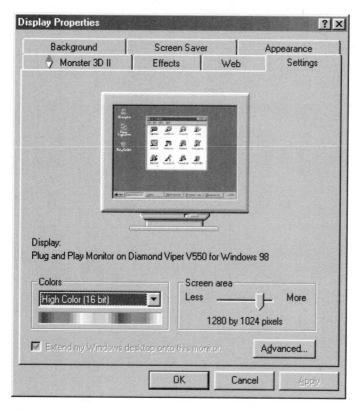

Figure 3-23 The Windows 98 *Display Properties* dialog.

3. This brings up the specific properties for your display adapter. Click the *Adapter* tab (Figure 3-24) to review the adapter settings and basic adapter/driver information. Click the *Change* button to update the adapter drivers.

4. The *Update Device Driver Wizard* will start (similar to Figure 3-12) and identify the device being updated (i.e., "Diamond Viper V550 PCI" adapter). Click *Next*. You can then select whether to search for a new driver or display all the drivers in a specific location (Figure 3-13).

5. Now specify the locations where Windows will search for new drivers. As you saw in Figure 3-14, you can search a floppy disk, CD-ROM, a Microsoft Windows Update (Web download), or specify some other location (i.e., an Iomega Zip drive).

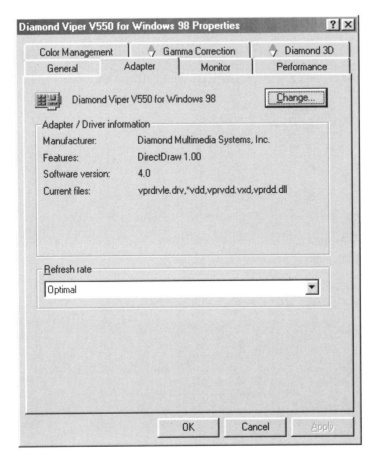

Figure 3-24 The Windows 98 *Adapter* tab.

6. If updated drivers are found in the location you specify, you'll be able to choose the best driver from a list and install it. However, if there are no other drivers to choose from (or you're already using the best available driver), you'll see a message such as the one shown in Figure 3-15.

7. To view or choose an alternate driver, click the "*Install one of the other drivers*" radio button, then click the *View List* button. A *Select Other Driver* dialog will appear (Figure 3-16). Highlight the desired file and click *OK*, or click *Cancel* to abort.

8. When a new driver is selected, click the *Finish* button to install the driver, then reboot the system if necessary.

UPDATING PRINTERS MANUALLY

Although the newest generation of printers are PnP-compatible and can be identified automatically, most traditional printers must be specified under Windows 95/98 manually. You may also need to reinstall printers that you remove or replace printer drivers periodically as new drivers become available. These tasks can be accomplished through the *Printers* icon as specified below:

1. Click the *Start* button, point to *Settings,* and then click *Printers.*

2. This opens the *Printers* dialog (Figure 3-25). Double-click *Add Printer* and then click *Next.*

3. Click *Local Printer* or *Network Printer* as appropriate (in Figure 3-26; for most end users, you'd choose *Local Printer*) and then click *Next.*

NOTE If you click *Network Printer,* you are prompted for the network path for the printer. If you do not know the correct path, click *Browse* or check with your network administrator. Click either *Yes* or *No* as appropriate in the *"Do you print from MS-DOS based programs?"* area, and then click *Next.*

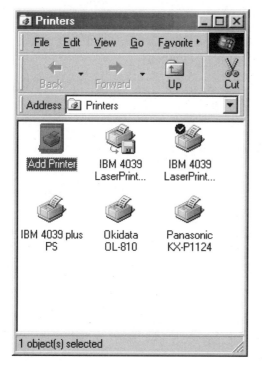

Figure 3-25 The *Printers* dialog.

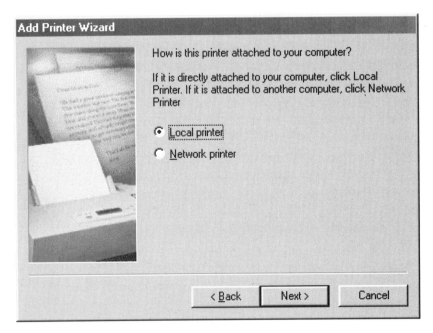

Figure 3-26 The *Add Printer Wizard* dialog.

4. Click the appropriate manufacturer and model for your printer (Figure 3-27). If you have specific drivers (or new/upgraded drivers) for your printer, click the *Have Disk* button and specify the path to those new drivers; otherwise, click *Next*.

5. If you chose to install a local printer, click the correct port (Figure 3-28). If you need to configure the printer port, click the *Configure Port* button; then click *Next*.

6. Type a name for the printer (or accept the default name) and then click either *Yes* or *No* in the "*Do you want your Windows-based programs to use this printer as the default printer?*" area. Click *Next*.

7. To print a test page, click *Yes,* then click *Finish*. If the test page prints correctly, you can be certain that the printer should be ready to operate under Windows.

DISABLING A PnP DEVICE

Ordinarily, Windows 95/98 identifies devices, assigns resources, and loads drivers for all the PnP devices it finds. From time to time (especially during

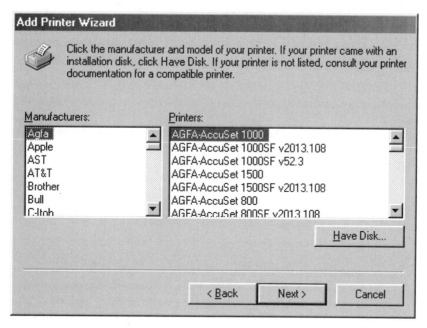

Figure 3-27 Selecting a printer make and model.

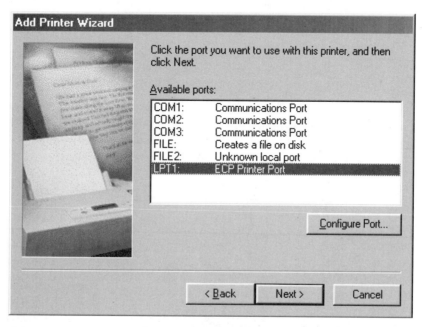

Figure 3-28 Selecting a port for the new printer.

troubleshooting), it may be necessary to "disable" a device—in effect, *disabling* a device prevents Windows from loading drivers or allocating resources associated with the device, but does not physically "remove" the device from your system. This is a particularly handy trick when checking for resource assignment problems:

1. Click the *Start* button, point to *Settings,* and then click *Control Panel.*

2. Double-click the *System* icon in the *Control Panel.*

3. Select the *Device Manager* tab, highlight the device you want to disable, and then click the *Properties* button (or just double-click the device of interest).

4. For Windows 95, on the *General* tab, click the "*Original Configuration (Current)*" check box (under the *Device usage* area) to clear it and then click *OK*. For Windows 98, check the "*Disable in this hardware profile*" check box in the *Device usage* area (Figure 3-29) and then click *OK*.

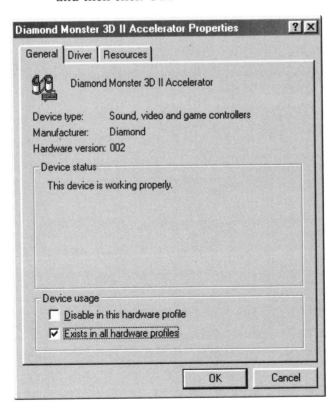

Figure 3-29 Checking device usage under Windows 98 device properties.

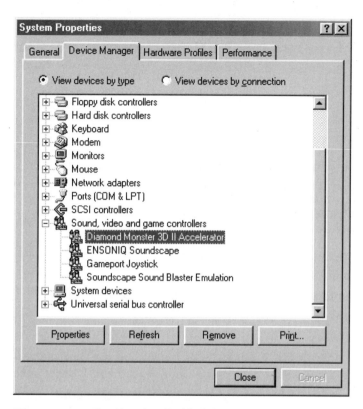

Figure 3-30 Checking the disabled device.

5. You may need to reboot the system in order to free the resources, but the neutralized device should no longer be available. The device should now appear in the *Device Manager* with a red "X" in front of it (as in Figure 3-30).

NOTE You can easily reenable the device later either by returning to the *Device properties* dialog for that device and clearing the *"Disable in this hardware profile"* box or by simply clicking the *Enable Device* button that appears in the *Device status* area.

REMOVING A PnP OR LEGACY DEVICE

There will be times (especially during troubleshooting) where it may be necessary to remove a device entirely from the Windows 95/98 platform in order to free resources otherwise assigned to the device. Normally, Windows 95/98 should free the resources of a PnP device simply by "disabling" it (see previous section, "Disabling a PnP Device"), or when the device is physically removed. But legacy cards (and a few pesky PnP cards) may need to be physically "removed" from the PC before their assigned resources can be freed for reassignment to other devices. To free resource settings used by disabled hardware:

1. Click *Start, Settings,* and *Control Panel.* Click the *System* icon and select the *Device Manager* tab.

2. In the hardware list, click the plus sign (+) next to the type of hardware and then click the device that must be removed.

3. Click the *Remove* button (Figure 3-30) and then click *OK.* You'll be asked to confirm the device removal (Figure 3-31).

4. Click the *Start* button and then click *Shut Down.* Click *OK.* When the message appears saying it is safe to do so, turn off and unplug your computer, and then remove the physical hardware device from inside the computer.

NOTE If you simply want the device to be redetected/reinstalled, use the *Remove* button to delete the device, but leave the device installed. Reboot the PC without removing the device. It should be redetected and its drivers should be reinstalled.

NOTE PnP device resources are freed automatically when you disable or remove a device. To see if resources are free after the device is disabled—but *before* physically removing the device—double-click the device in the hardware list in *Device Manager* and then click the *Resources* tab.

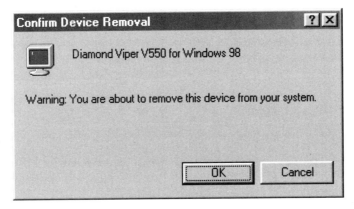

Figure 3-31 Confirming device removal under Windows 98.

CHECKING RESOURCE ASSIGNMENTS

Whether you're installing a new device, upgrading an existing device, or troubleshooting a resource conflict, chances are that you'll need to make a quick determination of which resources are in use and which (if any) are available in the system. Fortunately, the Windows 95/98 *Device Manager* provides a convenient summary of that information:

1. Click the *Start* button, point to *Settings,* and then click *Control Panel.*

2. Double-click the *System* icon in the *Control Panel.*

3. Select the *Device Manager* tab, then double-click the *Computer* entry at the top of the device list. The *Computer Properties* dialog will appear (Figure 3-32). By default, you'll see the summary of *Interrupt* (IRQ) assignments. Simply scroll down the list to examine each assignment.

4. To view other resources, click the *DMA, I/O,* or *Memory* radio button and scroll down the list.

5. Click *OK* or *Cancel* to leave the *Computer Properties* dialog.

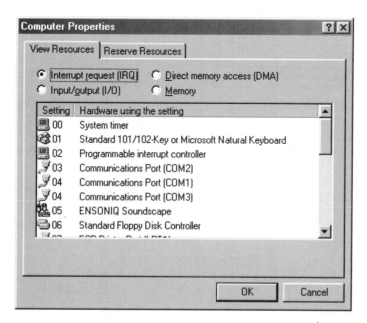

Figure 3-32   Inspecting resource assignments.

CHANGING RESOURCE ASSIGNMENTS

Plug-and-Play systems generally do an excellent job of assigning resources, but it's not a foolproof process (especially if there are still legacy devices in the system). When trouble or confusion occurs with resource assignments, you may need to tweak resources manually through the Windows *Device Manager.* In most cases, you can use the *Device Manager* to adjust IRQs, DMA channels, I/O ports, and memory ranges. A typical adjustment process is outlined below:

1. Click the *Start* button, point to *Settings,* and then click *Control Panel.*

2. Double-click the *System* icon in the *Control Panel.*

3. Select the *Device Manager* tab, highlight the device you want to disable (Figure 3-33), and then click the *Properties* button (or just double-click the device of interest).

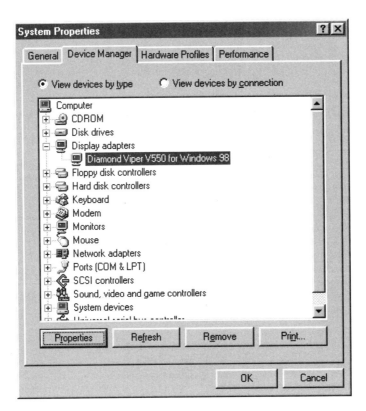

Figure 3-33 Selecting a device to modify.

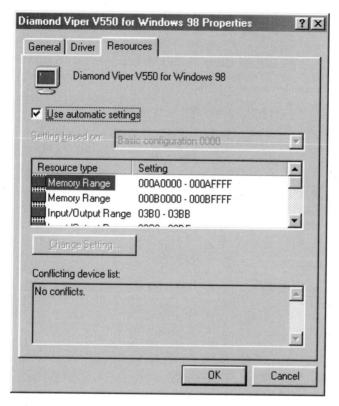

Figure 3-34 Reviewing a device's resource assignments.

4. Once the *Device Properties* dialog appears, select the *Resources* tab (Figure 3-34) to review the resources being allocated to the device. If there's a conflict, you should see a brief discussion of it in the *Conflicting Device List* area.

5. Normally, the "*Use automatic settings*" box is always checked. Before you try reassigning resources, you'll need to uncheck this box. You'll notice that the "*Setting based on*" list and *Change Setting* button will no longer appear grayed out.

6. Scroll up and down the list of resources until you locate the assignment that needs to be changed. Highlight the desired resource and click the *Change Setting* button. For the purposes of this example, we'll try adjusting a memory range.

7. The *Edit Memory Range* dialog box will appear (Figure 3-35). The original setting will be listed on the "Value" line. You can then

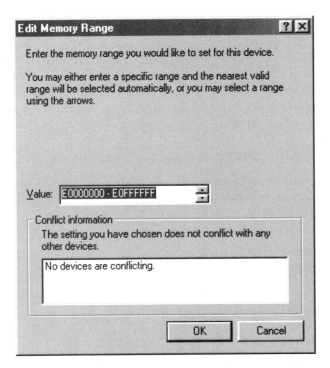

Figure 3-35 Entering new resource assignments.

enter the new range to be used. If your new setting conflicts with any other devices, a report will appear in the *Conflict information* area. When the new range is satisfactory, click *OK*.

NOTE You can use this same technique to change IRQ, DMA, I/O, and memory assignments. If you select a resource other than a memory range, the corresponding dialog box will appear to accept the new setting(s). When working with legacy devices, be sure the device's jumper settings correspond to the new resource settings that you're entering.

8. Once the new resource has been entered, it may be necessary for you to reboot the system.

Legacy Notes

Since legacy devices do not report their resource assignments to Windows, be careful to ensure that the resource assignments "listed" under Windows match the actual jumper assignments made on the legacy device itself. For example, just changing the resources of a legacy device in the *Device Man-*

ager is not enough. You must shut down the PC, reconfigure the physical device as required, then reenter the *Device Manager* and alter the resource assignments to match.

Managing USB Devices Under Windows 98

The Universal Serial Bus (USB) is poised to become a premier external interface for the PC (as well as the new Apple iMac). It allows features such as hot detection and disconnection, autodetection and configuration, automatic driver installation, and support for up to 128 external PC devices. USB also supports a moderate data throughput of up to 12 Mbps, so a diverse range of peripheral devices can be employed. Although USB architecture has been available on motherboards for a few years now, the introduction of Windows 98 (and its comprehensive USB support) has captured the enthusiasm and support of the PC industry. Insiders often refer to USB as "Plug-and-Play outside of the box"—greatly simplifying the connection of many different devices. This part of the chapter highlights a few basic elements of USB management.

GETTING STARTED WITH USB

You'll need four essential elements to use USB: (1) a motherboard with a USB BIOS, (2) a motherboard with one or two USB ports (typically located near the serial and parallel ports), (3) a USB-compliant operating system such as Windows 95 OSR2.5 or Windows 98, and (4) at least one USB peripheral device. Most late-model Pentium MMX and current Pentium II motherboards provide the necessary USB BIOS and at least one USB port. If you don't already have Windows 98, you might seriously consider an upgrade before firing up your USB system (Windows 98 provides much broader USB support than any OSR version of Windows 95). USB is designed to support a wide range of devices such as:

◀ Keyboards

◀ Trackballs

◀ Joysticks

◀ Speakers

◁   Scanners

◁   Printers

◁   Modems

◁   Cameras

Undoubtedly, this list will grow as USB continues to mature.

Enabling USB

If all the elements for USB are in place on your PC, you'll need to enable USB support through your CMOS Setup (such as the "*USB IRQ*" entry in Figure 1-6). After you enable USB and restart Windows 98, you may be asked to insert the Windows CD after the new USB hardware is identified. Once the USB support has been installed, you'll see an entry for a "*Universal serial bus controller*" (as in Figure 3-36). Below the controller's entry, you'll probably find an entry for the motherboard's specific bus controller

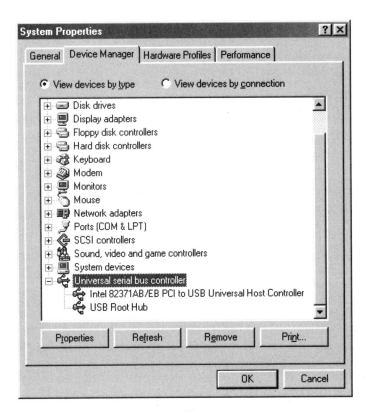

Figure 3-36 Checking the *Device Manager* for USB support.

device (i.e., the *"Intel 82371 AB/EB PCI to USB Universal Host Controller"*) and the USB port itself (i.e., the *"USB Root Hub"*). At this point, you can attach USB devices to the motherboard's USB port.

CONNECTING AND DISCONNECTING USB DEVICES

USB is one of the first practical "hot" Plug-and-Play connection schemes to appear on the PC, so connecting devices should be as simple as plugging the device into any available four-pin USB port. For a single USB device (i.e., a USB keyboard or mouse/trackball), you can connect the device directly to a USB port on the motherboard. If you want to remove or swap the USB device, just disconnect the plug and connect the new device—this can be done with the PC *on* and Windows 98 running.

NOTE Although USB is ideally designed to provide drivers and power to all USB devices, many high-end USB devices (i.e., scanners) will require their own device drivers and power supply. When the new USB device is detected and identified, you'll be asked to install the drivers from an installation diskette or CD. In some cases, the new USB driver will require you to reboot the system.

Using a USB Hub

USB devices work on a "tiered star" (a hub-and-spoke)—rather than a "daisy chain"—connection scheme, so if you're planning on connecting more than one USB device, you'll need to connect a USB hub such as the Peracom Quad USB Hub (*www.peracom.com*) first. You'd attach the hub to your motherboard's USB port, then connect USB devices to USB ports on the hub. As with other USB devices, you can connect the hub "hot," and Windows 98 will automatically detect and install drivers for it. LEDs on the hub will illuminate to tell you when the ports have initialized and are ready to accept USB devices.

Powered vs. Unpowered Hubs

Each device you connect to a USB port requires a certain amount of power in order to operate. Ideally, the USB provides this power. In actual practice, an "unpowered" hub (which is powered from the USB port) will accept low-power devices such as keyboards or mice. For more demanding devices such as digital cameras, you'll need to use a "powered" hub that employs a small AC power adapter to supplement the requirements of your USB devices. High-power devices (such as USB scanners or printers) will actually provide their own AC adapters or AC line cords. When you "power" a hub, it will normally reinitialize the hub and any devices (or subsequent hubs) attached to it, so expect the hub and devices to be momentarily redetected.

NOTE Since the hub must reinitialize when power is applied, a brief interruption in communication will occur. This can cause errors with certain devices that are communicating over the USB at that moment. Be sure your USB devices are idle before applying power to any hub.

Managing Infrared Devices Under Windows 98

One of the most troublesome aspects of using peripherals is the actual connection to the PC. Cables can be pricey (especially for good-quality cables) and they do not tolerate flexing very well. The use of infrared (or "Ir") connections helps to overcome connection problems by replacing physical cables with infrared receivers and transmitters. Infrared devices are particularly handy with printers or for basic PC-to-PC communication without the hassle of a direct cable. If your PC is equipped with an infrared port, note that this part of the chapter covers the essentials of "Ir Management" under Windows 98.

NOTE Infrared controls and tools will appear only when Windows 98 is installed on motherboards with an Ir module installed; otherwise, you should skip this section.

UNDERSTANDING INFRARED MONITOR

For systems equipped with an infrared transmitter/receiver module, you can use the *Infrared Monitor* (or *IrMon*) utility as the main interface between you and your system's infrared activity. IrMon serves four main functions:

1. It reports what infrared devices are within range of your system.

2. It reports whether your system is communicating with an infrared device (and the efficiency of that communication).

3. It allows you to tailor how infrared activity and status are reported.

4. It allows you to select what type(s) of infrared activity to allow.

Normally, IrMon will be running on systems fitted with infrared support. If IrMon is not running (or you have to terminate it and restart it later), you can open IrMon by double-clicking the *Infrared* icon in your *Control Panel*.

Placing IrMon in the System Tray

If you work with infrared devices frequently, it may be helpful to have IrMon on the Taskbar (located in your System Tray). Simply open IrMon by double-clicking the *Infrared* icon in *Control Panel*, select the *Preferences* tab, then check the box "*Display the Infrared Monitor icon on the taskbar.*" Click *OK* to select the change. If you decide to remove IrMon from the System Tray later, just clear the "*Display the Infrared Monitor icon on the taskbar*" box.

Enabling/Disabling Infrared Communication

You can use IrMon to enable or disable infrared communication with your PC. Just right-click the *Infrared* icon in your System Tray (or double-click the *Infrared* icon in *Control Panel*). To enable infrared communication, check the box "*Enable infrared communication.*" To disable infrared communication, make sure that box is unchecked.

NOTE When infrared communication is disabled, the *"Search for devices within range"* and *"Enable Plug-and-Play"* options in *Infrared Monitor* are also turned off.

Enabling/Disabling Infrared Plug-and-Play

Infrared devices often support Plug-and-Play, so when a PnP infrared device comes in range of your PC, the system will automatically recognize and use the device. You can use IrMon to enable or disable support for infrared Plug-and-Play devices. Just right-click the *Infrared* icon in your System Tray (or double-click the *Infrared* icon in *Control Panel*). To enable infrared Plug-and-Play operation, check the box "*Enable Plug-and-Play.*" To disable infrared Plug-and-Play support, make sure that box is unchecked. Remember that this option is available only if the infrared support is turned on and the system is set to search for infrared devices. If an infrared device is not Plug-and-Play–compliant but still in range and operational, you may need to add it through the *Add New Hardware* wizard in your *Control Panel.*

Reporting Infrared Communication Status with Sounds

Infrared Monitor will report when new devices come into range or when communication is interrupted. Just right-click the *Infrared* icon in your System Tray (or double-click the *Infrared* icon in *Control Panel*). Click the *Preferences* tab, then check the box "*Play sounds when available devices come within range and when communication is interrupted.*" If you do not want to be informed when communication status changes, just clear this check box.

NOTE If your computer has a sound card, you can double-click the *Sounds* icon in *Control Panel* to change which sounds are assigned to the infrared system events.

Searching for Infrared Devices

If you have Plug-and-Play–compliant infrared devices, you can configure *Infrared Monitor* to automatically scan for devices that are in range. Right-click the *Infrared* icon in your System Tray or double-click the *Infrared* icon in *Control Panel*. Select the *Options* tab, then check the box "*Search for and provide status for devices within range.*" Set the time interval to a fairly low value (i.e., 3 seconds). If that check box isn't available, be sure the "*Enable infrared communication*" box is checked. Click the *Apply* button, then select the *Status* tab. Now reposition the infrared devices until *Infrared Monitor* confirms that each device is within acceptable range.

CHAPTER 4

PC Plug-and-Play Troubleshooting

Plug-and-Play provides a quick and convenient means of adding internal (and some external) devices to your PC. Ideally the new device is detected automatically, assigned adequate resources, provided with the correct driver, and put into service—however, things don't always work this cleanly in the Plug-and-Play world. Hardware conflicts are still quite common, and many issues remain in the proper detection and configuration of Plug-and-Play devices. This chapter provides you with a standard troubleshooting protocol for handling conflicts, then covers a wealth of practical PnP troubleshooting procedures. This chapter also outlines the considerations and processes for upgrading a system BIOS, which might be necessary to support Plug-and-Play on some older PCs.

Standard Conflict Troubleshooting

One of the biggest problems with conflict troubleshooting is that every conflict situation is a bit different. Variations in PC motherboards, BIOS, installed devices, and available resources often reduce conflict troubleshooting to a hit-or-miss process. Even the most experienced technicians can find themselves stymied by a pesky conflict. Fortunately, conflict troubleshooting can be accomplished quickly and easily using the tools provided by Windows 95 and Windows 98—namely the *Device Manager*. This part of the chapter provides a step-by-step process that you can use for conflict resolution under Windows 95/98.

NOTE The steps described below should be read like a flowchart. You'll find many references that will take you back and forth to various steps throughout this section, so don't be confused if you find yourself jumping around this section.

NOTE If you find that an ISA-bus device (even an ISA PnP device) suffers from resource conflicts (or cannot be installed due to resource conflicts), use a PCI-bus version of that device instead.

STEP 1: GETTING STARTED

Begin by starting the *Device Manager* in Windows 95/98:

1. Click the *Start* button, then select *Settings*, then click *Control Panel.*

2. Double-click the *System* icon, then click on the *Device Manager* tab (Figure 4-1).

3. Make sure the *"View Devices By Type"* radio button is selected.

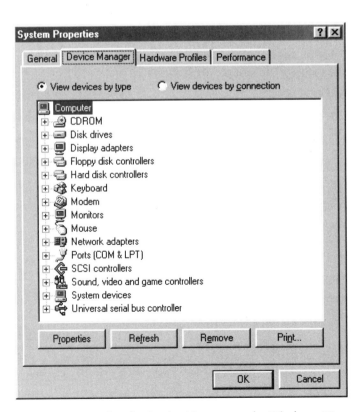

Figure 4-1   Starting the *Device Manager* under Windows 98.

NOTE **If the hardware that has the suspected conflict isn't visible in the list, click the plus sign (+) next to the type of hardware to see all the devices listed under it.**

Determine if any device was installed twice. Is the device you were installing (or that suffers from the conflict) listed *twice* in *Device Manager?*

◀ If the device is listed only *once,* go to Step 2.

◀ If the device is listed *twice* and there is *only* supposed to be one such device in the system, go to Step 3.

◀ If the device is listed *twice,* but there are *supposed* to be two such devices in the system (i.e., two video adapters for multimonitor support under Windows 98), go to Step 2.

STEP 2: DEVICE LISTED ONLY ONCE

When the device is listed only once, review the resource settings for the conflicting device:

1. Double-click on the hardware that shows a conflict.

2. In the *Device Usage* area, make sure that there is a check in the box next to the configuration marked "*Current.*" If the box isn't checked, check the box now. For Windows 98, make sure the check box(es) "*Disable in this hardware profile*" and "*Remove from this hardware profile*" are unchecked (Figure 4-2).

3. Click the *Resources* tab (if the device doesn't have a *Resources* tab, skip to Step 6).

Do you see a dialog box with resource settings (as in Figure 4-3)?

◀ If the dialog box with resource settings appears, go to Step 4.

◀ If the *Set Configuration Manually* button appears instead, go to Step 5.

◀ If your particular device doesn't have a *Resources* tab (i.e., a port or dial-up adapter), go to Step 6.

STEP 3: DEVICE LISTED TWICE

When you find a device is incorrectly entered more than once, remove *all* the duplicated device(s) and redetect/reinstall them again:

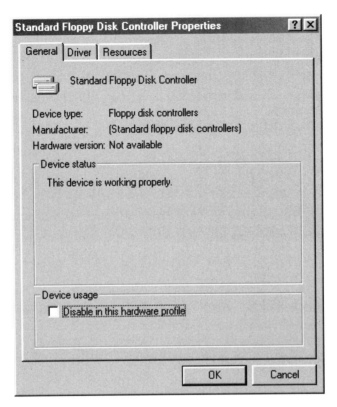

Figure 4-2 Checking *Device Usage* under Windows 98.

1. Remove *every* entry for the duplicated item from the hardware list. Click its name to highlight it and then click *Remove* (as in Figure 4-4). When you're finished, *no* instances of the conflicting hardware should be listed at all.

2. Click *OK*.

3. Now, while still within the *Control Panel*, double-click on the *Add New Hardware* icon. If you see a message that you already have a wizard open, click *Finish* in that wizard and *then* click the button in this step to start a new wizard.

4. Click *Next*.

5. Click the option to automatically detect your hardware and then click *Next*. Continue until you finish the wizard. For Windows 98, the *Add New Hardware Wizard* will check automatically for PnP devices (Figure 4-5). Simply click *Next* to proceed.

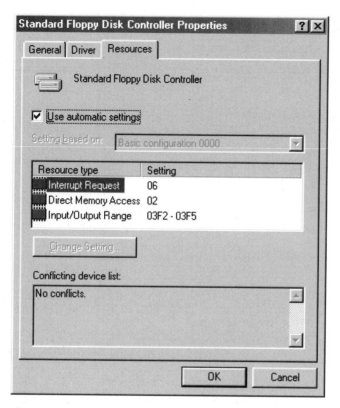

Figure 4-3 Examining the resource assignments for a selected device.

Did this fix the problem?

◁ If the conflict no longer appears (and only one instance of the device is listed), this should correct the problem and you should be done. Exit the *Control Panel* and restart Windows 95/98. Double-check the *Device Manager* after rebooting to see that only one instance of the device remains and that there are no further conflicts.

◁ If the conflict still appears even with one instance of the device, go back to Step 2.

NOTE If you cannot prevent additional detection of a device when Windows reboots, you may have duplicate device entries in your Windows Registry. Use REGEDIT to back up the Registry, then identify and remove any duplicate entries that may be forcing Windows to list a device more than once.

Figure 4-4   Removing a duplicated device entry.

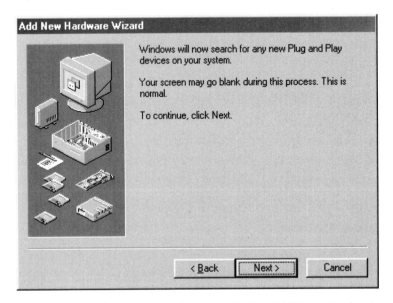

Figure 4-5   Redetecting PnP devices with the *Add New Hardware Wizard.*

STEP 4: RESOURCE SETTINGS APPEAR

Identify exactly *which* resources are causing the conflict:

1. In the *Conflicting device list* box (Figure 4-3), identify the hardware that is using conflicting resources.

Is more than one resource conflict listed?

◄ If *more than one* resource conflict is listed, go to Step 7.

◄ If *only one* conflict is listed, go to Step 8.

◄ If *no conflicts* are listed, or if one or more indications show *System Reserved* as the conflict, go to Step 9.

STEP 5: MANUAL BUTTON APPEARS

Determine *why* the resources are not displayed:

1. When the *Resources* tab shows a *Set Configuration Manually* button, it is either because the device has a conflict or other problem and is disabled or because the resource settings used by this device are working properly but they don't match any of the known configurations.

2. You can tell which situation applies by reading the text above the button.

Which text message do you see?

◄ If you see a message that says "*The device is conflicting, or the device is not currently enabled or has a problem,*" then go to Step 10.

◄ If you see a message that says "*The resource settings don't match any known configurations,*" there is *no* further solution to the problem. You should probably remove the conflicting device. You might try a similar device from another manufacturer.

STEP 6: THERE IS NO RESOURCES TAB

You have probably chosen the wrong device. Select the correct device:

1. Click *Cancel* to return to the hardware list.

2. Carefully double-click the hardware that has a conflict. In the *Device Usage* area, make sure that there is a check in the box next

to the configuration marked *"Current."* If the box isn't checked, check it now. For Windows 98, make sure the check box(es) *"Disable in this hardware profile"* and *"Remove from this hardware profile"* are unchecked (as in Figure 4-2).

3. Click the *Resources* tab.

Do you see a box with resource settings now?

◁ If the box with resource settings appears now, go back to Step 4.

◁ If you see a *Set Configuration Manually* button, go back to Step 5.

◁ If the resource settings still do not appear, there is *no* further solution to the problem. You should probably remove the conflicting device. You might try a similar device from another manufacturer.

STEP 7: MORE THAN ONE CONFLICT IS LISTED

At this point, you should determine just *how many* devices are listed as being *conflicting*.

◁ If you only see *one* device causing all the conflicts, go to Step 11.

◁ If *more than one* device is causing the conflicts, go to Step 12.

STEP 8: ONLY ONE CONFLICT IS LISTED

Look for a resource setting that doesn't conflict:

1. In the *Resource Settings* box, double-click the label of the resource setting that is *conflicting* (or highlight the label and click the *Change Setting* button). If you see a message that says *"You must clear the Use Automatic Settings box before you can change a resource setting,"* click OK to close the message and then clear the *Use Automatic Settings* check box and try again.

2. Scroll through the available resource settings provided or alter the resource setting manually (as in Figure 4-6).

3. For each setting, look at the *Conflict information* box to see if your new settings conflict with any other hardware.

4. If you find a free setting, click *OK*.

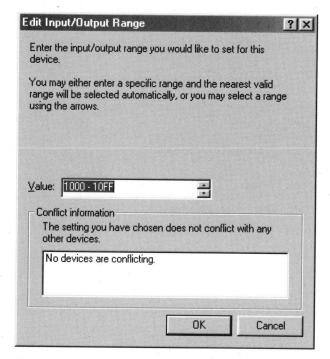

Figure 4-6 Entering new resource settings for a device.

Did you find a setting that doesn't conflict with any other hardware?

◀ If you *can* find a setting that does not conflict, go on to Step 13.

◀ If you *cannot* find a setting that does not conflict, skip to Step 14.

◀ If you see a message stating that the resource setting *cannot be modified,* skip to Step 15.

STEP 9: NO CONFLICTS ARE LISTED

If there are no conflicts listed in the *Conflicting device list* box, either you are not viewing resources for the correct device or the conflict has already been resolved (you need to restart your computer to allow Windows 95/98 to configure the hardware). Look at the top of the dialog box to see if you are viewing resources for the correct device.

There is *no* further solution to this problem. If restarting Windows 95/98 does not clear the problem, you may simply need to remove the conflicting device. Try a similar device from another manufacturer.

STEP 10: THE DEVICE IS CONFLICTING

Now you need to identify which hardware is conflicting:

1. Click the *Set Configuration Manually* button.

2. In the *Conflict information* box, identify the other hardware that is using the conflicting resources.

Is more than one resource conflict listed?

◁ If *more than one* resource conflict(s) is/are listed, skip to Step 16.

◁ If *only one* resource conflict is listed, go on to Step 17.

◁ If *no* conflicts are listed, go back to Step 9.

STEP 11: ONLY ONE DEVICE IS CONFLICTING

Do you want to disable the device that is causing all the conflicts?

◁ If you wish to simply disable the conflicting device (you will not be able to use it), skip to Step 18.

◁ If you *must* use the hardware that is causing the conflicts, go on to Step 17.

STEP 12: MORE THAN ONE DEVICE IS CONFLICTING

Look for resource settings that *don't* conflict:

1. In the *Resource Settings* box, double-click the label next to a resource setting that is *conflicting* (or highlight the label and click the *Change Setting* button). If you see a message that says "*You must clear the Use Automatic Settings box before you can change a resource setting,*" click *OK* to close the message and then clear the *Use Automatic Settings* box.

2. Scroll through the available resource settings provided or alter the resource setting manually (as in Figure 4-6).

3. For each setting, look in the *Conflict information* box to see if your new settings conflict with any other hardware.

4. When you find a free setting, click *OK*.

5. Repeat the preceding Steps 1–4 for each conflicting resource that you discover.

Did you find a free setting for *each* conflicting resource?

◄ If you *do* find free settings for each conflicting resource, go on to Step 19.

◄ If *some* (or all) resources are still conflicting, skip to Step 20.

◄ If you see a message indicating that the resource setting *cannot be modified,* go to Step 15.

STEP 13: THERE IS A FREE SETTING

When a free setting *is* available, change the configuration:

1. Enter the new setting value.

2. Make a note of the old and new settings to refer to later.

3. Click *OK.* If you see a message prompting you to restart your computer, click *No.*

NOTE If the setting you change relates to "legacy" devices, you may either have to change the jumpers on your hardware card to match the new setting(s) or have to run a configuration utility provided by your hardware manufacturer. If the jumper settings on your card aren't set properly, your hardware will not work, even if you resolved the conflict correctly. Refer to your hardware documentation for instructions on changing jumpers.

Restart your computer (and reconfigure the related "legacy" device if necessary):

1. Click *OK.*

2. You may see a message prompting you to restart your computer. Click *No.*

3. Click the *Start* button, click *Shut Down,* and then click *Yes.*

4. When Windows says it is safe to do so, turn off your computer so you can configure the hardware devices that you've changed.

This should correct the problem, and the hardware conflict should now be resolved once the PC is restarted.

STEP 14: ALL OTHER SETTINGS CONFLICT

You may need to remove hardware that you no longer need in order to free resources for the conflicting device(s). Identify hardware you no longer need:

1. Scroll through the available resource settings.
2. When a conflict appears in the *Conflicting device list* box, determine whether you still need to use the device that is causing the conflict.

Can you identify a hardware device that you no longer need to use?

◀ If you *can* disable the conflicting device, go on to Step 21.

◀ If you *cannot* disable the conflicting device, skip to Step 22.

STEP 15: RESOURCE SETTINGS CANNOT BE MODIFIED

View the resources for the other device:

1. In the *Conflicting device list* box (Figure 4-3), make a note of which device is using the resource that cannot be modified.
2. Click *Cancel*.
3. In the hardware list, find and double-click the device that is using the resource.

Does this device have a *Resources* tab?

◀ If a *Resources* tab *is* available, go on to Step 23.

◀ If a *Resources* tab *isn't* available, skip to Step 24.

STEP 16: THERE IS MORE THAN ONE CONFLICT

How many devices are listed as *conflicting*?

◀ If only *one* device is causing the conflicts, go back to Step 11.

◀ If *more* than one device is causing the conflicts, go back to Step 12.

STEP 17: THERE IS ONLY ONE CONFLICT

Look for a resource setting that *doesn't* conflict:

1. In the *Resource Settings* box, double-click the label next to the resource setting that is conflicting (or highlight the label and click the *Change Setting* button). If you see a message that says "*You must clear the Use Automatic Settings box before you can change a resource setting,*" click OK to close the message and then clear the *Use Automatic Settings* box.

2. Scroll through the available resource settings provided or alter the resource setting manually (as in Figure 4-6).

3. For each setting, look in the *Conflict information* box to see if your new settings conflict with any other hardware.

4. When you find a free setting, click OK.

Did you find a setting that doesn't conflict with any other hardware?

◁ If you manage to find a setting that does *not* conflict, return to Step 13.

◁ If you see a message indicating that the resource setting *cannot be modified,* jump back to Step 15.

◁ If all other settings conflict with other hardware, there is *no* further solution to the problem and you should probably remove the conflicting device. Try a similar device from a different manufacturer.

STEP 18: DISABLE CONFLICTING HARDWARE

Determine how best to disable the conflicting hardware:

1. On the hardware list, double-click the hardware that you want to disable. If you do not see the hardware list, click *Cancel* until you return to it (or close and restart the *Device Manager*).

2. In the *Device usage* area, click the box next to the configuration marked "*Current*" to remove the check mark. For Windows 98, check the box marked "*Disable in this hardware profile*" (Figure 4-7).

3. Click OK to confirm your decision to disable the device. You'll now see that the device is marked by a red "X" in the device list (Figure 4-8).

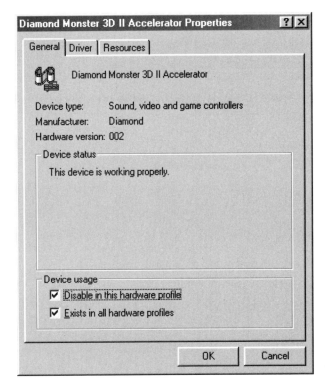

Figure 4-7 Disabling a device through the *Device Manager.*

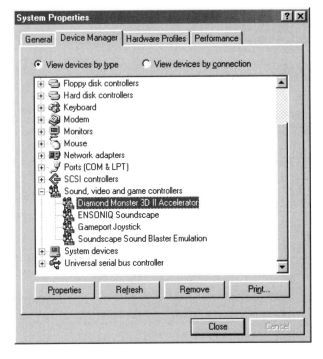

Figure 4-8 Identifying the disabled device.

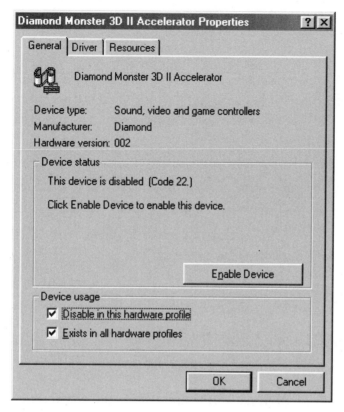

Figure 4-9   Reenabling the device under Windows 98.

4. Double-click the disabled entry again. Under Windows 98, you'll see an *Enable Device* button in the *Device status* area (Figure 4-9). You can reenable the PnP device again simply by clicking on the button.

NOTE For "legacy" devices under Windows, you may not be able to disable the device automatically—you will also need to remove the device.

Are you attempting to disable a PnP or "legacy" device?

◀ If you're disabling a PnP device, just removing it from the hardware profile should be sufficient, so go on to Step 19.

◀ If you're disabling a "legacy" device (or a PnP device won't release its resources), skip down to Step 25.

STEP 19: RESOURCES NOW SET WITHOUT CONFLICTS

Print out a report for each device you changed:

1. In the hardware list, click a device whose resource settings you changed while resolving the conflict. If you do not see the hardware list, click *OK* until you return to it (or simply close and restart the *Device Manager*).

2. Click *Print*.

3. Click the second option *to print the selected class or device.*

4. Click *OK*.

5. Repeat the preceding Steps 1–4 for each device that you changed during this troubleshooting process.

This should document the corrected problem, and you should be done.

STEP 20: SOME RESOURCES ARE STILL CONFLICTING

Set resources to conflict with only one device:

1. Double-click a resource that is still conflicting. If you see a message that says "*You must clear the Use Automatic Settings box before you can change a resource setting,*" click *OK* to close the message and then clear the *Use Automatic Settings* box.

2. Scroll through the available resource settings. For each value, write down the setting and the name of the hardware it conflicts with. Then click *Cancel*.

3. Repeat Steps 1 and 2 for each conflicting resource.

4. Looking at the list, see if you can change the resource settings so they conflict with only one device—*preferably* an unneeded device that you could disable or remove.

Are all conflicts with one device?

◁   If *all* the conflicts are with only one device, go back to Step 11.

◁   If resources still conflict with *more* than one device, there is *no* further solution to the problem, and you should probably remove the conflicting device. Try a similar device from another manufacturer.

STEP 21: DISABLE THE UNNEEDED DEVICE

Determine whether the hardware you want to disable is Plug-and-Play:

1. Select each resource setting that conflicts with the hardware you will disable and then click *OK*.

2. When the message appears saying the setting conflicts with another device, click *Yes* to continue.

3. Click *OK* until you return to the hardware list.

4. Click the plus sign (+) next to the type of hardware that you want to disable.

5. Double-click the hardware that you want to disable.

6. In the *Device Usage* area, click the box next to the configuration marked "*Current*" to remove the check mark. For Windows 98, check the box marked "*Disable in this hardware profile*" (i.e., Figure 4-7).

7. Click *OK* to confirm your decision to disable the device. You'll now see that the device is marked by a red "X" in the device list (Figure 4-8).

8. Double-click the disabled entry again. Under Windows 98, you'll see an *Enable Device* button in the *Device status* area (Figure 4-9). You can reenable the PnP device again simply by clicking on the button.

NOTE For "legacy" devices under Windows, you may not be able to disable the device automatically—you will also need to remove the device.

Are you attempting to disable a PnP or "legacy" device?

◁ If you're disabling a PnP device, just removing it from the hardware profile should be sufficient, so go on to Step 19.

◁ If you're disabling a "legacy" device (or a PnP device won't release its resources), skip down to Step 25.

STEP 22: ALL DEVICES ARE IN USE

Write down a list of all devices using resources:

1. Scroll through the resource settings. On a piece of paper, write down the name of each piece of conflicting hardware and its setting.

2. Click *Cancel* until you return to the hardware list (or simply close and restart the *Device Manager*).

Rearrange resource settings for conflicting hardware:

1. On the *Device Manager* hardware list, click the plus sign (+) next to the hardware type for the first item on your written list.

2. Double-click the hardware entry.

3. Click the *Resources* tab.

4. Double-click the resource setting that you wrote down. If you see a message that says "*You must clear the Use Automatic Settings box before you can change a resource setting,*" click *OK* to close the message and then clear the *Use Automatic Settings* box. Now double-click the resource to modify again.

5. Scroll through the available resource settings. For each setting, look in the *Conflict information* box to see if it conflicts with any other hardware.

6. If you find a free setting other than the one you wrote down, write down the new values, and continue.

7. If you do not find a free setting, repeat the preceding Steps 1–5 until you run out of hardware to try or you find a free setting.

Did you find a free resource setting?

◁ If you found free resources, go on to Step 26.

◁ If you could not locate free resources, skip to Step 27.

STEP 23: RESOURCE INFORMATION IS AVAILABLE

Check to see if the device can use a different resource:

1. Click the *Resources* tab.

2. In the *Resource Settings* box, double-click the resource setting that you need to free for the other device. If you see a message that says "*You must clear the Use Automatic Settings box before you can change a resource setting,*" click *OK* to close the message, then

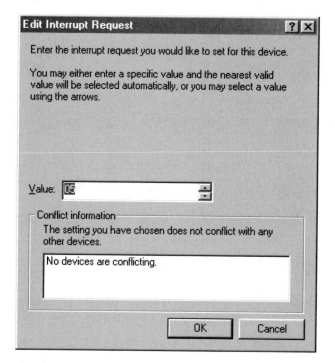

Figure 4-10 Selecting alternate resources for a device.

clear the *Use Automatic Settings* box and try double-clicking the resource again.

3. Scroll through the available resource settings (such as the IRQ assignment shown in Figure 4-10).

4. For each setting, look in the *Conflict information* box to see if it conflicts with any other hardware.

5. If you find a free setting, click *OK*. If you see a message prompting you to restart your computer, click *No* for now (you can restart later).

Did you find a free resource setting?

◄ If *Yes*, go on to Step 28.

◄ If *No* (or you determine that the resource settings cannot be modified, as in Figure 4-11), skip to Step 29.

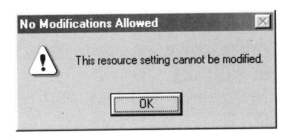

Figure 4-11 Determining when resource settings cannot be modified.

STEP 24: RESOURCE INFORMATION IS NOT AVAILABLE

Decide *which* device you should disable. Because *both* conflicting devices need to use the same resource setting, you must decide which device you want to use—and which device you want to live without (at least temporarily). You must disable and/or remove the other device.

It probably is easier to remove the device that had the original conflict. This is usually the *new* device that you've just tried adding to the system. If you choose to remove the *other* device, you may see a message telling you that you still have a conflict after completing the procedure. Just restart the procedure and continue to resolve the conflict.

Which device would you like to disable?

◁   If you'd rather disable the *original* device, go to Step 30.

◁   If you'd rather disable the *other* conflicting device, go to Step 31.

STEP 25: MANUAL BUTTON NOT AVAILABLE

You're freeing resources from a "legacy" device (or the PnP device will not release its resources). Disable the conflicting hardware by *removing* it from *Device Manager:*

1. On the hardware list, click the plus sign (+) next to the type of hardware that you want to disable. If you do not see the hardware list, click *Cancel* until you return to it (or simply close and restart the *Device Manager*).

2. Click the hardware you want to disable.

3. Click *Remove,* then click *OK.*

Go back to Step 19.

NOTE In many cases, you may have to physically remove a "legacy" device to prevent it from continuing to utilize resources assigned to other devices.

STEP 26: FREE RESOURCES ARE FOUND

You'll need to change the resource settings to utilize the free resources:

1. Save the new setting by clicking *OK* and then clicking *OK* again.

2. If you see a message about restarting your computer, click *No*.

3. In the *Device Manager* hardware list, double-click the hardware that first had the conflict.

4. Click the *Resources* tab to see the device's properties.

5. Double-click the resource that is conflicting. If you see a message that says "*You must clear the Use Automatic Settings box before you can change a resource setting,*" click *OK* to close the message, then clear the *Use Automatic Settings* box; now double-click the resource again.

6. Change the resource setting to the value you just freed. The *Conflict information* box may show a conflict with the other hardware that you just changed. If so, you may need to try other free resources (if any) until there are no conflicts.

7. Click *OK*. If you see a message, click *Yes* to continue.

Go to Step 19.

STEP 27: NO FREE RESOURCES ARE AVAILABLE

You must disable some hardware to relieve the conflict. Do you want to disable the hardware that caused the original conflict?

◀ If you want to disable the hardware that originally caused the conflict, go to Step 18.

◀ If you must use *all* of the hardware in the system, there is *no* further solution to the problem since the conflict cannot be resolved.

STEP 28: FREE SETTING IS FOUND

Determine whether there are any remaining conflicts:

1. Click *OK* to return to the hardware list in *Device Manager*.

2. Double-click the device that had the original conflict to access the device's properties.

3. Click the *Resources* tab.

4. See if there are any remaining conflicts listed in the *Conflicting Device List* box.

NOTE If the conflict you just resolved is listed, you can ignore it. It will no longer conflict after you restart your computer later.

Are there *still* conflicts listed?

◁ If all the resources are now set without any conflicts, go to Step 19.

◁ If some or all of the resources are still conflicting, go back to Step 20.

STEP 29: NO FREE SETTING FOUND

Decide *which* device you should disable. Because *both* conflicting devices need to use the same resource setting, you must decide which device you want to use—and which device you want to live without (at least temporarily). You must disable and/or remove the other device.

It probably is easier to remove the device that had the original conflict. This is usually the *new* device that you've just tried adding to the system. If you choose to remove the *other* device, you may see a message telling you that you still have a conflict after completing the procedure. Just restart the procedure and continue to resolve the conflict.

Which device would you like to disable?

◁ If you choose to disable the device with the *original* conflict, go on to Step 30.

◁ If you choose to disable the *other* device that it is conflicting with, skip to Step 31.

STEP 30: DISABLE ORIGINAL CONFLICTING DEVICE

Now determine whether you have to remove the card to disable the hardware:

1. On the *Device Manager* hardware list, double-click the hardware that you want to disable. If you do not see the hardware list, click *Cancel* until you return to it or close and restart the *Device Manager.*

2. In the *Device Usage* area, make sure that there is a check in the box next to the configuration marked *"Current."* If the box isn't checked, check it now. For Windows 98, check the box marked *"Disable in this hardware profile"* (i.e., Figure 4-7).

3. Click the *Resources* tab. If there is a *Set Configuration Manually* button, Windows 95 can free up resources for this hardware without your removing its card from your computer.

When you see a *Set Configuration Manually* button, and there are no resource settings listed in the box, you'll need to restart your computer.

1. Click *OK,* and then click *OK* again.

2. You may be prompted to restart your computer. Click *Yes.*

When you don't see a *Set Configuration Manually* button (i.e., no button is available), you'll need to disable the physical hardware by removing it from the system.

1. On the *Device Manager* hardware list, click the plus sign (+) next to the type of hardware that you want to disable. If you do not see the hardware list, click *Cancel* until you return to it or close and restart the *Device Manager.*

2. Click the hardware you want to disable.

3. Click *Remove,* and then click *OK.*

4. You may be prompted to restart your computer. You will have to remove the card for this hardware from your computer, so you need to shut down instead of restarting. Click *No.*

5. Click the *Start* button, click *Shut Down,* and then click *Yes.* When the message says it is safe to do so, turn off your computer and remove the card from your computer.

6. Restart your PC and check if your problem has been resolved.

This should correct the conflict and complete your troubleshooting procedure.

STEP 31: DISABLE OTHER CONFLICTING DEVICE

Determine whether you have to remove the card to disable the hardware:

1. On the *Device Manager* hardware list, double-click the hardware that you want to disable. If you do not see the hardware list, click *Cancel* until you return to it.

2. In the *Device Usage* area, click the box next to the configuration marked "*Current*" to remove the check mark. For Windows 98, check the box marked "*Disable in this hardware profile*" (i.e., Figure 4-7).

3. Click the *Resources* tab. If there is a *Set Configuration Manually* button, Windows 95 can free up resources for this hardware without your removing its card from your computer.

Do you see a *Set Configuration Manually* button?

◁ If you see the button, go on to Step 32.

◁ If you don't see the button, skip to Step 33.

STEP 32: DISABLE THE OTHER DEVICE

Determine whether there are any remaining conflicts:

1. Click *OK* to return to the *Device Manager* hardware list.

2. Double-click the device that had the original conflict.

3. Click the *Resources* tab.

4. See if there are any remaining conflicts listed in the *Conflicting Device List* box. If the conflict you just resolved is listed, you can ignore it. It will no longer conflict after you restart your computer later.

Are there still conflicts listed?

◁ If there are no further conflicts, go to Step 19.

◁ If one or more conflicts are still listed, go on to Step 34.

STEP 33: REMOVE THE OTHER DEVICE

Disable the offending hardware by removing it:

1. On the *Device Manager* hardware list, click the plus sign (+) next to the type of hardware that you want to disable. If you do not see the hardware list, click *Cancel* until you return to it.

2. Click the hardware you want to disable.

3. Click *Remove*.

Go to Step 19.

STEP 34: THERE ARE STILL SOME CONFLICTS

Try setting resources to conflict with only one device:

1. Double-click a resource that is still conflicting. If you see a message that says "*You must clear the Use Automatic Settings box before you can change a resource setting,*" click *OK* to close the message and then clear the *Use Automatic Settings* box.

2. Scroll through the available resource settings. For each value, write down the setting and the name of the hardware it conflicts with, then click *Cancel*.

3. Repeat Steps 1 and 2 for each conflicting resource.

4. Looking at the list, see if you can change the resource settings so they conflict with only one device—preferably one you could disable.

Are all conflicts now with one device?

◁ When all the conflicts are with only one device, go back to Step 11.

◁ If the resources still conflict with more than one device (or cannot be changed), there is *no* further solution to this problem, and you should probably remove the conflicting device. Try a similar device from a different manufacturer.

Troubleshooting PnP-Based Problems

Although hardware resource issues and conflicts make up many of the most common Plug-and-Play issues, there are many more problems that can plague a Plug-and-Play system. The system's BIOS version, its mother-board chipset, the installed PnP devices, and even the operating system version can all contribute to problems under Plug-and-Play. This part of the chapter highlights the most frequently encountered symptoms and solutions for PnP and USB port troubleshooting.

PnP BIOS SYMPTOMS

The first set of symptoms comes from the system's PnP BIOS during system startup. The BIOS POST conducts a thorough check of the PC hardware—including the Plug-and-Play system and PCI/PnP devices. This kind of startup testing is necessary to ensure that the PnP BIOS can recognize and allocate initial resources to PCI and PnP devices. If the BIOS detects trouble with the PCI/PnP system at start time, you'll probably see error messages similar to those listed below.

Symptom 1

Bad PnP serial ID checksum. The serial ID checksum of a Plug-and-Play card (or other internal device) is invalid. This typically means that the device is defective. Try replacing the offending expansion card or other device.

Symptom 2

Floppy disk controller resource conflict. The floppy disk controller (typically incorporated onto the motherboard) has requested a resource that is already in use by another device. You'll need to identify the conflicting device(s) and free the resources that are needed for the floppy disk controller.

Symptom 3

NVRAM checksum error, NVRAM cleared. The Extended System Configuration Data (ESCD) was reinitialized because of an NVRAM checksum error. Try rerunning the ISA Configuration Utility (ICU) to reenter any critical "legacy" resource assignments. If the problem persists, replace the CMOS RAM backup battery, replace the CMOS RAM IC (a.k.a. NVRAM), or replace the motherboard outright.

Symptom 4

NVRAM cleared by jumper. The "Clear CMOS" jumper on the motherboard has been moved to the "Clear" position and the system has been initialized. CMOS RAM (a.k.a. NVRAM) and the ESCD have been cleared and now must be reconfigured.

Symptom 5

NVRAM data invalid, NVRAM cleared. Invalid data have been found in the ESCD (which may mean that you have changed devices in the system). When this message is displayed, the BIOS has already rewritten the ESCD with current configuration data. Try rebooting the system—chances are that it will start normally.

Symptom 6

Parallel port resource conflict. The parallel port (typically incorporated onto the motherboard) has requested a resource that is already in use by another device. You'll need to identify the conflicting device(s) and free the resources that are needed by the parallel port.

Symptom 7

PCI error log is full. When errors are encountered with PCI devices during system startup, the errors are recorded to a log. This error means that the maximum number of errors (often more than 15 PCI conflict errors) have been detected and no additional PCI errors can be logged. You should deal with the PCI errors already contained in the log in order to reduce the total number of errors.

Symptom 8

PCI I/O port conflict. Two PCI/PnP devices have requested the same I/O address, resulting in a hardware resource conflict. Try freeing the I/O assignments needed to allow both devices to be configured properly. You may need to disable or remove one of the offending devices to allow the PC to boot normally.

Symptom 9

PCI IRQ conflict. Two PCI/PnP devices have requested the same interrupt setting (IRQ), resulting in a hardware resource conflict. Try freeing the

IRQ(s) needed to allow both devices to be configured properly. You may need to disable or remove one of the offending devices to allow the PC to boot normally.

Symptom 10

PCI memory conflict. Two PCI/PnP devices have requested the same memory range(s), resulting in a hardware resource conflict. Try freeing the memory space needed to allow both devices to be configured properly. You may need to disable or remove one of the offending devices to allow the PC to boot normally.

Symptom 11

Primary boot device not found. The primary boot device designated for your system (i.e., the hard disk drive, floppy disk drive, or CD-ROM drive) could not be found. This typically means that the device is not installed, installed incorrectly, or defective. Since many new device installations often cause loose cables (resulting in boot problems), check the installation and configuration of each boot device.

Symptom 12

Primary IDE controller resource conflict. The primary IDE device controller (typically incorporated onto the motherboard) has requested a resource that is already in use by another device. You'll need to identify the conflicting device(s) and free the resources that are needed for the primary IDE controller.

Symptom 13

Primary input device not found. The primary input device designated for your system (i.e., the keyboard, mouse, glide-pad, or other device) could not be found. This typically means that the device is not installed, installed incorrectly, or defective. Since many new device installations often cause loose cables, check the installation and configuration of all your input devices. Make sure that the input devices are also enabled in the CMOS Setup.

Symptom 14

Secondary IDE controller resource conflict. The secondary IDE device controller (typically incorporated onto the motherboard) has requested a resource that is already in use by another device. You'll need to identify the conflicting device(s) and free the resources that are needed for the secondary IDE controller.

Symptom 15

"Static device resource conflict" or *"System board device resource conflict."* A non-Plug-and-Play ("legacy") ISA card is configured for a resource that is already in use. Try reconfiguring the "legacy" ISA card to use other resources or try freeing the resources needed by the ISA card by reserving resources through an ICU or Windows *Device Manager*.

Symptom 16

Plug-and-Play configuration error. The system has encountered a problem in trying to configure one or more expansion cards. Start the CMOS Setup routine and check that any PnP options have been set correctly. If there are any "configuration utilities" included with your particular system (such as the ICU), try running those utilities to resolve any configuration issues.

STANDARD PnP SYMPTOMS

Of course, there are many more Plug-and-Play problems that are not detected or reported by the BIOS. In most cases, PnP problems will cause symptoms in the detection or allocation of system resources. You'll usually find these errors crop up in Windows with systemwide issues such as poor/erratic device performance or system lockups and crashes. The following symptoms outline many of the most common PnP problems under Windows 95/98.

Symptom 17

Windows 95/98 fails to recognize the computer as "Plug-and-Play." This type of problem often occurs with Intel OEM motherboards (such as those found in early Gateway 2000 systems). Windows does not recognize the computer as a Plug-and-Play platform—even though you receive a message during startup such as *"Intel PnP BIOS extensions installed."* Intel has developed some OEM motherboards that are equipped with a Plug-and-Play BIOS that does not contain the run-time services necessary to configure motherboard devices automatically—an example of such a motherboard is the Intel P5/90. Gateway 2000 (and possibly other OEMs) ship computers with the P5/90 motherboard. You'll need to upgrade the system BIOS to comply with the Plug-and-Play BIOS version 1.0a specification or later. Check with the motherboard (or system) manufacturer to obtain the very latest BIOS.

Symptom 18

You notice IRQ conflicts with PCI display adapters. When you install a PCI video adapter that is configured to use a particular interrupt (IRQ), Windows 95/98 may configure it to use another IRQ that is already in use by another device. Whereas PCI devices *can* share PCI IRQs, Windows does not support sharing PCI IRQs with other non-PCI devices (such as an Ultra-DMA/33 drive controller). Use the *Device Manager* to resolve the conflict by assigning a different IRQ to one of the conflicting devices (usually the new PCI video adapter).

NOTE This kind of behavior does not occur with ISA or VESA Local Bus VLB display adapters.

Symptom 19

The resources for disabled devices are not freed. Even though you disable a device in your computer's CMOS Setup, Windows 95/98 reenables the device and allocates its resources. Windows 95/98 may also reinstall a device that is removed from *Device Manager.* This happens because Windows detects Plug-and-Play devices regardless of the CMOS Setup. To prevent Windows from reactivating disabled hardware, you must disable the hardware in the computer's CMOS Setup *and* remove it from the "current configuration" under your Windows *Device Manager.* This frees the device's resources for other devices to use:

1. Click the *Start* button, select *Settings,* then click *Control Panel.*
2. Double-click the *System* icon.
3. Click the *Device Manager* tab, then double-click the device you want to disable in the hardware list.
4. Click the *General* tab, then click the "*Original Configuration (Current)*" check box to clear it. For Windows 98, make sure the "*Disable in this hardware profile*" box is checked (Figure 4-12).

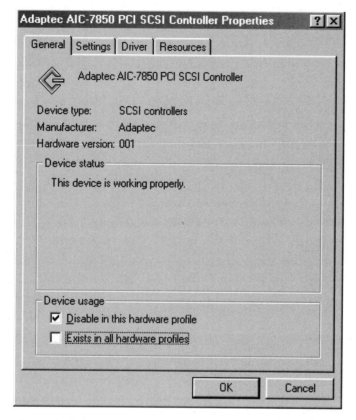

Figure 4-12   Freeing an unneeded device under Windows 98.

5. Click the *OK* button.

6. Restart Windows 95 when prompted. If Windows 98 does not need to restart, close any open windows and shut down/restart the system yourself.

7. Once you see the BIOS banner, immediately start the CMOS Setup routine and disable the device in the CMOS Setup.

8. Save the changes to CMOS, exit, and allow the system to reboot normally.

NOTE When you disable a device in *Device Manager,* you generally must restart your computer before you can reassign the device's resources to another device. If you're trying to disable a "legacy" device, you must physically shut down the PC and *remove* the device after disabling or removing it under Windows.

Symptom 20

An AST PnP BIOS is not registered as PnP. The AST Plug-and-Play BIOS is not registered as Plug-and-Play capable under Windows 95/98, and prevents the autodetection and use of PnP devices. This is usually because the AST PnP BIOS contains incorrect information in its 16-bit protected-mode entry point. When Windows detects this incorrect code in the AST BIOS, it will not recognize the BIOS as Plug-and-Play capable. You will need to contact AST for a BIOS upgrade.

Symptom 21

A PnP ISA adapter is not recognized automatically. If you insert a PnP ISA adapter in a computer whose motherboard does not contain PCI slots, Windows 95/98 may not recognize the new ISA adapter automatically. The *Device Manager* may also display a "PCI bus" entry with an exclamation point in a yellow circle, with the status "No Plug-and-Play ISA bus was found. (Code 29)." This problem is typically caused by a PnP BIOS that is not supported by Windows 95/98 on computers that have a PCI BIOS, but not a PCI bus. On PCI computers, it is usually the PCI driver that starts the PnP ISA driver. If the PCI driver fails, the ISA driver may not be loaded, and therefore PnP ISA adapters are not automatically recognized or configured. To add a PnP adapter so that Windows 95/98 automatically recognizes it, enable the ISA PnP bus manually:

1. In *Control Panel,* double-click the *Add New Hardware* icon and then click *Next.*
2. Click *No* and then click *Next.*
3. Click *System Devices* and then click *Next.*
4. Select *"ISA Plug and Play Bus"* from the list and then click *Next.*
5. Click *Finish.*
6. Restart your computer when you are prompted to do so.

You may also want to contact your computer manufacturer to see about obtaining an updated PnP BIOS that is supported by Windows 95/98.

Symptom 22

The computer no longer operates properly after docking or undocking. As an example, the keyboard or mouse may stop working. *Hot docking* and *hot undocking* refer, respectively, to inserting the computer (typically a laptop or other mobile PC) in a docking station or removing it from the docking station while the computer is running at full power. By contrast, *warm docking* refers to docking or undocking the computer while it is in suspend mode. Laptop or portable computers with a PnP BIOS can be hot or warm docked or undocked. In virtually all cases, this kind of symptom means the computer does not have a suitable PnP BIOS (this is mandatory for hot or warm docking and undocking). To correct this problem on a permanent basis, you'll need to upgrade the laptop's BIOS to a version that supports PnP. In the meantime, you can work around this problem by turning the computer off before you dock or undock it.

Symptom 23

Serial PnP devices are not recognized when an adapter is used to connect them. For example, when you use a 9-pin to 25-pin serial adapter with a serial PnP device (i.e., an external PnP modem), the device may not be enumerated by the configuration manager at startup. This is caused by the adapter—some 9-pin to 25-pin serial adapters do not connect the lines that pass the PnP initialization string (including adapters made by Microsoft before the release of Windows 95). Try another, more current, serial adapter. If the problem persists, add the PnP device manually using the *Add New Hardware Wizard* in the *Control Panel*.

Symptom 24

Windows 95/98 Setup hangs up when detecting SCSI controllers. This often happens with Adaptec SCSI controllers on the first reboot while PnP devices are being detected, and is known to happen when a SCSI hard disk is supported by an Adaptec AHA 2940, Adaptec 2940AU, or Adaptec 2940W controller. You can work around this problem by disabling the SCSI controller and allowing Setup to finish the PnP device detection (then enable the controller later):

1. Enable *PnP SCAM* support in the Adaptec SCSI controller's BIOS Setup.

2. Disable *BIOS Support For Int13 Extension* in the Adaptec SCSI controller's BIOS Setup.

3. Restart Windows 95/98, press the <F8> key when you see the "*Starting Windows . . .*" message, and then choose Safe Mode from the Startup menu.

4. In *Control Panel,* double-click the *System* icon, click the *Performance* tab, click *File System,* and then click the *Troubleshooting* tab (Figure 4-13).

5. Enable the following two options: "*Disable protect-mode hard disk interrupt handling*" and "*Disable all 32-bit protect-mode disk drivers.*"

6. Click *OK* and then click *OK* again.

7. When you are prompted to restart your computer, click *Yes* to continue with Setup.

8. After Windows is installed, return to the *Troubleshooting* tab and disable the options you enabled in Step 5.

Symptom 25

After installing an HP OfficeJet 300 printer, you encounter a "Fatal Exception Error" each time you run the Add New Hardware Wizard. You'll typically see Exception Errors 06, 0E, 0C, or 0D. This is because the "HP

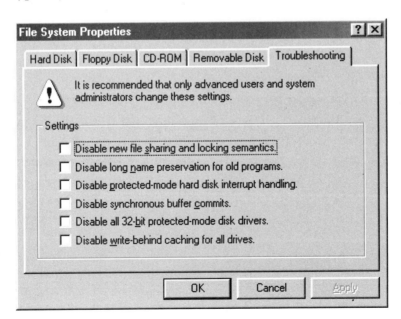

Figure 4-13 Troubleshooting the *File System.*

OfficeJet Series 300 Device Manager" contends with Windows 95/98 for control of PnP. The HP installation process sets up a shortcut in the Startup folder that runs "HPOJDMAN.EXE/AUTOPROMPT." This causes HPOJDMAN.EXE to run in the background. Start the *Close Program* dialog box by pressing <Ctrl> + <Alt> + <Delete>. Click HPOJDMAN in the list of tasks, and then click *End Task*. Check with HP (*www.hp.com*) for updated printer software utilities or remove the HP OfficeJet Series 300 Device Manager software.

Symptom 26

The PS/2 mouse is disabled after installing an ISA PnP device. For example, installing a SoundBlaster 16 "value" sound card disables the PS/2 mouse. This problem can occur on computers where the PnP BIOS (rather than Windows 95/98) assigns resources to ISA PnP devices. The PnP BIOS may assign IRQ 12 to the IDE drive and disable the mouse port. To correct this problem, disable the BIOS PnP support in the computer's CMOS Setup to allow Windows 95/98 to configure the hardware instead.

Symptom 27

When running the Add New Hardware Wizard, it doesn't detect a device that has been removed in Device Manager on a multiple-profile system. This is because removing a PnP device from one profile and leaving it in another causes a flag to be set in the registry to prevent the device from being enumerated on the next startup. This may also cause the *Add New Hardware Wizard* to bypass the device. The flag exists only in the profile in which the device was removed. To prevent this type of problem from occurring, *disable* the device in *Device Manager* instead of *removing* it. To disable a device, click the "*Disable In This Hardware Profile*" check box for the device in *Device Manager*. To restore (or redetect) the device, remove it from all profiles and then run the *Add New Hardware Wizard* or simply reboot the computer and allow the device to be autodetected.

Symptom 28

An extra serial port is displayed in the Device Manager. When you are using Windows 95 OSR 2 or 2.1, you may see an extra communications port in *Device Manager*. There is an exclamation point in a yellow circle next to the port. If you remove the port, it is redetected again the next time you restart your computer. The computer's PnP BIOS is probably reporting (incorrectly) that the COM ports are not using resources, though they were detected during Setup—this is a problem with Windows 95. Check with Microsoft (*www.microsoft.com*) for any available upgrades or patches, or upgrade to Windows 98.

Symptom 29

You cannot set up Windows 95 with a PnP program active. When you try to install Windows 95, you may receive the following error message:

```
A fatal exception OE has occured at 0028:xxxxxxxx in VxD VMM(06) + xxxxxxxx
```

Or, you may receive a *Vwin32* error message displayed on a blue screen, a *registry* error message, or a *general protection fault* (GPF) error message. This problem can occur if you have a PnP program active in memory when you try to install Windows 95. To work around this issue, install Windows 95 from a command prompt. Restart the computer. When you see the *"Starting Windows 95"* message, press the <F8> key, and then choose *Command Prompt Only* from the Startup Menu. At the command prompt, type:

```
<drive>:\setup.exe
```

where `<drive>` is the drive containing your original Windows 95 Setup disk or CD-ROM.

Symptom 30

An IBM ThinkPad doesn't support PnP under Windows. Chances are that the IBM ThinkPad required a BIOS update. The following IBM ThinkPad models are known to need specific BIOS versions:

◁ ThinkPad 750 family: 750/360/755 System Program Service Diskette version 1.20 or later.

◁ ThinkPad 755C/Cs and 360/355 family: 750/360/755 System Program Service Diskette version 1.20 or later.

◁ ThinkPad 755CE/CD, ThinkPad 755CX/CV, ThinkPad 755CDV: 755 System Program Service Diskette version 1.30 or later.

◁ ThinkPad 701C: 701C System Program Service Diskette version 3H or later.

◁ ThinkPad 340CSE and 370C: 340 System Program Service Diskette version 1.10 or later.

The following ThinkPad models require APM BIOS 1.1 or later and PnP BIOS 1.0a or later in order for these features to work correctly with Windows:

◁ ThinkPad 755C/Cs

◁ ThinkPad 360/355 family

◁ ThinkPad 755CE/CD/CX/CV/CDV

◁ ThinkPad 340CSE

◁ ThinkPad 370C

◁ ThinkPad 701C

◁ ThinkPad 530CS

The following ThinkPad models require APM BIOS version 1.0 to work correctly with Windows. There is *no* PnP BIOS support for these models:

◁ ThinkPad 750 family

◁ ThinkPad 340 monochrome display system

◁ ThinkPad 230Cs

To obtain an updated BIOS or System Program Service Diskette for an IBM ThinkPad computer, contact IBM (*www.ibm.com*).

Symptom 31

A PnP pointing device is not detected. When you connect a PnP pointing device (i.e., Microsoft PnP serial mouse, Microsoft EasyBall, or Microsoft IntelliMouse), the new device may not be detected by Windows 95/98. Running the *Add New Hardware Wizard* does not correct the problem. This is almost always because the registry entries for your *previous* pointing device were not properly removed from the Registry. This problem is known to occur when your previous pointing device was a Microsoft, Microsoft-compatible, or Logitech mouse. To work around this problem, use the *Registry Editor* (REGEDIT) to remove the registry entries for your previous pointing device. Remove the following Registry keys:

```
Hkey_Local_Machine\System\CurrentControlSet\Services\Class\Mouse\<nnnn>
```

where <nnnn> is an incremental four-digit number starting at 0000. Also remove the following Registry keys (if they exist):

```
Hkey_Local_Machine\Enum\Root\Mouse\<nnnn>
```

where <nnnn> in an incremental four-digit number starting at 0000. Remove all Registry keys under the following registry key (if they exist):

```
Hkey_Local_Machine\Enum\Serenum
```

Remove the following Registry key (if it exists):

```
Hkey_Local_Machine\Software\Logitech\Mouseware
```

Use the right mouse button to click *My Computer* and then click *Properties* on the menu that appears. Click the *Device Manager* tab. Click each serial pointing device and then click *Remove*. Click *OK,* then restart Windows. When you restart Windows, the attached pointing device will be detected and the appropriate drivers will be installed.

NOTE Before you edit the Registry, you should first make a backup copy of the Registry files (SYSTEM.DAT and USER.DAT). Both are hidden files in the \Windows folder.

Symptom 32

The PnP printer is redetected every time Windows 95 starts. This occurs even when the printer is already installed. When you start Windows 95, the following message may be displayed:

```
New Hardware Found
<device>
Windows has found new hardware and is installing the software for it
```

This problem is known to occur with Hewlett-Packard 4L and Hewlett-Packard DeskJet 660C PnP printers, and is usually caused by damage to the following Registry key:

```
Hkey_Local_Machine\Enum\Lptenum
```

Remove the Registry key and then restart your computer. When Windows starts, it will detect the printer and install support for it. Once the printer is installed, it will no longer be detected each time you start Windows.

NOTE Before you edit the Registry, you should first make a backup copy of the Registry files (SYSTEM.DAT and USER.DAT). Both are hidden files in the \Windows folder.

Symptom 33

After installing Windows 95/98, none of the APM features were installed. You may also note that there is no "battery meter" for laptops. Some computers and BIOS revisions have known incompatibilities with the APM 1.1 specification; you are probably running Windows 95/98 on such a computer. As a result, the hardware "suspend" functions of your computer should still function correctly, but you cannot use the Windows 95/98 APM features. Windows 95/98 turns off APM support *completely* on the following computers:

- AMIBIOS 07/08/1994
- AMIBIOS 07/08/94
- any Gateway ColorBook >1.0 w/SystemSoft BIOS
- any Gateway ColorBook with APM 1.0
- AST Ascentia 900N
- Canon Innova 150C
- DECpc LPv+ 1.00
- DECpc LPv+ 1.01
- DECpc LPv+ 1.02
- NCR/AT&T 3150
- Ultra laptop 486sx33
- Wyse Forte GSV 486/66
- Zenon P5/90

Windows 95/98 turns off power status polling (so you do not see a battery meter) on the following computers:

- IBM ThinkPad 500
- LexBook
- WinBook

Windows 95/98 uses APM 1.0 mode on NEC Versa and AT&T Globalyst systems with APM 1.1 BIOS and no Plug-and-Play BIOS. The following IBM ThinkPad computers support APM 1.1:

◁ ThinkPad 755C

◁ ThinkPad 360/355 Family

◁ ThinkPad 755CE/CD/CX/CV/CDV

◁ ThinkPad 340CSE

◁ ThinkPad 370C

◁ ThinkPad 701C

◁ ThinkPad 530CS

The following IBM ThinkPad computers work with Windows 95/98, but only APM BIOS 1.0 is supported:

◁ ThinkPad 750 family

◁ ThinkPad 340 (monochrome)

◁ ThinkPad 230Cs

The ASUS PCI/I P55SP4 motherboard with a SiS 5511/5512/5513 chipset and an Award BIOS has been known to exhibit similar problems (the battery meter may appear on the Taskbar when it should not). This problem should be fixed with PnP BIOS version 0110 (11/21/95) for revision 1.2 and 1.3 motherboards. Revision 1.4 motherboards have this fix using PnP BIOS version 0303 (11/21/95).

Symptom 34

The Device Manager reports a "PCI-to-ISA Bridge Conflict." The *Device Manager* displays a PCI-to-ISA bridge entry with an exclamation point in a yellow circle—indicating that there is a resource conflict. This problem is typically caused by a PnP BIOS that reports *both* a PCI and an ISA bus, but only an ISA bus is present, so there is no actual conflict. You'll need to update your system's PnP BIOS to a version with better detection and reporting capability.

Symptom 35

The PnP BIOS is disabled on a laptop or notebook computer. When you install Windows 95/98 on a dockable notebook computer with a PnP BIOS, you see no "Eject PC" command on the *Start* menu when the notebook computer is docked in a docking station. Also, no PnP BIOS node is displayed in *System Devices* under the *Device Manager*. This problem was known to occur on IBM ThinkPad (360/750/755 series) dockable notebook computers with a PnP BIOS, and occurs because early versions of dockable notebook computers with PnP BIOS are not fully compatible with Windows 95/98. When a PnP BIOS is disabled in Windows 95/98, certain features (such as warm docking) no longer work. To make your dockable notebook computer compatible with Windows 95/98, contact the manufacturer of your notebook computer and obtain the most recent PnP BIOS.

NOTE In general, a PnP BIOS dated after 7/1/95 is compatible with Windows 95/98.

Symptom 36

The sound device on a DEC HiNote Ultra isn't working. When you install Windows 95/98 over an existing Windows for Workgroups 3.1x or Windows 3.1x installation on a DEC HiNote Ultra computer with a PnP BIOS, the sound device no longer works properly. Also, the wrong sound device is installed in Windows. This is a PnP BIOS problem—early versions of the DEC HiNote Ultra shipped with a PnP BIOS are not compatible with Windows 95/98. Contact DEC and obtain the most recent PnP BIOS for the DEC HiNote Ultra.

Symptom 37

Device resources are not updated in a "forced" configuration. You'll notice that an exclamation point appears over a resource icon in *Computer Properties* in *Device Manager,* or that changes you make to the resources assigned to a PnP device in the computer's CMOS Setup are not reflected in the "Settings" column in *Computer Properties* under *Device Manager.* This is because the device is using a "forced" configuration instead of an automatic configuration. To remove a forced configuration and allow the PnP device to be fully configurable by the computer's BIOS and Windows 95/98, set the device to use automatic settings:

1. Double-click the *System* icon in *Control Panel.*
2. Click the *Device Manager* tab.
3. Double-click the device and then click the *Resources* tab.
4. Click the "*Use Automatic Settings*" check box to select it (i.e., Figure 4-3).
5. Click *OK.*

NOTE A "forced" configuration overrides any BIOS or ROM settings (even if Windows 95/98 knows the device is currently consuming a different set of resources). If you move a device to a different set of resources, you must update the forced configuration manually. When you are diagnosing hardware problems, it is a good idea to look for forced configurations and remove them.

Symptom 38

Restarting the computer causes the PC to hang. This often happens when you try to restart your computer using the *"Restart the computer"* option in the *Shut Down Windows* dialog box. This problem can occur on computers with a BIOS that expects IRQ 12 to be used by a PS/2-style mouse port, but instead have a software-configurable hardware device (such as a PnP adapter) using IRQ 12. To work around this problem, either reserve IRQ 12 in *Device Manager* or change the IRQ for the software-configurable device in *Device Manager.* You may also want to consider upgrading the BIOS in the computer to a later version. To reserve an IRQ with *Device Manager:*

1. In the *Control Panel,* double-click the *System* icon.
2. On the *Device Manager* tab, double-click *Computer.*
3. On the *Reserve Resources* tab (Figure 4-14), click the *Interrupt Request (IRQ)* option, and then click *Add.*
4. In the *Value* box, click the IRQ you want to reserve.
5. Click *OK* until you return to *Control Panel.*

Symptom 39

Adding a PCI device to a Dell Dimension causes the system to hang in Windows 95/98. The BIOS in the Dell computer has probably configured the new PCI device to use IRQ 10, but another legacy device installed in the system is already configured to use IRQ 10. Although Windows 95/98 is designed to recognize resource conflicts such as this, this particular conflict causes the computer to hang before the Windows *Configuration Manager* recognizes that the conflict exists. Although the PCI bus is normally a PnP-compatible bus, the BIOS in Dell Dimension computers statically allocates IRQ 10 to a new PCI device—there is no way to disable this behavior. To work around this problem, configure the existing legacy device to use an IRQ *other* than IRQ 10.

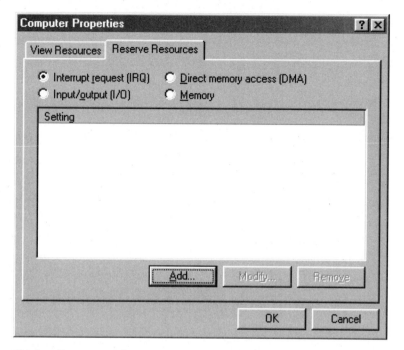

Figure 4-14 Reserving system resources.

Symptom 40

You cannot configure disabled devices in the Device Manager. When you're using a PnP BIOS, you may not be able to configure (through *Device Manager*) a device that has been disabled in the BIOS—even though the BIOS supports configuring devices for the next time the computer starts. When you click the device in *Device Manager* and then click *Properties*, you see a message such as:

```
The device has been disabled in the hardware. In order to use this
device, you must re-enable the hardware. See your hardware documentation
for details (Code 29).
```

This is a problem with Windows. You'll need to enable the device in the BIOS *before* you try to configure it in *Device Manager*.

Symptom 41

A Toshiba T4900 laptop doesn't switch from LCD to external monitor. If you place a Toshiba T4900 computer into its docking station while Windows 95/98 is running (a "warm dock" operation), the display may not switch from the LCD screen to the external monitor. Toshiba's PnP BIOS does not switch the display properly between the LCD screen and an external monitor. For a short-term workaround, press the <F5> key to manually toggle the display between the LCD screen and the external monitor. In the meantime, contact Toshiba for a PnP BIOS upgrade.

Symptom 42

A third port is detected with a CMD PCI dual-port IDE controller. When using a CMD PCI Dual-Port IDE controller (with at least *one* device on both the primary and secondary port), the *Device Manager* displays a third port. This "false" third port is displayed with an exclamation point inside a yellow circle. This happens because the PnP BIOS in your computer is erroneously reporting that a third port is present. Windows 95/98 does not allocate any resources to the third port and the existence of the third port in *Device Manager* should not cause any problems; however, if you want to disable the third port, follow these steps:

1. Use the right mouse button to click *My Computer,* then click *Properties* on the menu that appears.
2. Click the *Device Manager* tab.
3. Click the third port, then click *Properties.* Note that you may need to expand a branch of the hardware tree by double-clicking the branch, or by clicking the plus sign (+) to the left of the branch, before you can click the port.
4. Click the *"Original Configuration (Current)"* check box to clear it, then click *OK.* Reboot the PC if necessary.

INFRARED SYMPTOMS UNDER WINDOWS 98

Infrared technology has provided a convenient tool for short-range wireless communication between PnP PCs and peripheral devices. Although infrared communication has proven popular, there are still a number of problems that can arise. This part of the chapter highlights several of the more common infrared issues that you should be familiar with.

Symptom 43

An infrared device is in range, but the PC will not detect its presence. There are many possible reasons why a PC may not detect an infrared device. First make sure that the PC's infrared system has been enabled and see that the remote infrared device is turned on and enabled for infrared communication. Also check the Infrared Monitor utility to verify that the "search interval" is not set too high (otherwise, it may seem as if the PC never checks for infrared devices).

Double-check the infrared device to see that it is actually in range and see that there are no obstacles blocking the infrared activity (even dirt, grease, or dust on the infrared covers can cause unwanted interference). If you're working in a sunlit room, make sure that direct sunlight (which is rich in infrared) is not shining on either end of the infrared link. Finally, if there are other non-IrDA devices nearby, see that none of them is attempting to communicate.

Symptom 44

You cannot print to an infrared printer. This is usually caused by a minor oversight in the setup of your infrared link. Verify that the printer is turned on and in range of the PC and make sure nothing is blocking the communications path. Also check the PC's Infrared Monitor application and see that infrared communication is enabled. Finally, check that the printer is assigned to the PC's infrared printer port.

Symptom 45

You notice that an infrared device frequently seems to go out of range. In most cases, intermittent infrared communication is caused by physical factors. Keep both infrared devices still (movement or vibration can sometimes cause intermittent communication). Try moving the infrared devices closer together and see that there are no obstructions between the devices. Clean the infrared windows of dust, grease, or grime, and see that there is no direct sunlight shining on either infrared device (try shading the devices from sunlight). Finally, if one of the devices is using a battery-powered infrared transceiver, make sure that the batteries are fresh or fully charged.

Symptom 46

You find that infrared communication has been interrupted. This is not an intermittent problem. If communication is interrupted, it is usually because something has moved between the infrared devices or one of the devices has been moved. Remove the obstruction or move the device back into range. If there is no obstruction (and the devices are in range), check to see if direct sunlight (or another infrared device) is interfering with the infrared communication.

Symptom 47

Infrared communication takes place, but it is not efficient. Efficiency of infrared communication is affected by several factors that can cause inter-mittent behavior or frequent interruptions:

◄ *Movement*—make sure the devices are not moving or vibrating in any way.

◄ *Range*—try moving the infrared devices closer together.

◄ *Sunlight*—try shading the devices from direct sunlight or turn off bright nearby lighting.

◄ *Obstructions*—check for and remove any partial obstructions between infrared devices. Also try cleaning the infrared windows.

USB SYMPTOMS

In spite of its great promise, the pathway toward USB has been *anything* but straightforward. Chipset issues, BIOS versions, and operating system bugs (along with a surprisingly slow introduction of USB peripherals by the PC industry) continue to present serious problems for USB users. This part of the chapter examines many of the more common USB symptoms that you may encounter.

Symptom 48

Pressing <Ctrl> + <Alt> + <Del> on the USB keyboard has no effect. This problem has been reported when connecting the Microsoft Natural Keyboard Elite (version 1.0) to the Universal Serial Bus (USB) port on a computer running Windows 98. According to Microsoft, this is a problem with Windows 98 itself and should be corrected in the final release. To correct the problem in the meantime, either revert to a version of OSR 2.x or exchange the keyboard for another model (or use a conventional keyboard). In some cases, the CMOS Setup may offer a switch to enable a USB keyboard. If such a switch is available, be sure it's enabled.

Symptom 49

You cannot log on to Windows 98 through the USB keyboard. This problem has been reported with the Microsoft Natural Keyboard Elite (version 1.0) under Windows 98. The keyboard does *not* respond the first time you try to log on. This occurs because you must log on to Windows 98 *before* Windows can detect the keyboard and install the drivers needed to use it. Use the following steps to work around the problem:

1. Shut down and turn off your computer.
2. Connect the keyboard to the USB port on the computer.
3. Connect a PS/2 keyboard to a PS/2 port on the computer.
4. Use the PS/2 keyboard to log on to Windows 98. Windows 98 then detects the keyboard and installs the proper drivers.
5. Shut down and turn off the computer again.
6. Disconnect the PS/2 keyboard.
7. Restart the computer and use the USB keyboard to log on to Windows 98 normally.

NOTE As with Symptom 48, your CMOS Setup may be recent enough to enable a USB keyboard under BIOS and DOS before Windows loads. If this option is available, be sure it's enabled.

Symptom 50

Windows 95 OSR 2.1 hangs while a USB device is "hot inserted." Under some conditions, plugging a USB device into the PC can cause an overcurrent condition. The problem is that Windows 95 OSR 2.1 does not clear the overcurrent status of the USB hardware, which in turn causes Windows 95 to service the same overcurrent error multiple times, thereby hanging up the system. This is a problem with Windows 95 OSR 2.1. OSR 2.5 should fix this problem by updating Windows 95 with the following files:

```
OPENHCI.SYS    2/17/98 31,280 (version 4.03.1217)
USBHUB.SYS     2/17/98 28,448 (version 4.03.1217)
```

This problem should also be corrected with the release of Windows 98.

Symptom 51

The computer hangs after attempting to "resume" from a power-saving mode. This is a known problem, which occurs frequently under Windows 95 OSR 2.1 and can manifest itself in two general scenarios:

1. First, the system may hang if you use the PC's "sleep" button to manually place the PC into a power-saving mode; use the "sleep" button again to resume normal operation.

2. Second, the system may hang if it automatically switches to a "sleep" mode (or other power-saving mode) after some period of inactivity; then you use the "sleep" button to resume normal operation.

This is a problem with Windows 95 OSR 2.1. OSR 2.5 should fix this problem by updating Windows 95 with the following file:

```
USBHUB.SYS    8/29/97 28,448 (version 4.03.1215)
```

This problem should also be corrected with the release of Windows 98.

Symptom 52

You experience docking and power management trouble with mobile USB-equipped PCs. There are three general problem modes that can occur when using the USB driver in Windows 95 OSR 2.1 with a USB-equipped mobile PC:

1. The PC's "hot docking" feature of the mobile PC may function only intermittently (if at all).

2. The automatic power-saving modes (i.e., "sleep" or "suspend") may not work properly on some mobile PC models.

3. When entering a power-saving mode, the CPU clock is not properly slowed or stopped by the power management software.

This is a problem with Windows 95 OSR 2.1. OSR 2.5 should fix this problem by updating Windows 95 with the following file:

```
UHCD.SYS     8/13/97 39,872 (version 4.03.1215)
```

This problem should also be corrected with the release of Windows 98.

Symptom 53

You find that the PC hangs when working with USB. This is a known problem under Windows 95 OSR 2.1. The USB-equipped computer may hang in any of several known situations:

- If a mobile PC's PC Card controller is in CardBus mode and the PC is docked to a port replicator, the PC may hang when undocking. This is a known problem with USB-equipped Toshiba portables.

- When suspending and resuming a PC's operation with a USB mouse (such as a Logitech USB mouse), the PC may not complete its resume process successfully.

- When disabling a USB Root Hub device in the Device Manager while PC Card sockets are enabled, either the system may hang or a "Fatal Exception Error 0E" may appear.

- When rapidly installing and removing a USB game pad (such as an ALPS USB game pad), either the PC may hang or a "Fatal Exception Error 0E" may appear.

This is a problem with Windows 95 OSR 2.1. OSR 2.5 should fix this problem by updating Windows 95 with the following file:

```
OPENHCI.SYS   7/17/97 31,248 (version 4.03.1214)
```

Some Toshiba portable computers also require the following updated file for Windows 95 OSR 2.1:

```
CBSS.VXD      6/13/97 16,249 (version 4.00.1117)
```

This problem should also be corrected with the release of Windows 98.

Symptom 54

During the setup of OSR 2.1, you find that the VMM32.VXD file is missing or damaged. This problem occurs when rebooting the PC after installing OSR 2.1 and may prevent you from restarting Windows 95. This error can occur if the VMM32.VXD file was not rebuilt properly (or was damaged)—resulting in an error message suggesting that "*VMM32.VXD is missing or corrupt.*" The rebuilding of the VMM32.VXD file was unsuccessful, preventing Windows 95 from booting properly and processing the RunOnce section of the Registry. This error can also occur when the addition of USB support causes a conflict with the system and Windows 95 is unable to boot normally. To correct the problem, you'll need to use either of the following procedures:

If the VMM32.VXD file is missing or damaged. You must uninstall OSR 2.1 using the OSR 2.1 real-mode uninstall tool (REM.PSS) on the installation disk:

1. Restart the computer and press <F8> when you see *"Starting Windows 95."*

2. Choose *"Safe Mode Command Prompt Only"* from the Startup menu.

3. Copy the REM.PSS file to the root folder of the boot drive as "REMUSB.BAT" (do not copy it to REM.BAT because "Rem" is a reserved command and it will not function).

4. Type REMSUB to restore the original files that were renamed with an .o20 extension.

5. To complete the uninstall process, restart your computer and use the *Add/Remove Programs* tool in *Control Panel* to remove the program *"WDM/USB Supplement."*

6. Delete the REMSUB.BAT file from the root folder of the boot drive.

7. Restart the computer normally, then try reinstalling OSR 2.1 from a known-good source disk.

If Windows 95 cannot boot because of a conflict. If there is a conflict between Windows 95 and USB support, follow these steps:

1. Restart the computer and press <F8> when you see *"Starting Windows 95."*

2. Choose *"Safe Mode"* from the Startup menu.

3. Rename the DETROIT.BAT file to AUTOEXEC.BAT. The DETROIT.BAT file is actually your original AUTOEXEC.BAT file that was renamed by the OSR 2.1 Setup process.

4. Troubleshoot the conflict while in the Safe Mode or delete OSR 2.1 as shown previously.

Symptom 55

You find that a USB peripheral may not function properly in any USB port. For example, this is a known problem with the Compaq USB camera.

When you attempt to use a Compaq USB camera with an OpenHCI (OHCI) USB host controller, the camera may not be detected and probably will not work properly.

This means your particular USB peripheral was probably designed and developed for use on the Intel Universal HCI (UHCI) USB host controller, and is *not* supported on an OHCI controller. OHCI host controllers employ optimization, which allows multiple transactions to be submitted within a single frame. By comparison, the UHCI host controller sends only a single transaction per frame. This means the peripheral (i.e., the Compaq USB camera) cannot respond to a second transaction within a single frame.

Such a PC-specific peripheral cannot be used on other PCs; for more information, you'll need to contact the peripheral maker for any patches or workarounds.

Symptom 56

Your USB keyboard does not operate in DOS. Chances are that this is a fault of the BIOS. Without a USB-aware operating system (such as Windows 98 or Windows NT 5.0), USB keyboards rely on the system BIOS for support. If the BIOS does not directly support USB keyboards, your keyboard won't work under DOS. You'll receive a *"Keyboard Error"* or *"Keyboard Not Present"* error message when you start the computer. Check with the motherboard or system maker for available BIOS upgrades. In the meantime, there are generally two ways to work around this issue.

1. First, you can replace the USB keyboard with a PS/2 model outright. Shut down Windows 95/98 and turn off the computer. Disconnect the USB keyboard and remove the USB adapter. Connect a PS/2 keyboard to a PS/2 port on the computer and then restart the computer.

2. Second, you can use a "dual keyboard" strategy. If you have a PS/2 keyboard available, shut down Windows 95/98 and turn off the computer. Plug the PS/2 keyboard into a PS/2 port on the computer (leaving the USB keyboard attached), then restart the computer. You can then use the PS/2 keyboard in DOS and use the USB keyboard in Windows.

BIOS Update Guide

As you reviewed the many PnP-related symptoms discussed earlier, you probably noticed that a large number of problems could be traced to the system BIOS. Updating the BIOS (especially on older systems) is often the fastest and most complete means of correcting PnP support issues. This means you should have some understanding of how to perform a BIOS upgrade. This part of the chapter outlines the procedure for basic BIOS upgrades and offers some troubleshooting tips in the event your upgrade hits a snag.

FLASHING THE BIOS

"Flash" BIOS represents the newest class of BIOS ROM ICs, typically found in fast i486 and virtually all Pentium, Pentium MMX, and Pentium II PCs. A flash BIOS is essentially an *electrically erasable programmable read-only memory* (EEPROM)—that is, the IC can be erased and reprogrammed right on the motherboard. Rather than worry about warehousing and shipping new BIOS ICs, a BIOS or motherboard manufacturer can provide updated BIOS code as a downloadable file directly from an Internet Web site. The name of the file is typically coupled to a particular motherboard; for example, updating the flash BIOS on an AMI Atlas ISA/PCI Pentium motherboard requires a file named S721P.ROM. If this file name is not used, the BIOS will not be reprogrammed. The AMI Excalibur PCI-II ISA/PCI Pentium motherboard requires the filename S722P.ROM. When attempting a flash procedure, follow the points below:

◁ First, you *must* have a flash BIOS IC in the computer. If the IC does not use "flash" technology, you won't be able to reprogram it—instead, you'll need to replace the BIOS IC outright.

◁ Make a complete backup of your system hard drive(s) in the event of drive problems after the flash process is complete.

◁ Make a complete record of all CMOS Setup settings before flashing the BIOS. In many cases, you'll need to restore or tweak the CMOS Setup again after performing the flash upgrade. Pay particular attention to the hard-drive geometry settings.

◁ Record the current BIOS version number and/or release date and verify that you do not already have this version running on your system.

◁ When downloading the flash file (usually several BIOS data files, a flashing utility, and brief documentation all compressed into a single .ZIP file), be certain to download *only* the flash package for your exact PC make and model.

NOTE Downloading and flashing the INCORRECT BIOS upgrade can render your computer unbootable—forcing you to replace the physical BIOS IC.

A BASIC FLASH PROCEDURE

◁ Create a "clean," bootable floppy disk with any version of DOS or as a Windows 95/98 Startup Disk.

◁ Copy the downloaded .ZIP file containing your flash package to the diskette and decompress the .ZIP file into its constituent files (usually an .EXE file as the flashing utility, a .BIN or .ROM file as the new BIOS data file, and one or more .TXT files as the documentation).

NOTE NEVER attempt to flash a BIOS by running the flash utility from a hard drive. Proceed from the floppy drive only.

◁ You may need to set the "Flash Enable" jumper on the motherboard. If so, turn off the PC, locate this jumper (refer to the documentation for your system), and set it.

◁ Reboot the PC and start your CMOS Setup to verify that the PC will boot from the floppy drive first. This is usually indicated as a "Boot Order" or "Boot Sequence" of A:/C:.

◁ Once the PC boots "clean" from the bootable diskette, start the flashing utility such as:

```
A:\> awdflash    <Enter>
```

◁ When the flash program starts, it may ask you for the name of the .BIN or .ROM file you wish to use as an upgrade. Type in the *exact* name of this file when prompted to do so. In some cases, the flash utility will automatically use the only available source file.

◁ Many flash utilities will query you to back up your current BIOS. If you have this opportunity, make a backup copy of the current BIOS before proceeding. Enter the file name to save and proceed. In some cases, the flash program will assign a backup file name automatically (i.e., BACKUP.BIN).

◁ You will then be asked if you are sure you wish to continue; answer *Yes*.

◁ Once the flash process begins, you'll usually see a "Progress Indicator" at the bottom of the display that will keep track of the flashing process.

IMPORTANT NOTE **It is critical that you do NOT power down or reset the PC while the flash process is proceeding. Doing so will interrupt the flash process and leave your BIOS corrupt and *unrecoverable*.**

◁ When the "Progress Indicator" has stopped (or the flash process has otherwise concluded), you'll probably see a message such as *"Please cycle power or reset this machine."*

◁ Turn your computer *completely off*—your new BIOS is installed and is ready to use.

◁ If you had to set a "Flash Enable" jumper on the motherboard, reset it now before restoring power to the PC.

◁ Remove the bootable diskette from the system.

◁ Restart the computer now—the new BIOS version will be shown on the display screen. You're done with the BIOS upgrade.

◁ In most cases, you'll need to restore your CMOS Setup parameters before you can utilize the PC.

If there is an error at any point in the reprogramming process, you may hear one or more beeps. Table 4-1 outlines the beeps and descriptions for AMI flash BIOS. These are not beep codes in the classical sense, but flash BIOS procedural errors. Keep in mind that the flash BIOS procedures outlined here may vary for your particular system.

TABLE 4-1   AMI Flash Programming Beep Messages

Beeps	Meaning
None	No error. Successful completion
Continuous Single Beep	No floppy disk in drive A:
Five Beeps	Needed .ROM program not present on floppy disk
Seven Beeps	Floppy read error
Six Beeps	BIOS file-size error
Eight Beeps	The expected flash EEPROM is not present
Continuous Two Beeps	Problem erasing the flash EEPROM
Continuous Three Beeps	Problem programming the flash EEPROM
Continuous Four Beeps	BIOS is not able to reset the CPU

TROUBLESHOOTING BIOS UPGRADES

Ideally, a "flash" BIOS upgrade can be accomplished quickly and easily, and upgrades are rarely plagued by problems; however, BIOS upgrade problems can and do occur, and can be quite serious under the right circumstances. This part of the chapter looks at a series of common BIOS upgrade symptoms and solutions.

Symptom 57

The PC does not boot after upgrading the BIOS. This is the classic problem that most frequently haunts technicians. When you've replaced the physical BIOS ICs, double-check the IC(s) for proper orientation and installation. Make sure that all of the pins are inserted into the socket and that none of the DIP pins have been bent under the IC's body. If you're replacing "even and odd" BIOS ICs, make sure that you have not accidentally transposed the even and odd IC locations. If the problem persists, try replacing the original BIOS ICs. If the original IC(s) work, you may have defective or improper replacement IC(s).

If you've flashed the BIOS, chances are that your problem is a little stickier. You've either flashed the *wrong* BIOS version or the flash process failed for some reason. In either case, there's nothing you can do except to replace the BIOS IC. You'll need to contact the system or motherboard manufacturer for a replacement.

Symptom 58

You accidentally reset or powered down the PC during a BIOS flash, and now the PC won't start. The great weakness of flash BIOS is that it cannot be interrupted once the flash process is underway; otherwise, the BIOS will be left "partially programmed" and totally corrupted. Your only course of action here is to replace the BIOS IC outright. You'll need to contact the system or motherboard manufacturer for a replacement.

Symptom 59

The BIOS upgrade proceeded properly, but now the system behaves erratically or other errors appear. There are several potential causes here. Most of the time, you've either flashed the wrong BIOS version (probably for a system using an *almost* identical motherboard), or the BIOS was corrupted during the flash process. If you made a backup copy of the original BIOS file during the flash process, repeat the process and restore the original BIOS version. If the system works, you can verify that you downloaded the correct flash file (and repeat the upgrade if possible). If you cannot restore the original BIOS, or the problems persist, replace the BIOS IC. If the problem occurs when replacing physical ICs, chances are that you've installed the BIOS for the wrong PC or motherboard, and you'll need to replace the original BIOS ICs until you get the proper replacements.

Symptom 60

The BIOS upgrade proceeded properly, but system performance seems poor. This is a frequent (but little-discussed) complaint with BIOS upgrades. In many cases, a new BIOS will require you to restore or tweak your CMOS Setup for proper performance. If you recorded your original CMOS Setup contents before attempting your upgrade, you can enter the CMOS Setup and compare the current settings to the original ones—chances are that one or more performance-oriented settings have been disabled in order to ensure proper system booting. Here are some points for quick tweaking (remember that not all of these features may be available in all BIOS versions)—for fastest booting:

◁ Set the "Boot Sequence" to C:/A:.

◁ Set the "Boot Up Floppy Drive Seek" to DISABLED.

◁ Set the "Boot Up System Speed" to HIGH.

◁ Set the "Quick Power-on Self Test" to ENABLED.

For highest overall system performance:

◁ ENABLE all shadowing unless you are using an adapter that absolutely requires that shadowing be disabled for a specified address. Video shadow will increase the video speed.

◁ Set "Auto Configuration" to DISABLE.

◁ Reduce all of the memory timings to their minimum values.

◁ ENABLE the "Turbo Read Lead Off."

◁ ENABLE the "Speculative Lead Off."

◁ ENABLE the "Turn Around Insertion."

◁ Increase the ISA Speed by setting the ISA Clock to PCICLK/3.

◁ Lower 8- and 16-Bit Recovery times to 1 (one) each.

◁ Set the "System BIOS Cacheable" to Enable.

◁ Set the "Video BIOS Cacheable" to Enable.

◁ L2 Cache Cacheable Size—If you are installing 64 MB of RAM or more, set to 512 MB (64 MB is the default).

◁ Pipeline Cache Timing—Set to FASTEST if there is only 256-KB total pipeline cache (FASTER is the default).

NOTE When tweaking BIOS settings in the CMOS Setup, be sure to change only *one* parameter at a time, then retest the system's performance each time.

Symptom 61

You see a message such as "Update ESCD Successfully" on boot up. This is not really an error, but more of an informational message. The ESCD (Extended System Configuration Data) is a method that the BIOS uses to store resource information for both PNP and non-PNP devices. The reason it shows this message is that the system has at least one ISA card in it and it is running Windows 95/98. The ESCD boot-up sequence arranged by Windows 95/98 is different from the ESCD boot-up sequence arranged by the BIOS. So on boot-up, the system BIOS will attempt to update the ESCD; this will in no way affect system performance.

Symptom 62

You just upgraded the BIOS, and now can't boot from the A: drive. Otherwise, the A: drive seems to be working normally. In virtually all cases, the updated BIOS defaulted the CMOS Setup to a "Boot Sequence" of C:/A: instead of A:/C:, so the system isn't even checking the floppy drive at startup. Start your CMOS Setup and tweak the "Boot Sequence" to A:/C:, then save your changes and try the system again. Also verify that you actually have a working bootable floppy disk in the drive.

Symptom 63

You get a message saying "Incompatible BIOS translation detected - unable to load disk overlay." This typically happens when you upgrade a BIOS to support Logical Block Addressing (LBA), but the hard drive in your system is already using overlay software such as *Disk Manager.* Since overlay software and LBA are usually incompatible, you'll need to either disable LBA in the CMOS Setup or remove the overlay software from the hard drive. Since you probably upgraded the BIOS to support LBA anyway, chances are that you'll want to remove the overlay software:

- ◁ Back up the hard drive before proceeding.
- ◁ Boot the system from a bootable floppy disk.
- ◁ Run FDISK and delete all partitions on the hard drive.
- ◁ Reboot and check with FDISK to be sure that all the partitions on the drive have been removed.
- ◁ You can repartition and reformat the drive, then restore your files from a backup.

If you cannot remove all partitions from the hard drive with FDISK, you can use the following procedure to erase the master boot record (MBR) on the hard drive. (Note that this procedure will render *all* data on the drive inaccessible. Be sure to back up the system completely before proceeding.) You'll need the DEBUG utility on your bootable diskette before proceeding:

```
A:\> debug          <Enter>
F 200 L200 0
a 100
mov ax,301
mov bx,200
```

```
mov cx,1
mov dx,0080          ;Note: use 0081 for second fixed disk
int 13
int 3
(enter a blank line here)
G=100
q
```

The drive should now have no partitions on it. Reboot and use FDISK to partition the drive, and FORMAT to reformat each partition. You can then restore the operating system and recover files from your backup.

CMOS Settings for PCI and PnP

Plug-and-Play (PnP) and the PCI (Peripheral Component Interconnect) bus are two tightly related features designed not only to ease the configuration burden of PC devices but also to provide those devices with a high-performance bus capable of working directly with the CPU and main memory. However, Plug-and-Play and PCI features must be configured properly in the CMOS Setup in order to ensure trouble-free operation. This appendix explains the options used to configure PCI slots and PnP behavior in many different CMOS Setup routines.

NOTE The selections below represent a cross section of many different BIOS makers. Not all of the entries listed will appear in every CMOS Setup routine.

Latency Timer (PCI Clocks)

This entry controls the length of time an agent on the PCI bus can hold the bus when another device has requested it. Since the PCI bus runs faster than the ISA bus, the PCI bus must be slowed during interactions with it. This setting allows you to define how long the PCI bus will delay for a transaction between the given PCI slot and the ISA bus. This number depends on the PCI master device in use, and ranges from 0 to 255. The default is often 66, but 40 is a good place to start. Smaller values result in faster access to the bus (with better response times), but bandwidth and data throughput become lower. Normally, you'd leave this setting alone unless you're working with latency-sensitive devices (i.e., audio cards or network cards with small buffers).

PCI Slot x INTx

Use this entry to assign PCI interrupts (INT#s) to specific PCI slots.

◄ *Edge/Level Select.* Once an interrupt is assigned with *"PCI Slot x INTx,"* this option programs PCI IRQs to single-edge or logic level triggering modes. Most PCI cards use level triggering, whereas most ISA cards use edge triggering. However, try selecting edge triggering for PCI IDE.

PCI Device, Slot 1/2/3

This feature enables I/O and memory cycle decoding for PCI slots. There are three options: (1) Enable (enables the device as a slave PCI device); (2) En Master (enables the device as a master PCI device); and (3) Use Default Latency Timer. If this is enabled (yes) you don't need to set the Latency Timer value.

Slot X Using INT#

This entry selects an interrupt (INT#) channel for a PCI slot; there are four (A, B, C, and D) for each one—that is, each PCI bus slot supports interrupts A, B, C, and D. INT#A is allocated automatically, and you would use #B, #C, and #D only if the PCI card needs to use more than one (PCI) interrupt service. For example, select #D if your PCI card needs four interrupts. Often, it is simplest to use the Auto mode.

Xth Available IRQ

This feature selects (or "maps") an IRQ for one of the available INT#s (A, B, C, or D). There are 11 selections (3, 4, 5, 6, 7, 9, 10, 11, 12, 14, 15). First available IRQ means the BIOS will assign this IRQ to the first PCI slots (order is 1, 2, 3, 4), and so on. N/A means the particular IRQ has been assigned to the ISA bus, and is therefore not available to a PCI slot.

PCI IRQ Activated By

This feature lists the method by which the PCI bus recognizes an IRQ request (Level or Edge). Use the default entries unless advised otherwise by your PCI device manufacturer or if you have a PCI device that recognizes only one of these methods.

Configuration Mode

This entry sets the method by which information about "legacy" cards is conveyed to the system:

◄ *Use ICU.* The BIOS depends on information provided by Plug-and-Play software (such as the Configuration Manager or ISA Configuration Utility). Select this only if you have the utilities needed.

◄ *Use Setup Utility.* The BIOS depends on information provided in the CMOS Setup routine—don't use configuration utilities.

ISA Shared Memory Size

This option sets a block of system memory that will not be shadowed. This feature should normally be disabled unless you have an ISA card that uses the upper memory area. If you enable this feature you'll also need to configure the following:

◄ *ISA Shared Memory Base Address.* Enter the base address here. If you choose 64 K, you can choose only D000h or below.

IRQ 3–IRQ 15

These entries are used to list what IRQs are in use (or reserved) by ISA "legacy" cards. If you don't use specific IRQs, set the respective entries to "*Available*"; otherwise, set "*Used by ISA Card,*" which means that nothing else can use it.

PCI IDE Prefetch Buffers

This feature allows you to enable or disable a set of prefetch buffers in the PCI IDE controller. You may need to disable this feature with an operating system (such as Windows NT) that doesn't use the BIOS to access the hard disk and doesn't disable interrupts when completing a programmed I/O operation. Disabling also prevents errors with faulty PCI-IDE interface chips that can corrupt data on the hard disk (as can happen with true 32-bit operating systems). You can usually leave this feature disabled.

PCI IDE 2nd Channel

Disable this feature if you're not using the 2nd channel on the PCI IDE card. This frees up IRQ 15; otherwise, you will lose IRQ 15 on the ISA slots.

PCI IDE IRQ Map To

This option allows you to configure your system to the type of IDE disk controller. An ISA device is assumed. If you have a PCI IDE controller, this setting allows you to specify which slot has the controller and which PCI INT# (A, B, C, or D) is associated with the connected hard drives. Note that this refers to the hard disk rather than individual partitions. Since each IDE controller supports two drives, you can select the INT# for each. Also note that the primary channel has a lower interrupt than the secondary channel. There are four modes:

1. *PCI-Auto.* If the IDE is detected by the BIOS on one of the PCI slots, then the appropriate INT# channel will be assigned to IRQ 14.
2. *PCI-Slot X.* If the IDE is not detected, you can manually select the slot.
3. *Primary IDE INT#, Secondary IDE INT#.* This assigns 2 INT# channels for primary and secondary channels (if supported).
4. *ISA.* This option assigns no IRQs to PCI slots. Use this mode for PCI IDE cards that connect IRQs 14 and 15 directly from an ISA slot using a table from a legacy paddle board.

PCI Bus Parking

This is a sort of bus mastering—a device parking on the PCI bus has full control of the bus for a short time. This feature improves performance when that device is being used, but excludes others. Try enabling this feature with network cards and hard disk controllers.

IDE Buffer for DOS and Windows

When enabled, this feature provides IDE read-ahead and posted-write buffers, so you can increase throughput to and from IDE devices by buffering reads and writes. However, this feature may actually slow older devices, so it should be disabled.

IDE Master (Slave) PIO Mode

This option changes the IDE data transfer speed: Modes 0–4 or Auto. Rather than have the BIOS issue commands to effect transfers to or from the disk drive, PIO allows the BIOS to tell the controller what it wants and then lets the controller and the CPU perform the complete task by themselves. Modes 1–4 are available for EIDE systems, but set to Auto for an automatic configuration.

HCLK PCICLK

This entry allows you to set the host CLK/PCI CLK divider. The options are: AUTO, 1-1, and 1-1.5.

PCI-ISA BCLK Divider

This entry allows you to set the PCI Bus CLK/ISA Bus CLK divider. The options are: AUTO, PCICLK1/3, PCICLK1/2, and PCICLK1/4.

PCI Write-Byte-Merge

This feature is sometimes called "CPU-to-PCI Byte Merge." When enabled, this allows data sent from the CPU to the PCI bus to be held in a buffer. The chipset will then write the data in the buffer to the PCI bus when appropriate.

CPU-to-PCI Read Buffer

This feature is sometimes called "PCI-to-CPU Write Buffer." When enabled, up to four double-words (Dwords) can be read from the PCI bus without interrupting the CPU. When disabled, a write buffer is not used and the CPU read cycle will not be completed until the PCI bus signals that it is ready to receive the data. Enabling the buffer is best for system performance.

CPU-to-PCI Read-Line

When this feature is enabled (on), more time will be allocated for data setup with faster CPUs. This feature may be required only if you add an Intel OverDrive processor to your 486-class system.

CPU-to-PCI Read-Burst

When this feature is enabled (on), the PCI bus will interpret CPU read cycles as the PCI burst protocol, meaning that back-to-back sequential CPU memory read cycles addressed to the PCI will be translated into fast PCI burst memory cycles. Performance is improved, but some nonstandard PCI adapters (i.e., VGA adapters) may experience problems.

PCI-to-DRAM Buffer

When enabled, this feature improves PCI-to-DRAM performance by allowing data to be stored if a destination is busy. Buffers are needed for this feature because the PCI bus is separate from the CPU.

Latency for CPU-to-PCI Write

This is the delay time before a CPU writes data to the PCI bus.

PCI Cycle Cache Hit

This option defines how the cache is refreshed during PCI operation. Normal refresh will produce a cache refresh during normal PCI cycles. Fast refresh will produce a cache refresh without a PCI cycle for CAS. Fast performance is usually better.

Use Default Latency Timer Value

This option determines whether the default value for the Latency Timer will be loaded or the succeeding Latency Timer Value will be used. If *Yes* is selected (default), no further programming is needed for the Latency Timer Value.

Latency Timer Value

This is the maximum number of PCI bus clocks that the master may burst. A longer latency time gives the CPU more of a chance to control the bus.

Latency from ADS# Status

This feature allows you to configure how long the CPU waits for the Address Data Status (ADS). It determines the CPU-to-PCI Post write speed. When set to 3T, this is 5T for each double-word. With 2T (default), it is 4T per double-word. For a quad-word (Qword) PCI memory write, the rate is 7T (2T) or 8T (3T). The default should be correct, but if you add a faster CPU to your system, you may find it necessary to increase it. The choices are: 3T—three CPU clocks, or 2T—two CPU clocks (Default).

PCI Master Latency

This option sets the time that a PCI master can control the bus. If your PCI master controls the bus for too long, there is less time for the CPU to control it. A longer latency time gives the CPU more time to control the PCI bus.

Max. Burstable Range

This is the maximum bursting length for each asserting FRAME#. Longer burst durations should improve performance.

CPU-to-PCI Burst Memory Write

When enabled, back-to-back sequential CPU memory write cycles to PCI are translated to PCI burst memory write cycles; otherwise, each single write to PCI will have an associated FRAME# sequence. Keeping this feature enabled is best for performance, but some nonstandard PCI cards (i.e., VGA adapters) may have problems.

CPU-to-PCI Post-Memory Write

This feature enables up to four double-words (Dwords) of data to be posted to PCI; otherwise, not only is buffering disabled, but completion of CPU writes is limited (the CPU write does not complete until the PCI transaction completes). Keeping this feature enabled is best for performance.

CPU-to-PCI Write Buffer

This feature is the same as "CPU-to-PCI Read Buffer," only for writing.

PCI-to-ISA Write Buffer

When this feature is enabled, the system will temporarily write data to a buffer so the CPU is not interrupted. When disabled, the memory write cycle for the PCI bus will be directed to the slower ISA bus. As a result, keeping this feature enabled is best for performance.

DMA Line Buffer

This feature allows DMA data to be stored in a buffer so PCI bus operations are not interrupted. Disabled means that the line buffer for DMA is in single-transaction mode. Enabled allows it to operate in an 8-byte transaction mode for greater efficiency. This feature should be enabled for best system performance.

ISA Master Line Buffer

ISA master buffers are designed to isolate the slower ISA I/O operations from the PCI bus for better performance. Keeping this feature disabled means the buffer for ISA master transaction is in single-mode. Enabling this feature means it is in 8-byte mode, which increases the ISA master's performance.

CPU/PCI Post-Write Delay

This is the delay time before the CPU writes data into the PCI bus.

Post-Write CAS Active

This is the pulse width of the CAS# signal when the PCI master writes to DRAM.

PCI Master Accesses Shadow RAM

This feature enables the shadowing of a ROM on a PCI master for better performance.

Enable Master

This feature enables the selected device as a PCI bus master, and checks whether the card is capable of performing as a PCI master.

AT/ISA Bus Clock Frequency

This is the AT bus speed in a PCI system. Select a divisor that will give you a bus speed closest to 8.33 MHz (depending on the speed of the PCI bus).

Base I/O Address

This entry lists the base of the I/O address range from which the PCI device resource requests are satisfied.

Base Memory Address

This entry lists the base of the 32-bit memory address range from which the PCI device resource requests are satisfied.

Parity

When enabled, this feature allows parity checking of PCI devices.

ISA Linear Frame Buffer

This feature enables a buffer if you use an ISA card that features a linear frame buffer (i.e., a second video card for AutoCAD). The buffer address will be set automatically.

ISA VGA Frame Buffer Size

Also known as "ISA LFB Size," this feature allows you to use a VGA frame buffer and 16 MB of RAM at the same time—the system will allow access to the graphics card through a "hole" in its own memory map. In other words, access to addresses within this "hole" will be directed to the ISA bus instead of main memory. This feature should be set to disabled unless you're using an ISA card with more than 64 KB of memory that needs to be accessed by the CPU *and* you are not using the Plug-and-Play utilities. If you have less than 8 MB of memory, or use MS-DOS, this feature will be ignored.

Residence of VGA Card

This option lists whether the VGA card resides on a PCI or VL bus. Today, the default is PCI.

Memory Map Hole Start/End Address

This entry determines where the hole starts and depends on the ISA LFB Size. If you can change it, the base address should be 16 MB, minus the buffer size. See "ISA VGA Frame Buffer Size."

Memory Hole Size

This entry defines the size of the memory "hole." Options are: 1 MB, 2 MB, 4 MB, 8 MB, and disabled. These are the amounts below 16 MB that are assigned to the AT bus and reserved for ISA cards.

Memory Hole Start Address

This entry defines where the memory "hole" starts. The selections are from 1 MB to 15 MB. This entry is not used if the memory hole is disabled.

Byte Merging

This feature allows writes to sequential memory addresses to be merged into one PCI-to-memory operation, which increases performance for older applications that write to video memory in bytes rather than words. This feature is not supported well on all PCI video cards. Enable this feature unless you encounter graphics problems.

Byte Merge Support

This feature is a variation of Byte Merging: 8- or 16-bit data traveling from the CPU to the PCI bus are held in a buffer where they are accumulated, or merged, into 32-bit data, giving faster overall performance. In this case, enabling this feature means that CPU-PCI writes are buffered.

Multimedia Mode

This feature enables or disables palette snooping for multimedia cards.

Video Palette Snoop

This feature controls how a PCI graphics card can "snoop" write cycles to an ISA video card's color palette registers. *Snooping* essentially means interfering with a device. This is a powerful performance option, so disable it only if: an ISA card connects to a PCI graphics card through a VESA connector; the ISA card connects to a color monitor, and the ISA card uses the RAMDAC on the PCI card; and Palette Snooping (RAMDAC shadowing) is not operative on the PCI card.

PCI/VGA Palette Snoop

This feature alters the VGA palette setting while graphic signals pass through the feature connector of a PCI VGA card and are processed by an MPEG card. VGA snooping is used by multimedia video devices (i.e., video capture boards) to look ahead at the video controller (VGA device) to see what color palette is currently in use. Enable this feature if you have MPEG connections through the VGA feature connector (this means you can adjust PCI/VGA palettes); otherwise, go ahead and disable the feature.

Snoop Filter

Also known as "Cache Snoop Filter," this feature saves the need for multiple inquiries to the same line if it was checked previously. When enabled, cache snoop filters ensure data integrity (cache coherency) while reducing the snoop frequency to a minimum.

E8000 32K Accessible

This 64-KB area of upper memory is used for BIOS purposes on PS/2s, 32-bit operating systems, and Plug-and-Play. This setting allows the second 32-KB page to be used for other purposes when not needed (in the same way that the first 32-KB page of the F range is useable after boot up has finished).

PCI Arbiter Mode

Devices gain access to the PCI bus through arbitration. There are two modes, mode 1 (default) and mode 2. The idea is to minimize the time it takes to gain control of the bus and move data. Generally, mode 1 should be sufficient, but try mode 2 if you encounter problems with PCI bus access.

Stop CPU When PCI Flush

When this feature is enabled, the CPU will be stopped when the PCI bus is being flushed of data. Disabling this feature (default) allows the CPU to continue processing, giving somewhat greater system performance.

Stop CPU at PCI Master

When this feature is enabled, the CPU will be stopped when the PCI bus master is operating on the bus. Disabling this feature (default) allows the CPU to continue processing, giving somewhat greater system performance.

I/O Cycle Recovery

When enabled, the PCI bus will be allowed a recovery period for back-to-back I/O (which slows back-to-back data transfers)—it's like adding wait-states to the PCI bus, so disable this feature (default) for best performance.

I/O Recovery Period

This feature sets the length of time for the "I/O Cycle Recovery." The range is from 0–1.75 microseconds (μs) in 0.25-μs intervals.

Action When W Buffer Full

This feature sets the behavior of the system when the write buffer is full. By default, the system will immediately retry (rather than wait for it to be emptied).

Fast Back-to-Back

When this feature is enabled, the PCI bus will interpret CPU read cycles as the PCI burst protocol, meaning that back-to-back sequential CPU memory read cycles addressed to the PCI will be translated into the fast PCI burst memory cycles. By default the feature is enabled.

CPU Pipelined Function

This feature allows the system controller to signal the CPU for a new memory address even before all data transfers for the current cycle are complete, which results in increased data throughput. The default is usually disabled, so pipelining is off.

Primary Frame Buffer

When this feature is enabled, the system can use unreserved memory as a primary frame buffer. Unlike the VGA frame buffer, this would reduce overall available RAM for applications. The default is usually disabled.

M1445RDYJ to CPURDYJ

This feature determines whether the PCI ready signal is to be synchronized by the CPU clock's ready signal or bypassed (default).

VESA Master Cycle ADSJ

This feature allows you to increase the length of time the VESA Master has in order to decode bus commands. Typical choices are Normal (default) and Long.

LDEVJ Check Point Delay

This feature allows you to select how much time is allocated for checking bus cycle commands. These commands must be decoded to determine whether a local bus device access signal (LDEVJ) is being sent or an ISA device is being addressed. Increasing the delay increases stability (especially in the VESA subsystem), while very slightly degrading the performance of the ISA subsystem. Settings are in terms of the feedback clock rate (FBCLK2) used in the cache/memory control interface:

- 1 FBCLK2 = One clock
- 2 FBCLK2 = Two clocks (default)
- 3 FBCLK2 = Three clocks

CPU Dynamic-Fast-Cycle

This feature gives you faster access to the ISA bus. When the CPU issues a bus cycle, the PCI bus examines the command to determine if a PCI agent claims it; if not, then an ISA bus cycle is initiated. The Dynamic-Fast-Cycle then allows for faster access to the ISA bus by decreasing the latency (or delay) between the original CPU command and the beginning of the ISA cycle.

CPU Memory Sample Point

This feature allows you to select the cycle check point (which is where memory decoding and cache hit/miss checking take place). Each selection indicates that the check takes place at the end of a CPU cycle, with one wait-state indicating more time for checking to take place than zero wait-states. A longer check time allows for greater stability at the expense of some performance.

LDEV# Check Point

The VESA local device (LDEV#) check point is where the VL-bus device decodes the bus commands and checks for errors, within the bus cycle itself:

◀ 0 Bus cycle point T1 (default)
◀ 1 During the first T2
◀ 2 During second T2
◀ 3 During third T2

Local Memory Check Point

This entry allows you to select between two techniques for decoding and error checking local bus writes to DRAM during a memory cycle:

1. Slow = Extra wait-state; better checking (default)
2. Fast = No extra wait-state used

FRAMEJ Generation

When the PCI-VL bus bridge is acting as a PCI Master and receiving data from the CPU, a fast CPU-to-PCI buffer will be enabled if this selection is also enabled. Using the buffer allows the CPU to complete a write even though the data have not been delivered to the PCI bus. This reduces the number of CPU cycles involved and speeds overall processing:

◁ Normal Buffering not employed (Default)

◁ Fast Buffer used for CPU-to-PCI writes

PCI-to-CPU Write Pending

This feature sets the behavior of the system when the write buffer is full. By default, the system will immediately retry (but you can set it to wait for the buffer to be emptied before retrying).

Delay for SCSI/HDD

This option is also sometimes called "SCSI Boot Delay." This is the length of time (in seconds) that the BIOS will wait for the SCSI hard disk to be ready for operation. If the hard drive is not ready, the PCI SCSI BIOS might not detect the hard drive correctly. The range is from 0–60 seconds.

Master IOCHRDY

When this feature is enabled, it allows the system to monitor for a VESA master request to generate an I/O channel ready (IOCHRDY) signal.

VGA Type

This entry is used when the video BIOS is being shadowed. The BIOS uses this information to determine which bus to use. Choices are Standard (default), PCI, ISA/VESA.

PCI Master Timing Mode

This entry gives you the ability to choose between two timing modes, 0 (default) and 1.

PCI Arbit. Rotate Priority

Typically, the system manages (or arbitrates) access to the PCI bus on a first-come-first-served basis. When priority is rotated, once a device gains control of the bus, it is assigned the lowest priority and every other device is moved up one in the priority queue. This helps to prevent any one device from monopolizing the PCI bus.

I/O Cycle Post-Write

When this feature is enabled (default), data being written during an I/O cycle will be buffered for faster performance.

PCI Post-Write Fast

When this feature is enabled (default), data being written during an PCI cycle will be buffered for faster performance.

CPU Master Post-W/R Buffer

When the CPU operates as a bus master for either memory access or I/O, this entry controls its ability to use a high-speed posted write buffer. Choices are N/A, 1, 2, and 4 (default).

CPU Master Post-WR Burst Mode

When the CPU operates as a bus master for either memory access or I/O, this entry controls its ability to use a high-speed burst mode for posted writes to a buffer.

CPU Master Fast Interface

This entry enables or disables what is known as a "fast back-to-back" interface when the CPU operates as a bus master. When enabled, consecutive reads/writes are interpreted as the CPU high-performance burst mode.

PCI Master Post-W/R Buffer

When a PCI device operates as a bus master for either memory access or I/O, this entry controls its use of a high-speed posted write buffer. Choices are N/A, 1, 2, and 4 (default).

PCI Master Burst Mode

When a PCI device operates as a bus master for either memory access or I/O, this entry controls its use of a high-speed burst mode for posted writes to a buffer.

PCI Master Fast Interface

This feature enables or disables what is known as a "fast back-to-back" interface when a PCI device operates as a bus master. When enabled, consecutive reads/writes are interpreted as the PCI high-performance burst mode.

CPU Master DEVSEL# Time-out

When the CPU initiates a master cycle using an address (target) that has not been mapped to PCI/VESA or ISA space, the system will monitor the DEVSEL (device select) pin for a period of time to see if any device claims the cycle. This entry allows you to determine how long the system will wait before timing-out. Choices are 3 PCICLK, 4 PCICLK, 5 PCICLK, and 6 PCICLK (default).

PCI Master DEVSEL# Time-out

When a PCI device initiates a master cycle using an address (target) that has not been mapped to PCI/VESA or ISA space, the system will monitor the DEVSEL (device select) pin for a period of time to see if any device claims the cycle. This entry allows you to determine how long the system will wait before timing-out. Choices are 3 PCICLK, 4 PCICLK (default), 5 PCICLK, and 6 PCICLK.

IRQ Line

If you have installed a device requiring an IRQ service into the given PCI slot, use this entry to inform the PCI bus which IRQ it should initiate. Choices range from IRQ 3 through IRQ 15.

Fast Back-to-Back Cycle

When this feature is enabled, the PCI bus will interpret CPU read or write cycles as PCI burst protocol, meaning that back-to-back sequential CPU memory read/write cycles addressed to the PCI will be translated into fast PCI burst memory cycles.

State Machines

The chipset uses four state machines to manage specific CPU and/or PCI operations—each can be thought of as a highly optimized process center designed to handle specific operations. Generally, each operation involves a master device and the bus it wishes to employ. The four state machines are: (1) CPU master to CPU bus (CC); (2) CPU master to PCI bus (CP); (3) PCI master to PCI bus (PP); and (4) PCI master to CPU bus (PC). Each state machine has the following settings:

◁ *Address 0 WS.* This refers to the length of time the system will delay while the transaction address is decoded. When enabled, there will be no delay.

◁ *Data Write 0 WS.* The length of time the system will delay while data are being written to the target address. When enabled, there will be no delay.

◁ *Data Read 0 WS.* The length of time the system will delay while data are being read from the target address. When enabled, there will be no delay.

Onboard PCI/SCSI BIOS

You should enable this feature if your system motherboard had a built-in SCSI controller attached to the PCI bus and you want to boot from it.

PCI I/O Start Address

The I/O devices make themselves accessible by occupying an address space. This allows you to make additional room for older ISA devices by defining the I/O start address for the PCI devices.

Memory Start Address

This feature is for devices with their own memory, which use part of the CPU's memory address space, allowing you to determine the starting point in memory where PCI device memory will be mapped.

VGA 128-K Range Attribute

When this feature is enabled, it allows the chipset to apply features such as CPU-to-PCI Byte Merge and CPU-TO-PCI Prefetch to be applied to VGA memory range A0000H–BFFFFH. When enabled, the VGA receives CPU-to-PCI functions; when disabled, the system retains the standard VGA interface.

CPU-to-PCI Write Posting

The Intel 450GX/KX "Orion" chipset maintains its own internal read and write buffers that are used to help compensate for the speed differences between the CPU and the PCI bus. When this feature is enabled, writes from the CPU to the PCI bus will be buffered; when disabled (default), the writes will not be buffered and the CPU will be forced to wait until the write is completed.

CPU Read Multiple Prefetch

A prefetch occurs during a process (i.e., reading from the PCI bus or memory) when the chipset peeks at the next instruction and actually begins the next read. The Intel 450GX/KX "Orion" chipset has four read lines. A multiple prefetch means the chipset can initiate more than one prefetch during a process. By default, the feature is disabled.

CPU Line Read Multiple

A line read means that the CPU is reading a full cache line. When a cache line is full it holds 32 bytes (eight Dwords) of data. Because the line is full, the system knows exactly how much data it will be reading and doesn't need to wait for an end-of-data signal, freeing it to do other things. When this feature is enabled, the system is allowed to read more than one full cache line at a time; the default is disabled.

CPU Line Read Prefetch

When this feature is enabled, the system is allowed to prefetch the next read instruction and initiate the next process.

CPU Line Read

This feature enables or disables (default) full CPU line reads.

CPU Burst Write Assembly

The Intel 450GX/KX "Orion" chipset maintains four posted write buffers. When this feature is enabled, the chipset can assemble long PCI bursts from the data held in them. By default, the feature is disabled.

VGA Performance Mode

When this feature is enabled, the VGA memory range of A0000–B0000 will use a special set of performance features. This feature has little or no effect using video modes beyond the standard VGA most commonly used for Windows, OS/2, UNIX, and so on, but this memory range is heavily used by games such as DOOM.

Snoop Ahead

This feature is applicable only if the cache is enabled. When enabled, PCI bus masters can monitor the VGA palette registers for direct writes and translate them into PCI burst protocol for greater speed, which can enhance the performance of multimedia video.

DMA Line Buffer Mode

This feature allows DMA data to be stored in a buffer so as not to interrupt the PCI bus. When the Standard mode is selected, the line buffer is in single-transaction mode. When the Enhanced mode is selected, the feature allows it to operate in 8-byte transaction mode.

Master Arbitration Protocol

This is the method by which the PCI bus determines which bus master device gains access to the bus.

PCI Clock Frequency

This entry allows you to set the clock rate for the PCI bus, which can operate between 0–33 MHz. CPUCLK/3 means the PCI bus was operating at 11 MHz (33/3 = 11). The typical entries are:

- CPUCLK/1.5   CPU speed/1.5 (default)
- CPUCLK/3   CPU speed/3
- 14 MHz   14 MHz
- CPUCLK/2   CPU speed/2

Max. Burstable Range

This feature sets the size of the maximum range of contiguous memory, which can be addressed by a burst from the PCI bus.

I/O Recovery Time

This is a programmed delay that allows the PCI bus to exchange data with the slower ISA bus without data errors. Settings are in fractions of the PCI BCL:

- 2 BCLK = Two BCLKs (default)
- 4 BCLK = Four BCLKs
- 8 BCLK = Eight BCLKs
- 12 BCLK = Twelve BCLKs

PCI Concurrency

When this feature is enabled, more than one PCI device can be active at a time. With Intel chipsets, it allocates memory bus cycles to a PCI controller while an ISA operation (such as bus-mastered DMA) is taking place, which normally requires constant attention. This involves turning on additional read and write buffering in the chipset. The PCI bus can also obtain access cycles for small data transfers without the delays caused by renegotiating bus access for each part of the transfer, so the feature is meant to improve performance and consistency.

PCI Streaming

Data are typically moved to and from memory and between devices in discrete chunks of limited sizes, because the CPU is involved. On the PCI bus, data can be *streamed*—that is, much larger chunks can be moved without the CPU being used. This feature should be enabled for best performance.

PCI Bursting

When this feature is enabled, consecutive writes from the CPU will be regarded as a PCI Burst cycle. This feature should normally be enabled.

PCI (IDE) Bursting

This is similar to "PCI Bursting," but this one enables burst mode access to video memory over the PCI bus. The CPU provides the first address and consecutive data are transferred at one word per clock. The device must support burst mode.

Burst Copy-Back Option

When this feature is enabled, if a cache miss occurs, the chipset will initiate a second, burst cache line fill from main memory to the cache—the goal being to maintain the status of the cache.

Preempt PCI Master Option

When this feature is enabled, PCI bus operations can be preempted by certain system operations, such as DRAM refresh, and so on; otherwise, they can take place concurrently.

IBC DEVSEL# Decoding

This feature allows you to set the type of decoding used by the ISA Bridge Controller (IBC) to determine which device to select. The longer the decoding cycle, the better chance the IBC has to correctly decode the commands. Choices are Fast, Medium, and Slow (default).

Keyboard Controller Clock

This entry sets the speed of the keyboard controller (PCICLKI = PCI bus speed). Typical options are:

- ◀ 7.16 MHz (default)
- ◀ PCICLKI/2 1/2 PCICLKI
- ◀ PCICLKI/3 1/3 PCICLKI
- ◀ PCICLKI/4 1/4 PCICLKI

CPU Pipeline Function

This feature allows the system controller to signal the CPU for a new memory address even before all data transfers for the current cycle are complete, resulting in increased throughput. Enabled means that address pipelining is active.

PCI Dynamic Decoding

When this feature is enabled, the system can remember the PCI command that has just been requested. If subsequent commands fall within the same address space, the cycle will be automatically interpreted as a PCI command.

Master Retry Timer

This feature sets how long the CPU master will attempt a PCI cycle before the cycle is unmasked (terminated). The choices are measured in PCICLKs, values of which are 10 (default), 18, 34, or 66 PCICLKs.

PCI Pre-Snoop

Pre-snooping is a technique by which a PCI master can continue to burst to the local memory until a 4-K page boundary is reached rather than just a line boundary. This feature can be enabled.

CPU/PCI Write Phase

This feature determines the turnaround between the address and data phases of the CPU master to PCI slave writes. Choices are 1 LCLK (default) or 0 LCLK.

PCI Preempt Timer

This entry sets the length of time before one PCI master preempts another when a service request has been pending. Typical entries are:

◁ Disabled   No preemption (default)

◁ 260 LCLKs   Preempt after 260 LCLKs

◁ 132 LCLKs   Preempt after 132 LCLKs

◁ 68 LCLKs   Preempt after 68 LCLKs

◁ 36 LCLKs   Preempt after 36 LCLKs

◁ 20 LCLKs   Preempt after 20 LCLKs

◁ 12 LCLKs   Preempt after 12 LCLKs

◁ 5 LCLKs   Preempt after 5 LCLKs

CPU-to-PCI POST/BURST

Data from the CPU to the PCI bus can be posted (buffered by the controller) and/or burst. This entry sets the methods used:

◁ POST/CON.BURST. Posting and bursting supported (default).

◁ NONE/NONE. Neither supported.

◁ POST/NONE. Posting but not bursting supported.

PCI CLK

This feature determines whether the PCI clock is tightly synchronized with the CPU clock or is asynchronous. If your CPU, motherboard, and PCI bus are running at multiple speeds of each other (i.e., Pentium 120, 60 MHz, and 30-MHz PCI bus), choose to synchronize.

Plug-and-Play ID Code Table

General Device Categories

PNP0xxx	System devices
PNP8xxx	Network adapters
PNPAxxx	SCSI, proprietary CD adapters
PNPBxxx	Sound, video capture, multimedia
PNPCxxx–Dxxx	Modems

Device ID Codes

Device ID	Description
	System Devices—PNP0xxx—*Interrupt Controllers*
PNP0000	AT Interrupt Controller
PNP0001	EISA Interrupt Controller
PNP0002	MCA Interrupt Controller
PNP0003	APIC
PNP0004	Cyrix SLiC MP Interrupt Controller
	System Devices—PNP0xxx—*Timers*
PNP0100	AT Timer
PNP0101	EISA Timer
PNP0102	MCA Timer
	System Devices—PNP0xxx—*DMA*
PNP0200	AT DMA Controller
PNP0201	EISA DMA Controller
PNP0202	MCA DMA Controller
	System Devices—PNP0xxx—*Keyboards*
PNP0300	IBM PC/XT Keyboard Controller (83-key)
PNP0301	IBM PC/AT Keyboard Controller (86-key)
PNP0302	IBM PC/XT Keyboard Controller (84-key)

Device ID Codes (*Continued*)

Device ID	Description
	System Devices—PNP0xxx—*Keyboards*
PNP0303	IBM Enhanced (101/102-key, PS/2 mouse support)
PNP0304	Olivetti keyboard (83-key)
PNP0305	Olivetti keyboard (102-key)
PNP0306	Olivetti keyboard (86-key)
PNP0307	Microsoft Windows keyboard
PNP0308	General Input Device Emulation Interface (GIDEI) legacy
PNP0309	Olivetti keyboard (A101/102-key)
PNP030A	AT&T 302 keyboard
PNP030B	Reserved (by Microsoft)
PNP0320	Japanese 106-key keyboard A01
PNP0321	Japanese 101-key keyboard
PNP0322	Japanese AX keyboard
PNP0323	Japanese 106-key keyboard 002/003
PNP0324	Japanese 106-key keyboard 001
PNP0325	Japanese Toshiba Desktop keyboard
PNP0326	Japanese Toshiba Laptop keyboard
PNP0327	Japanese Toshiba Notebook keyboard
PNP0340	Korean 84-key keyboard
PNP0341	Korean 86-key keyboard
PNP0342	Korean Enhanced keyboard
PNP0343	Korean Enhanced keyboard 101b
PNP0343	Korean Enhanced keyboard 101c
PNP0344	Korean Enhanced keyboard 103
	System Devices—PNP0xxx—*Parallel Devices*
PNP0400	Standard LPT printer port
PNP0401	ECP printer port
	System Devices—PNP0xxx—*Serial Devices*
PNP0500	Standard PC COM port
PNP0501	16550A-compatible COM port
PNP0502	Multiport serial device (nonintelligent 16550)
PNP0510	Generic IrDA-compatible device
PNP0511	Generic IrDA-compatible device
	System Devices—PNP0xxx—*Disk Controllers*
PNP0600	Generic ESDI/IDE/ATA-compatible hard disk controller
PNP0601	Plus Hardcard II
PNP0602	Plus Hardcard IIXL/EZ
PNP0603	Generic IDE supporting Microsoft Device Bay Specification
PNP0700	PC standard floppy disk controller
PNP0701	Standard floppy controller supporting MS Device Bay Spec.

Device ID Codes (*Continued*)

Device ID	Description
	System Devices—PNP0xxx—Early Sound Systems
PNP0802	Microsoft Sound System device (now obsolete; use PNPB0xx instead)
	System Devices—PNP0xxx—Display Adapters
PNP0900	VGA Compatible
PNP0901	Video Seven VRAM/VRAM II/1024i
PNP0902	8514/A Compatible
PNP0903	Trident VGA
PNP0904	Cirrus Logic Laptop VGA
PNP0905	Cirrus Logic VGA
PNP0906	Tseng ET4000
PNP0907	Western Digital VGA
PNP0908	Western Digital Laptop VGA
PNP0909	S3 Inc. 911/924
PNP090A	ATI Ultra Pro/Plus (Mach 32)
PNP090B	ATI Ultra (Mach 8)
PNP090C	XGA Compatible
PNP090D	ATI VGA Wonder
PNP090E	Weitek P9000 Graphics Adapter
PNP090F	Oak Technology VGA
PNP0910	Compaq QVision
PNP0911	XGA/2
PNP0912	Tseng Labs W32/W32i/W32p
PNP0913	S3 Inc. 801/928/964
PNP0914	Cirrus Logic 5429/5434 (memory mapped)
PNP0915	Compaq Advanced VGA (AVGA)
PNP0916	ATI Ultra Pro Turbo (Mach64)
PNP0917	Reserved (by Microsoft)
PNP0918	Matrox MGA
PNP0919	Compaq QVision 2000
PNP091A	Tseng W128
PNP0930	Chips & Technologies Super VGA
PNP0931	Chips & Technologies Accelerator
PNP0940	NCR 77c22e Super VGA
PNP0941	NCR 77c32blt
PNP09FF	Plug-and-Play Monitors (VESA DDC)
	System Devices—PNP0xxx—Peripheral Buses
PNP0A00	ISA Bus
PNP0A01	EISA Bus
PNP0A02	MCA Bus
PNP0A03	PCI Bus
PNP0A04	VESA/VL Bus
PNP0A05	Generic ACPI Bus
PNP0A06	Generic ACPI Extended-IO Bus (EIO bus)

Device ID Codes (*Continued*)

Device ID	Description
System Devices—PNP0xxx—*Real-Time Clock, BIOS, Motherboard Devices*	
PNP0800	AT-style speaker sound
PNP0B00	AT Real-Time Clock
PNP0C00	Plug-and-Play BIOS
PNP0C01	System Board
PNP0C02	General ID for reserving resources required by Plug-and-Play mother-board registers
PNP0C03	Plug-and-Play BIOS Event Notification Interrupt
PNP0C04	Math Coprocessor
PNP0C05	APM BIOS (Version independent)
PNP0C06	Reserved for identification of early Plug-and-Play BIOS implementation
PNP0C07	Reserved for identification of early Plug-and-Play BIOS implementation
PNP0C08	ACPI system board hardware
PNP0C09	ACPI Embedded Controller
PNP0C0A	ACPI Control Method Battery
PNP0C0B	ACPI Fan
PNP0C0C	ACPI power button device
PNP0C0D	ACPI lid device
PNP0C0E	ACPI sleep button device
PNP0C0F	PCI interrupt link device
PNP0C10	ACPI system indicator device
PNP0C11	ACPI thermal zone
PNP0C12	Device Bay Controller
PNP0C13	Plug-and-Play BIOS (used when ACPI mode cannot be used)
System Devices—PNP0xxx—*PCMCIA Controller Chipsets*	
PNP0E00	Intel 82365–compatible PCMCIA Controller
PNP0E01	Cirrus Logic CL-PD6720 PCMCIA Controller
PNP0E02	VLSI VL82C146 PCMCIA Controller
PNP0E03	Intel 82365–compatible CardBus controller
System Devices—PNP0xxx—*Mice*	
PNP0F00	Microsoft Bus Mouse
PNP0F01	Microsoft Serial Mouse
PNP0F02	Microsoft InPort Mouse
PNP0F03	Microsoft PS/2-style Mouse
PNP0F04	Mouse Systems Mouse
PNP0F05	Mouse Systems 3-Button Mouse (COM2)
PNP0F06	Genius Mouse (COM1)
PNP0F07	Genius Mouse (COM2)
PNP0F08	Logitech Serial Mouse
PNP0F09	Microsoft BallPoint Serial Mouse
PNP0F0A	Microsoft Plug-and-Play Mouse

Device ID Codes (*Continued*)

Device ID	Description
	System Devices—PNP0xxx—*Mice*
PNP0F0B	Microsoft Plug-and-Play BallPoint Mouse
PNP0F0C	Microsoft-compatible Serial Mouse
PNP0F0D	Microsoft-compatible InPort-compatible Mouse
PNP0F0E	Microsoft-compatible PS/2-style Mouse
PNP0F0F	Microsoft-compatible Serial BallPoint-compatible Mouse
PNP0F10	Texas Instruments QuickPort Mouse
PNP0F11	Microsoft-compatible Bus Mouse
PNP0F12	Logitech PS/2-style Mouse
PNP0F13	PS/2 Port for PS/2-style Mouse
PNP0F14	Microsoft Kids Mouse
PNP0F15	Logitech bus mouse
PNP0F16	Logitech SWIFT device
PNP0F17	Logitech-compatible serial mouse
PNP0F18	Logitech-compatible bus mouse
PNP0F19	Logitech-compatible PS/2-style Mouse
PNP0F1A	Logitech-compatible SWIFT Device
PNP0F1B	HP Omnibook Mouse
PNP0F1C	Compaq LTE Trackball PS/2-style Mouse
PNP0F1D	Compaq LTE Trackball Serial Mouse
PNP0F1E	Microsoft Kids Trackball Mouse
PNP0F1F	Reserved (by Microsoft Input Device Group)
PNP0F20	Reserved (by Microsoft Input Device Group)
PNP0F21	Reserved (by Microsoft Input Device Group)
PNP0F22	Reserved (by Microsoft Input Device Group)
PNP0F23	Reserved (by Microsoft Input Device Group)
PNP0FFF	Reserved (by Microsoft Systems)
	System Devices—PNP8xxx—*Network Adapters*
PNP8001	Novell/Anthem NE3200
PNP8004	Compaq NE3200
PNP8006	Intel EtherExpress/32
PNP8008	HP EtherTwist EISA LAN Adapter/32 (HP27248A)
PNP8065	Ungermann-Bass NIUps or NIUps/EOTP
PNP8072	DEC (DE211) EtherWorks MC/TP
PNP8073	DEC (DE212) EtherWorks MC/TP_BNC
PNP8078	DCA 10 MB MCA
PNP8074	HP MC LAN Adapter/16 TP (PC27246)
PNP80C9	IBM Token Ring
PNP80CA	IBM Token Ring II
PNP80CB	IBM Token Ring II/Short
PNP80CC	IBM Token Ring 4/16Mbs
PNP80D3	Novell/Anthem NE1000

Device ID Codes (*Continued*)

Device ID	Description
	System Devices—PNP8xxx—*Network Adapters*
PNP80D4	Novell/Anthem NE2000
PNP80D5	NE1000 Compatible
PNP80D6	NE2000 Compatible
PNP80D7	Novell/Anthem NE1500T
PNP80D8	Novell/Anthem NE2100
PNP80DD	SMC ARCNETPC
PNP80DE	SMC ARCNET PC100, PC200
PNP80DF	SMC ARCNET PC110, PC210, PC250
PNP80E0	SMC ARCNET PC130/E
PNP80E1	SMC ARCNET PC120, PC220, PC260
PNP80E2	SMC ARCNET PC270/E
PNP80E5	SMC ARCNET PC600W, PC650W
PNP80E7	DEC DEPCA
PNP80E8	DEC (DE100) EtherWorks LC
PNP80E9	DEC (DE200) EtherWorks Turbo
PNP80EA	DEC (DE101) EtherWorks LC/TP
PNP80EB	DEC (DE201) EtherWorks Turbo/TP
PNP80EC	DEC (DE202) EtherWorks Turbo/TP_BNC
PNP80ED	DEC (DE102) EtherWorks LC/TP_BNC
PNP80EE	DEC EE101 (Built-In)
PNP80EF	DECpc 433 WS (Built-In)
PNP80F1	3Com EtherLink Plus
PNP80F3	3Com EtherLink II or IITP (8- or 16-bit)
PNP80F4	3Com TokenLink
PNP80F6	3Com EtherLink 16
PNP80F7	3Com EtherLink III
PNP80F8	3Com Generic EtherLink Plug-and-Play Device
PNP80FB	Thomas Conrad TC6045
PNP80FC	Thomas Conrad TC6042
PNP80FD	Thomas Conrad TC6142
PNP80FE	Thomas Conrad TC6145
PNP80FF	Thomas Conrad TC6242
PNP8100	Thomas Conrad TC6245
PNP8105	DCA 10 MB
PNP8106	DCA 10 MB Fiber Optic
PNP8107	DCA 10 MB Twisted Pair
PNP8113	Racal NI6510
PNP811C	Ungermann-Bass NIUpc
PNP8120	Ungermann-Bass NIUpc/EOTP
PNP8123	SMC StarCard PLUS (WD/8003S)
PNP8124	SMC StarCard PLUS With On Board Hub (WD/8003SH)
PNP8125	SMC EtherCard PLUS (WD/8003E)

Device ID Codes (*Continued*)

Device ID	Description
	System Devices—PNP8xxx—*Network Adapters*
PNP8126	SMC EtherCard PLUS With Boot ROM Socket (WD/8003EBT)
PNP8127	SMC EtherCard PLUS With Boot ROM Socket (WD/8003EB)
PNP8128	SMC EtherCard PLUS TP (WD/8003WT)
PNP812A	SMC EtherCard PLUS 16 With Boot ROM Socket (WD/8013EBT)
PNP812D	Intel EtherExpress 16 or 16TP
PNP812F	Intel TokenExpress 16/4
PNP8130	Intel TokenExpress MCA 16/4
PNP8132	Intel EtherExpress 16 (MCA)
PNP8137	Artisoft AE-1
PNP8138	Artisoft AE-2 or AE-3
PNP8141	Amplicard AC 210/XT
PNP8142	Amplicard AC 210/AT
PNP814B	Everex SpeedLink/PC16 (EV2027)
PNP8155	HP PC LAN Adapter/8 TP (HP27245)
PNP8156	HP PC LAN Adapter/16 TP (HP27247A)
PNP8157	HP PC LAN Adapter/8 TL (HP27250)
PNP8158	HP PC LAN Adapter/16 TP Plus (HP27247B)
PNP8159	HP PC LAN Adapter/16 TL Plus (HP27252)
PNP815F	National Semiconductor Ethernode *16AT
PNP8160	National Semiconductor AT/LANTIC EtherNODE 16-AT3
PNP816A	NCR Token-Ring 4Mbs ISA
PNP816D	NCR Token-Ring 16/4Mbs ISA
PNP8191	Olicom 16/4 Token-Ring Adapter
PNP81C3	SMC EtherCard PLUS Elite (WD/8003EP)
PNP81C4	SMC EtherCard PLUS 10T (WD/8003W)
PNP81C5	SMC EtherCard PLUS Elite 16 (WD/8013EP)
PNP81C6	SMC EtherCard PLUS Elite 16T (WD/8013W)
PNP81C7	SMC EtherCard PLUS Elite 16 Combo (WD/8013EW or 8013EWC)
PNP81C8	SMC EtherElite Ultra 16
PNP81E4	Pure Data PDI9025-32 (Token Ring)
PNP81E6	Pure Data PDI508+ (ArcNet)
PNP81E7	Pure Data PDI516+ (ArcNet)
PNP81EB	Proteon Token Ring (P1390)
PNP81EC	Proteon Token Ring (P1392)
PNP81ED	Proteon ISA Token Ring (1340)
PNP81EE	Proteon ISA Token Ring (1342)
PNP81EF	Proteon ISA Token Ring (1346)
PNP81F0	Proteon ISA Token Ring (1347)
PNP81FF	Cabletron E2000 Series DNI
PNP8200	Cabletron E2100 Series DNI
PNP8209	Zenith Data Systems Z-Note
PNP820A	Zenith Data Systems NE2000-compatible

Device ID Codes (*Continued*)

Device ID	Description
System Devices—PNP8xxx—Network Adapters	
PNP8213	Xircom Pocket Ethernet II
PNP8214	Xircom Pocket Ethernet I
PNP821D	RadiSys EXM-10
PNP8227	SMC 3000 Series
PNP8228	SMC 91C2 controller
PNP8231	Advanced Micro Devices AM2100/AM1500T
PNP8263	Tulip NCC-16
PNP8277	Exos 105
PNP828A	Intel '595-based Ethernet
PNP828B	TI2000-style Token Ring
PNP828C	AMD PCNet Family cards
PNP828D	AMD PCNet32 (VL version)
PNP8294	IrDA Infrared NDIS driver (Microsoft-supplied)
PNP82BD	IBM PCMCIA-NIC
PNP82C2	Xircom CE10
PNP82C3	Xircom CEM2
PNP8321	DEC Ethernet (All Types)
PNP8323	SMC EtherCard (All Types except 8013/A)
PNP8324	ARCNET Compatible
PNP8326	Thomas Conrad (All Arcnet Types)
PNP8327	IBM Token Ring (All Types)
PNP8385	Remote Network Access Driver
PNP8387	RNA Point-to-point Protocol Driver
PNP8388	Reserved (for Microsoft Networking components)
PNP8389	Peer IrLAN infrared driver (Microsoft-supplied)
PNP8390	Generic network adapter
System Devices—PNPAxxx—SCSI and Proprietary CD Adapters	
PNPA002	Future Domain 16-700–compatible controller
PNPA003	Panasonic proprietary CD-ROM adapter (SBPro/SB16)
PNPA01B	Trantor 128 SCSI controller
PNPA01D	Trantor T160 SCSI controller
PNPA01E	Trantor T338 Parallel SCSI controller
PNPA01F	Trantor T348 Parallel SCSI controller
PNPA020	Trantor Media Vision SCSI controller
PNPA022	Always IN-2000 SCSI controller
PNPA02B	Sony proprietary CD-ROM controller
PNPA02D	Trantor T13b 8-bit SCSI controller
PNPA02F	Trantor T358 Parallel SCSI controller
PNPA030	Mitsumi LU-005 Single Speed CD-ROM controller + drive
PNPA031	Mitsumi FX-001 Single Speed CD-ROM controller + drive
PNPA032	Mitsumi FX-001 Double Speed CD-ROM controller + drive

Device ID Codes (*Continued*)

Device ID	Description
	System Devices—PNPBxxx—*Sound, Video-Capture, and Multimedia*
PNPB000	Sound Blaster 1.5–compatible sound device
PNPB001	Sound Blaster 2.0–compatible sound device
PNPB002	Sound Blaster Pro–compatible sound device
PNPB003	Sound Blaster 16–compatible sound device
PNPB004	Thunderboard-compatible sound device
PNPB005	AdLib-compatible FM synthesizer device
PNPB006	MPU401 compatible
PNPB007	Microsoft Windows Sound System–compatible sound device
PNPB008	Compaq Business Audio
PNPB009	Plug-and-Play Microsoft Windows Sound System Device
PNPB00A	MediaVision Pro Audio Spectrum (Trantor SCSI Enabled, Thunder Chip Disabled)
PNPB00B	MediaVision Pro Audio 3D
PNPB00C	MusicQuest MQX-32M
PNPB00D	MediaVision Pro Audio Spectrum Basic (no Trantor SCSI, Thunder Chip Enabled)
PNPB00E	MediaVision Pro Audio Spectrum (Trantor SCSI Enabled, Thunder Chip Enabled)
PNPB00F	MediaVision Jazz-16 chipset (OEM Versions)
PNPB010	Auravision VxP500 chipset—Orchid Videola
PNPB018	MediaVision Pro Audio Spectrum 8-bit
PNPB019	MediaVision Pro Audio Spectrum Basic (no Trantor SCSI, Thunder Chip Disabled)
PNPB020	Yamaha OPL3–compatible FM synthesizer device
PNPB02F	Joystick/Game port
	System Devices—PNPCxxx-Dxxx—*Modems*
PNPC000	Compaq 14400 Modem
PNPC001	Compaq 2400/9600 Modem

PC Preventive Maintenance

For most users, the purchase or construction of a new PC is a substantial investment of both time and money. But after the money is spent and the PC is in our home or office, few PC users ever take the time to *maintain* their PC. Routine maintenance is an important part of PC ownership and can go a long way toward keeping your computer's hardware *and* software error-free. Proper routine maintenance can also help to avoid costly visits to your local repair shop. This appendix provides you with a comprehensive, step-by-step procedure for protecting and maintaining your personal computer investment.

Protecting Your Data

It's interesting to note that the data recorded on our computers are often far more valuable than the actual cost of a new drive. But if the drive fails, your precious data are usually lost along with the hardware. Months (perhaps years) of records and data could be irretrievably lost with the failure of just a few bytes on a hard drive. One of the first steps in any routine maintenance plan is to make regular *backups* of not only the contents but also the configuration of your system. Backups ensure that you can recover from any hardware glitch, accidental file erasure, or virus attack.

STEP 1: FILE BACKUPS

File backups are important for all types of PC users from major corporations to occasional home users. By creating a "copy" of your system files (or even just a part of them), you can restore the copy and continue working in the event of a disaster. Before you proceed with any type of system checks, consider performing a file backup.

What You Need

To back up your files, you will need two items: (1) a backup drive and (2) backup software. The actual choice of backup drive is really quite open. Tape drives such as the Iomega Ditto drive (*www.iomega.com*) or the MicroSolutions 8000t 8-GB "Backpack" drive (*www.micro-solutions.com*) are the traditional choices, but other high-volume removable media drives such as Iomega's 100-MB Zip drive, their 1-GB Jaz drive, or the SyQuest 1.5-GB EZ-Flyer drive (*www.syquest.com*) are very popular. You may choose an internal or external version of a drive, but you might consider an *external* parallel port drive because it is portable—it can be shared between any PCs.

You'll also need some backup software to format the media, and handle your backup and restore operations. If you're using Windows 95, try the native Backup applet (click on *Start, Programs, Accessories, System Tools,* and *Backup*). If Backup doesn't suit your needs, many drives ship with a backup utility on diskette. Just make sure that the backup drive and backup software are compatible with one another.

Types of Backups

Backups generally fall into two categories: incremental and complete. Both types of backups offer unique advantages and disadvantages. An *incremental* backup records just the "differences" from the last backup; this usually results in a faster backup procedure and uses less tape (or other media), but restores take longer because you need to walk through each "increment" in order. A *complete* backup records the drive's full contents, which takes much longer and uses a lot more media, but restores are easier. Many PC users employ a combination of complete and incremental backups. For example, you might start with a complete backup on January 1, then make incremental backups each week until the end of February; by

March 1, you'd make another complete backup, and start the incremental backup process again.

Backup Frequency

Perhaps the most overlooked issue with backups is the frequency—how often should backups be performed? The answer to that question is not always a simple one because everyone's needs are different. Major corporations with busy order entry systems may back up several times each day, whereas individual home users may not even consider backups to be necessary. The standard that I use is this: Can you afford to lose the data on this drive? If the answer is "no," it's time to back up.

File Backup Tips

Regardless of how you choose to handle file backups, there are some tips that will help you get the most from your backup efforts:

◄ Keep the backup(s) in a secure location (such as a fireproof safe or cabinet).

◄ Keep the backup(s) in a different physical location away from the original PC.

◄ Back up consistently—backups are useless if they are out of date.

◄ If time is a factor, start with a complete backup, then use incremental backups.

◄ Use a parallel port tape drive (or other "backup" drive) for maximum portability between PCs.

STEP 2: CMOS BACKUPS

All PCs use a sophisticated set of configuration settings—everything from "Date" and "Time" to "Video Palette Snoop" and "Memory Hole"—which define how the system should be operated. These settings are stored in a small amount of very low power memory called *CMOS RAM* (you can learn more about CMOS Setup variables in Appendix A). Each time the PC starts, motherboard BIOS reads the CMOS RAM and copies the contents into low system memory—also known as the *BIOS Data Area* or BDA. While system power is off, CMOS RAM contents are maintained with a small battery. If this battery goes dead, CMOS contents can be lost. In most cases, this will prevent the system from even starting until you reconfigure the CMOS Setup from scratch. By making a backup of the CMOS Setup, you can restore lost settings in a matter of minutes. CMOS backups are simply printed screens of your CMOS Setup pages.

What You Need

The one item that you'll need to perform a CMOS backup is a *printer*—it really doesn't matter what kind of printer (i.e., dot-matrix, ink jet, or laser). The printer should be attached to the PC's parallel port. After starting the CMOS Setup routine, visit each page of the setup and use the <Print Screen> key to "capture" each page to the printer. Since every BIOS is written differently, be sure to check for submenus that might be buried under each main menu option.

CMOS Backup Tips

CMOS backups are quick and simple, but you'll get the most benefit from a CMOS backup by following the pointers below:

◁ Make it a point to print out *every* CMOS Setup page.

◁ Keep the printed pages taped to the PC's housing or with the system's original documentation.

◁ You should back up the CMOS Setup whenever you make a change to the system's configuration.

Cleaning

Now that you've backed up the system's vital information, you can proceed with the actual maintenance procedures. The first set of procedures concerns exterior cleaning. This may hardly sound like a glamorous process, but you'd be surprised how quickly dust, pet hair, and other debris can accumulate around a computer. You'll need four items for cleaning: (1) a mild ammonia-based cleaner (a little ammonia in water will work just as well); (2) a supply of paper towels or clean lint-free cloths; (3) a canister of electronics-grade compressed air, which can be obtained from any electronics store; and (4) a small static-safe vacuum cleaner.

NOTE Avoid the use of ordinary household vacuum cleaners. The rush of air tends to generate significant amounts of static electricity along plastic hoses and tubes, which can accidentally damage the sensitive electronics in a PC.

NOTE NEVER use harsh or industrial-grade cleaners around a PC. Harsh cleaners often contain chemicals that can damage the finish of (or even melt) the plastics used in PC housings. Use a highly diluted ammonia solution *only.*

As a rule, exterior cleaning can be performed every four months (three times per year) or as required. If the PC is operating in dusty, industrial, or other adverse environments, you many need to clean the system more frequently. Systems operating in clean office environments may need to be cleaned only once or twice each year. Always remember to turn off the computer and unplug the AC cord from the wall outlet before cleaning.

STEP 3: CLEAN THE CASE

Use a clean cloth lightly dampened with ammonia cleaner to remove dust, dirt, or stains from the exterior of the PC. Start at the top and work down. Add a little bit of extra cleaner to remove stubborn stains. You'll find that the housing base is typically the dirtiest (especially for tower systems). When cleaning, be careful not to accidentally alter the CD-ROM volume or sound card master volume controls. Also do not dislodge any cables or connectors behind the PC.

NOTE Always dampen a clean towel with cleaner—NEVER spray cleaner directly onto any part of the computer.

STEP 4: CLEAN THE AIR INTAKE

While cleaning the case, pay particular attention to the air intake(s), which are usually located in the front (or front sides) of the housing. Check for accumulations of dust or debris around the intakes, or caught in an intake filter. Clean away any accumulations from the intake area, then use your static-safe vacuum to clean the intake filter if possible—you may need to remove the intake filter for better access. If the intake filter is washable, you may choose to rinse the filter in simple soap and water for best cleaning (remember to dry the filter thoroughly before replacing it). Of course, if there is no intake filter, simply clean around the intake area.

STEP 5: CLEAN THE SPEAKERS

Multimedia speakers offer a countless number of ridges and openings that are just perfect for accumulating dust and debris. Use your can of compressed air to gently blow out the speaker's openings. Do not insert the long, thin air nozzle into the speaker—you can easily puncture the speaker cone and ruin it. Instead, remove the long nozzle and spray air directly from the can. Afterward, use a clean cloth lightly dampened with ammonia solution to remove any dirt or stains from the speaker housings.

STEP 6: CLEAN THE KEYBOARD

Keyboards are open to the environment, so dust and debris readily settle between the keys. Over time, these accumulations can jam keys or cause repeated keystrokes. Attach the long, thin nozzle to your can of compressed air and use the air to blow through the horizontal gaps between key rows. Be careful—this will kick up a lot of dust—so keep the keyboard away from your face. Afterward, use a clean cloth lightly dampened with ammonia solution to remove dirt or stains from the keys and keyboard housing. If any keys seem unresponsive or "sticky," you can remove the corresponding keycap and spray a bit of good-quality electronic contact cleaner into the key assembly, then gently replace the keycap.

NOTE Do not remove the <Enter> key or <Space Bar>. These keys are held in place by metal brackets that are *extremely* difficult to reattach once the key is removed. Only the most experienced technicians should work with these keys.

STEP 7: CLEAN THE MONITOR

There are several important issues when cleaning a monitor: ventilation, case, and CRT. Monitors rely on vent openings for proper cooling. Use your vacuum cleaner to carefully remove any accumulations of dust and debris from the vents underneath the case, as well as those on top of the case. Make sure that none of the vent openings is blocked by paper or other objects (this can restrict ventilation and force the monitor to run hot).

Next, use a clean cloth lightly dampened with ammonia solution to clean the monitor's plastic case. There is active circuitry directly under the top vents, so under no circumstances should you spray cleaner directly onto the monitor housings. Do *not* use ammonia or any chemicals to clean the CRT face. The CRT is often treated with antiglare and other coatings, and even mild chemicals can react with some coatings. Instead, use clean tap water *only* to clean the CRT face. Be sure to dry the CRT face completely.

STEP 8: CLEAN THE MOUSE

Like the keyboard, a mouse is particularly susceptible to the dust and debris carried from the mouse pad up into the mouse ball and rollers. When enough foreign matter has accumulated, you'll find that the mouse cursor hesitates or refuses to move completely. Loosen the retaining ring and remove the mouse ball. Clean the mouse ball using a clean cloth and an ammonia solution. Dry the mouse ball thoroughly and set it aside with the retaining ring. Next, locate three rollers inside the mouse (an "X" roller, a "Y" roller, and a small "pressure" roller). Use a clean cloth dampened with ammonia solution to clean all of the rollers completely. Use your can of compressed air to blow out any remaining dust or debris that may still be inside the mouse. Finally, replace the mouse ball and secure it into place with its retaining ring.

External Check

Now that the system is clean, it's time to perform a few practical checks of the system interconnections and take care of some basic drive maintenance. Gather a small regular screwdriver (i.e., a "jeweler's" screwdriver) along with a commercial floppy drive cleaning kit; in addition, if your system uses a tape drive, arrange to have a tape drive cleaning kit on hand. If you cannot locate the appropriate cleaning kits, you can use isopropyl alcohol and long electronics-grade swabs. A handheld degaussing coil is recommended, but may not be necessary. For this part of the maintenance routine, you'll need to power up the PC.

These checks should be performed every four months (three times per year) or as required. If the PC is operating in dusty, industrial, or other adverse environments, you many need to check the system more frequently. Systems operating in clean office environments may need to be checked only once or twice each year.

STEP 9: CHECK CABLES

There are a myriad of external cables interconnecting the computer to its peripheral devices. You should examine each cable and verify that it is securely connected. If the cable can be secured to its connector with screws, make sure that the cable is secured properly. As a minimum, check for the following cables:

- AC power cable for the PC
- AC power cable for the monitor
- AC power cable for the printer
- AC/DC power pack for an external modem (if used)
- Keyboard cable
- Mouse cable
- Joystick cable (if used)
- Video cable to the monitor
- Speaker cable(s) from the sound board
- Microphone cable to the sound board (if used)
- Serial port cable to external modem (if used)
- Parallel port cable to printer
- RJ11 telephone line cable to internal or external modem (if used)

STEP 10: CLEAN THE FLOPPY DRIVE

In spite of their age, floppy disks remain a reliable and highly standardized media—every new PC sold today still carries a 3.5″ 1.44-MB floppy drive. However, floppy disks are "contact" media—the read/write heads of the floppy drive actually come into contact with the floppy disk. This contact transfers some of the magnetic oxides from the floppy disk to the drive's read/write heads. Eventually, enough oxides can accumulate on the read/write heads to cause reading or writing problems with the floppy drive. You should periodically clean the floppy drive to remove any excess oxides.

Cleaning can be accomplished in several ways—you can either use a prepackaged cleaning kit or swab the read/write heads with fresh isopropyl alcohol. You can obtain prepackaged cleaning kits from almost any store with a computer or consumer electronics department. With a cleaning kit, you simply dampen a mildly abrasive cleaning diskette with cleaning solution (typically alcohol-based), then run the cleaning diskette in the drive for 15–30 seconds. You can often get 10 to 20 cleanings from a cleaning diskette before discarding it.

If you don't have a cleaning kit handy, you can use a thin fabric swab dampened in fresh isopropyl alcohol and gently scrub between the read/write heads. Remember to turn off and unplug the PC before attempting a manual cleaning. Repeat the scrubbing with several fresh swabs, then use a dry swab to gently dry the heads. Allow several minutes for any residual alcohol to dry before turning the PC back on.

STEP 11: CLEAN THE TAPE DRIVE

As with floppy drives, tape drives are also "contact" media—the tape head is in constant contact with the moving tape. This causes oxides from the tape to transfer to the tape head and capstans, which can ultimately result in reading or writing errors from the tape drive. If a tape drive is present with your system, you should periodically clean the tape head(s) and capstans to remove any dust and excess oxides. You may be able to find a prepackaged drive cleaning kit for your particular tape drive; otherwise, you'll need to clean the tape drive manually.

Turn off and unplug the PC. Use a thin fabric swab dampened in fresh isopropyl alcohol to gently scrub the tape head(s) and capstan. Repeat the scrubbing with several fresh swabs, then use a dry swab to gently dry the tape head(s). Allow several minutes for any residual alcohol to dry before turning the computer back on.

NOTE This step is needed *only* if you have an internal or external tape drive with your system; if not, you can omit this step.

STEP 12: CHECK THE CD TRAY

Most CD-ROM drives operate using a "tray" to hold the CD. Try ejecting and closing the tray several times—make sure that the motion is smooth and that there is no hesitation or grinding, which might suggest a problem with the drive mechanism. While the tray is open, check for any accumulations of dust, pet hair, or other debris in the tray that might interfere with a CD. Clean the tray with a cloth lightly dampened in water *only*. Be sure the tray is completely dry before closing it again. Do not use ammonia or ammonia-based cleaners around the CD-ROM—prolonged exposure to ammonia vapors can damage a CD.

STEP 13: CHECK THE SOUND SYSTEM

Next, you should make sure that your sound system is set properly. Begin playing an ordinary audio CD in the CD-ROM drive. Check the sound board itself and locate the master volume control (not all sound boards have a physical volume knob). Make sure that the master volume is set at 75 percent or higher. If not, you may need to keep the speaker volume abnormally high, which can result in a hum or other noise in the speakers. If the sound board does not have a master volume control, check the board's "mixer" applet and see that the master volume is set properly. Once the sound board is set, you can adjust the speaker volume to achieve the best sound quality.

NOTE Speakers are magnetic devices that can interfere with the color purity of a monitor. Keep unshielded speakers at least 6 inches away from your monitor.

STEP 14: CHECK COLOR PURITY

Color monitors use a fine metal screen located just behind the CRT face in order to isolate the individual color pixels in the display. This ensures that stray electrons don't strike adjacent phosphors and cause incorrect colors. If part or all of this metal screen becomes magnetized, it will deflect the electron beams and cause color distortion. Normally, a color CRT is demagnetized (or degaussed) each time the monitor is turned on. This is accomplished through a degaussing coil located around the perimeter of the CRT face. However, if the CRT is subjected to external magnetic fields (such as unshielded speakers, motors, or other strong magnets), it may cause color problems across the entire CRT or in small localized areas.

Check the CRT for color purity by displaying an image of a known color (preferably white). Examine the image for discoloration or discolored areas. For example, if you display an image that you know is white, and it appears bluish (or there are bluish patches), chances are that you've got color purity problems.

There are three means of correcting color purity problems. First, try moving anything that might be magnetic (such as speakers) *away* from the monitor. Second, try degaussing the monitor by turning it off, waiting 30 seconds, then turning it on again. This allows the monitor's built-in degaussing coil to cycle. If the problem persists, wait 20–30 minutes and try cycling the monitor again. Finally, if the image is still discolored, you should take the monitor to a technician who can use a handheld degaussing coil.

Internal Check

At this point, we can move into the PC and perform some internal checks to verify that critical parts and cables are secure and that all cooling systems are working. Internal checks can usually be performed every six months (twice per year). Gather a small Phillips screwdriver and an anti-static wrist strap. Use your screwdriver to unbolt the outer cover. Remove the outer cover (be careful for sharp edges) and set it aside. Attach the wrist strap from your wrist to a good earth ground—this allows you to work safely inside the PC without the risk of accidental damage from electrostatic discharge (or ESD).

STEP 15: CHECK THE FANS

PCs tend to generate a substantial amount of heat during normal operation; this heat must be ventilated with fans. If one or more fans fail, excess heat can build up in the PC enclosure and result in system crashes or premature system failures. Now that the cover is off, your first check should be to see that all the fans are running. As a minimum, check the power supply fan, the case exhaust fan (both usually located at the rear of the enclosure), and the CPU heat sink/fan. Other PCs such as tower systems may sport even more fans. If any fans are not running, they should be replaced—or the system should be serviced by an experienced technician who can replace defective fans.

Pay particular attention to the CPU heat sink/fan. Virtually all Intel Pentium/Pentium MMX, AMD K5/K6, and Cyrix 6x86/M2 CPUs are fitted with a heat sink/fan. This fan *must* be running or the CPU runs a very real risk of overheating and failing. If you notice that the fan has stopped, you should have the heat sink/fan assembly replaced *as soon as possible*.

STEP 16: CLEAN FANS AND FILTERS

Turn off and unplug the PC, then examine the fans and exhaust filters for accumulations of dust or other debris. Use your static-safe vacuum to clean the fan blades. Clean away any accumulations from the exhaust area, then clean the exhaust filter if possible—you may need to remove the exhaust filter for better access. If the exhaust filter is washable, you may choose to rinse the filter in simple soap and water for best cleaning (remember to dry the filter thoroughly before replacing it). Of course, if there is no exhaust filter, simply clean around the exhaust area. Also vacuum away any other accumulations of dust that you may find on the motherboard or around the drives, but be very careful to avoid vacuuming up the little jumpers on the motherboard.

NOTE Remember that PC electronics are *extremely* sensitive to ESD, so make sure to use a static-safe vacuum inside the PC.

STEP 17: CHECK EXPANSION BOARDS

Most PCs use several expansion boards that are plugged into expansion slots on the motherboard—internal modems, video boards, SCSI adapters, and network cards are just a few types of expansion boards that you may encounter. Each expansion board must be inserted completely into its corresponding slot and the metal mounting bracket on the board should be secured to the chassis with a single screw. Make sure that every board is installed evenly and completely and see that the mounting bolts are snugged down.

STEP 18: CHECK INTERNAL CABLES

You'll notice that there are a large number of cables inside the PC. Each cable must be installed securely—especially the wide ribbon cable connectors that can easily be tugged off. Take a moment to check any wiring between the case and the motherboard such as the keyboard connector, power LED, on/off switch, drive activity LED, turbo switch, turbo LED, and so on. Next, check the following cables:

- Motherboard power connector(s)
- All four-pin drive power cables
- Floppy drive ribbon cable
- Hard drive ribbon cable
- CD-ROM ribbon cable (usually separate from the hard drive cable)
- CD four-wire audio cable (between the CD-ROM and sound board)
- SCSI ribbon cable (if used)
- SCSI terminating resistors (if used)

STEP 19: CHECK MEMORY

Memory is provided in the form of SIMMs (single inline memory modules), which simply clip into sockets on the motherboard. Loose SIMMs can cause serious startup problems for the PC. Examine each SIMM—verify that each is inserted properly into its socket and that both ends of each SIMM are clipped into place.

STEP 20: CHECK THE CPU

The CPU is the single largest IC on the motherboard and is installed into a ZIF (zero insertion force) socket for easy replacement or upgrade. Examine the CPU and see that it is inserted evenly into its socket. The ZIF socket lever should be in the "closed" position and locked down at the socket itself. Next check the CPU's heat sink/fan—it should sit flush against the top of the CPU. It should not slide around or be loose; if it is, the heat sink/fan should be secured or replaced.

STEP 21: CHECK THE DRIVE MOUNTING

The final step in your internal check should be to inspect the drive mountings. Each drive should be mounted in place with four screws—fewer screws may allow excessive vibration in the drive, which can lead to premature failure. Make sure that each drive has four mounting bolts and use your Phillips screwdriver to snug down each bolt.

NOTE Do not overtighten the bolts. This can actually warp the drive frame and cause errors or drive failure.

Drive Check

After the PC has been cleaned and checked inside and out, it's time to check the hard drive for potential problems. This involves checking the drive's file system, reorganizing files, and creating an updated boot disk. To perform a drive check, you'll need a copy of *ScanDisk* and *Defrag*. Since these utilities are already built into Windows 95, you can reboot the system and use those utilities directly. If you are more comfortable with running these utilities from DOS, create a "Startup Disk" and boot from that, then run *ScanDisk* and *Defrag* right from the startup disk. As a rule, you should perform the drive check very regularly—once a month is usually recommended, or whenever you make major additions or deletions from your system.

STEP 22: UPDATE THE BOOT DISK

Your PC should always have a boot disk that can start the system from a floppy drive in the event of an emergency. Windows 95 has the ability to create a "Startup Disk" automatically. If you have access to a Windows 95 system, use the following procedure to create a DOS 7.x startup disk:

◁ Label a blank diskette and insert it into your floppy drive.

◁ Click on *Start, Settings,* and *Control Panel.*

◁ Double-click on the *Add/Remove Programs* icon.

◁ Select the *Startup Disk* tab.

◁ Click on *Create Disk.*

◀ The utility will remind you to insert a diskette, then prepare the disk automatically. When the preparation is complete, test the diskette.

The preparation process takes several minutes and will copy the following files to your diskette: ATTRIB, CHKDSK, COMMAND, DEBUG, DRVSPACE.BIN, EDIT, FDISK, FORMAT, REGEDIT, SCANDISK, SYS, and UNINSTAL. All of these files are DOS 7.x-based files, so you can run them from the A: prompt.

STEP 23: RUN SCANDISK

The *ScanDisk* utility is designed not only to check your drive for file problems (such as lost or cross-linked clusters) but also to correct those problems. If you're running from the Startup Disk, start *ScanDisk* by typing:

```
A:\> scandisk      <Enter>
```

If you're running from Windows 95, click *Start, Programs, Accessories, System Tools,* and *ScanDisk.* Select the drive to be tested and start the test cycle. *ScanDisk* will report any problems and give you the option of repairing the problems.

STEP 24: RUN DEFRAG

Operating systems such as DOS and Windows 95 segregate drive space into groups of sectors called *clusters.* Clusters are used on an "as found" basis, so it is possible for the clusters that compose a file to be scattered across a drive. This forces the drive to work harder (and take longer) to read or write the complete file because a lot of time is wasted moving around the drive. The *Defrag* utility allows file clusters to be relocated together. If you're running from the Startup Disk, start *Defrag* by typing:

```
A:\> defrag       <Enter>
```

If you're running from Windows 95, click *Start, Programs, Accessories, System Tools,* and *Disk Defragmenter.* Select the drive to be tested and start the cycle. *Defrag* will relocate all the files on the disk so that all their clusters are together.

NOTE You can run *Defrag* any time, but you do not *need* to run *Defrag* until your disk is more than 10 percent fragmented.

Wrap Up

That concludes the maintenance procedure for your PC. Now you can replace the outer cover and bolt it back into place (be careful for sharp edges). After the enclosure is secure, reboot the system and perform a final test of some of the major applications—the system should perform exactly the same as it did before. By performing this routine maintenance, you can keep your PC running longer and save on expensive downtime or trips to the shop.

Glossary and Acronyms

Glossary

AGP (Accelerated Graphics Port)   A new 32-bit expansion bus designed for high-performance graphics oriented toward 3D visualization.

API (Application Programming Interface)   A programming module that provides a suite of standardized functions used by various different applications.

BIOS (Basic Input/Output System)   The low-level "programs" that are used to operate the PC's hardware (i.e., the motherboard and drives).

conflicts   Contention for system resources caused by either hardware or software.

configuration   The setup of a system's operating parameters, or the outfitting of a particular system.

direct memory access (DMA)   A means of transferring data directly between a drive and memory without the direct intervention of the CPU (see PIO).

Device Manager (DM)   The Windows 95/98 feature that allows users to examine, adjust, or remove devices in the system. The DM is accessed through the *System* icon in the *Control Panel.*

driver   A small program used to enable an operating system to access a certain piece of hardware. Typical examples include CD-ROM drivers or video drivers (also called a *device driver*).

ECU (EISA Configuration Utility)   The utility that must be run when setting up or configuring an EISA system (i.e., when an expansion board is inserted or removed).

EISA (Enhanced ISA)   The direct descendent of the ISA bus, which provides more data lines and control signals than ISA but is fully backward-compatible with ISA devices.

expansion devices   Devices that can be added to a PC as an upgrade or replacement part. Typical devices are video cards, modems, drive controllers, and so on.

GPF (General Protection Fault)   A Windows error that occurs when more than one program attempts to use the same memory area.

hardware resource conflict   The condition that occurs when devices attempt to use the same interrupts, DMA channels, I/O ports, or memory range.

hexadecimal   The base-16 number system commonly used to represent PC addresses and data.

ICU (ISA Configuration Utility)   The utility often used with DOS or pre-PnP systems to (1) assign resources to PnP devices and (2) reserve resources for legacy devices.

interrupt (IRQ)   A logical signal line that is asserted by an expansion device in order to demand the attention of the CPU (usually in response to some "real-world" event).

I/O (Input/Output)   A very low logical address in the PC where data can be read or written.

ISA (Industry Standard Architecture)   The classical 16-bit expansion bus first introduced with the IBM AT and now used mainly for low-bandwidth devices such as modems or sound cards.

jumpers   Physical connections on the motherboard or expansion devices that are used to select various features or functions (such as IRQ assignments).

legacy   A non-PnP device or a device that must be manually configured through the use of jumpers.

MCA (MicroChannel Architecture)   A 32-bit expansion bus architecture introduced with the IBM PS/2 line of computers, now considered obsolete.

PCI (Peripheral Component Interconnect)   A high-performance 32-bit expansion bus now considered standard on all current PCs.

PIO (Programmed I/O)   A means of transferring data between a drive and memory that uses the CPU to move data (see **DMA**).

Plug-and-Play (PnP) Devices that can be recognized and configured automatically by the BIOS and/or operating system, so jumpers are not necessary.

POST (Power On Self Test) The internal device testing performed by the system BIOS during the moments following system startup.

properties The characteristics, assignments, and drivers related to a particular device (accessed through the Windows *Device Manager*).

resources The interrupts, DMA channels, I/O ports, and memory space used to configure various expansion devices in the system.

resource conflict See hardware resource conflict.

SCSI (Small Computer System Interface) A versatile, high-performance PC interface used to connect a wide variety of internal and external devices to the PC.

software conflicts The contention between two or more pieces of software (usually between drivers or TSRs and the operating system or particular applications).

upgrade The process of improving a PC by adding new devices or replacing existing devices with similar newer ones.

USB (Universal Serial Bus) The new medium-speed external serial bus, which can easily connect many different types of devices to the PC.

Acronyms

AC	Alternating Current
AGP	Accelerated Graphics Port
AI	Artificial Intelligence
ALU	Arithmetic-Logic Unit (related to CPUs)
AM	Amplitude Modulation (related to modems)
AMD	Advanced Micro Devices, Inc.
AMI	American Megatrends Inc.
ANSI	American National Standards Institute
ASCII	American Standard Code for Information Interchange
ASIC	Application Specific Integrated Circuit
ASPI	Advanced SCSI Programming Interface
AT	Advanced Technology

ATA	AT bus Attachment
ATDM	Asynchronous Time Division Multiplexing (related to PC communication)
ATM	Asynchronous Transfer Mode (related to PC communication)
BBS	Bulletin Board System
BCC	Block Check Character
BCD	Binary Coded Decimal
BDA	BIOS Data Area
BE	Back End
BiCMOS	Bipolar Complementary Metal-Oxide Semiconductor
BIOS	Basic Input/Output System
BNC	Bayonet Nut Connector
BPS/bps	Bytes/bits Per Second
BSC	Binary Synchronous Communications (or Bi-Sync)
CAD	Computer Aided Design
CAM	Computer Aided Manufacturing; or Common Access Method (Committee)
CAS	Column Address Strobe (related to dynamic memory)
CCD	Charge Coupled Device (related to cameras and video capture)
CCITT	Consultative Committee of International Telephony and Telegraphy
CD	Carrier Detect
CDDI	Copper Distributed Data Interface
CD-ROM	Compact Disk Read-Only Memory
CGA	Color Graphics Adapter
CHS	Cylinder Head Sector
CISC	Complex Instruction-Set Computer
CMOS	Complementary Metal-Oxide Semiconductor
COM	Communication [Port]
CP/M	Control Program/Monitor
CPI	Clocks Per Instruction
CPU	Central Processing Unit
CQFP	Ceramic Quad-Flat Pack (related to IC packaging)
CR	Carriage Return (related to printers)

CRC	Cyclical Redundancy Check
CRQ	Command Response Queue
CRT	Cathode Ray Tube
CS	Chip Select
CSMA	Carrier Sense Multiple-Access (related to PC communication)
CSMA/CD	Carrier Sense Multiple-Access with Collision Detect
CSR	Command Status Register
CTS	Clear To Send
DAT	Digital Audio Tape
DC	Direct Current
DCD	Data Carrier Detect
DCE	Data Circuit-terminating Equipment (related to PC communication)
DD	Double Density
DEC	Digital Equipment Corporation
DES	Data Encryption Standard
DID	Direct Inward Dial
DIMM	Dual Inline Memory Module
DIN	Deutsche Industrie Norm
DIP	Dual-In-line Package (related to IC packaging)
DIS	Draft International Standard
DMA	Direct Memory Access
DOS	Disk Operating System
DPE	Data Parity Error
DPSK	Differential Phase Shift Keying (related to PC communication)
DRAM	Dynamic Random Access Memory
DS	Double Sided
DSP	Digital Signal Processor
DSR	Data Set Ready
DTC	Data Terminal Controller
DTE	Data Terminating Equipment (related to PC communication)
DTMF	Dual-Tone Multi-Frequency
DTR	Data Terminal Ready

EBCDIC	Extended Binary Coded Decimal Interchange Code
ECC	Error Correction Code
ECL	Emitter-Coupled Logic
ECO	Engineering Change Order
ECU	EISA Configuration Utility
EEPROM	Electrically Erasable Programmable Read-Only Memory
EGA	Enhanced Graphics Adapter
EIA	Electronic Industries Association
EISA	Enhanced Industry Standard Architecture
EMI	Electro-Magnetic Interference
EMS	Expanded Memory Specification
EOF	End Of File
EOL	End Of Line
EOS	Electrical Over-Stress
EPROM	Erasable Programmable Read-Only Memory
ESD	Electro-Static Discharge
ESDI	Enhanced Small Devices Interface
FAT	File Allocation Table
FCC	Federal Communications Commission
FDD	Fixed Disk Drive; or Floppy Disk Drive
FDDI	Fiber Distributed Data Interface
FDM	Frequency Division Multiplexing
FDX	Full-Duplex Transmission
FE	Front End
FEP	Front End Processor
FF	Form Feed (related to printers)
FIFO	First In–First Out
FILO	First In–Last Out (same as LIFO, Last In–First Out)
FM	Frequency Modulation (related to modems)
FPGA	Field Programmable Gate Array (related to IC packaging)
FPU	Floating Point Unit (related to microprocessors)
FRU	Field-Replaceable Unit
FSF	Free Software Foundation
FSK	Frequency Shift Keying (related to modems)
FTP	File Transfer Program

GAS	Gallium Arsenide
GFLOPS	Billions (10^9) of Floating Point Operations Per Second (or "GigaFlops")
GNU	Gnu's Not Unix
GUI	Graphical User Interface
HD	High Density
HDD	Hard Disk Drive
HDX	Half-Duplex Transmission
HFS	Hierarchical File System
HPFS	High Performance File System
HS	Helical Scan
IBM	International Business Machines Corp.
IC	Integrated Circuit
ICU	ISA Configuration Utility
IDC	Insulation Displacement Connector
IDE	Integrated Device Electronics; or Integrated Drive Electronics
IEEE	Institute of Electrical and Electronic Engineers
IMP	Interface Message Processor
I/O	Input/Output
IPC	Inter-Process Communication
IRQ	Interrupt Request
ISA	Industry Standard Architecture
ISDN	Integrated Services Digital Network
ISO	International Standards Organization
JFS	Journaled File System
kVA	KiloVolt-Amps
LAN	Local Area Network
LAPM	Link Access Procedure M
LBA	Logical Block Addressing
LCD	Liquid Crystal Display

LED	Light Emitting Diode
LF	Line Feed (related to printers)
LIM	Lotus/Intel/Microsoft Expanded Memory Manager Specification
LPT	Line Printer Terminal (or simply "Printer Port")
LRU	Least-Recently Used
LSB/lsb	Least Significant Byte/bit
LSI	Large Scale Integration
LUN	Logical Unit Number (related to SCSI)
MAN	Metropolitan Area Network
MB/Mb	Mega Bytes/bits
MBR	Master Boot Record
MCA	Micro Channel Architecture
MCGA	Multi-Color Graphics Array
MCM	Multi-Chip Module (related to IC packaging)
MFLOPS	Millions (10^6) of Floating Point Operations Per Second (or "MegaFlops")
MFM	Modified Frequency Modulated
MHz	Megahertz
MICR	Magnetic Ink Character Recognition
MIDI	Musical Instrument Digital Interface
MIMD	Multiple-Instruction Multiple-Data
MIPS	Millions of Instructions Per Second
MISD	Multiple-Instruction Single Data
MMU	Memory Management Unit
MMX	Multimedia Extension (related to advanced microprocessors)
MNP	Microcom Network Protocol (related to PC communication)
MODEM	Modulator/Demodulator
MOPS	Millions of Operations Per Second
MOS	Metal-Oxide Semiconductor
MP	Multi-Processor
MPP	Massively Parallel Processor
MSB/msb	Most Significant Byte/bit

MS-DOS	Microsoft Disk Operating System
MSI	Medium Scale Integration
MTBF	Mean Time Between Failure
NBS	National Bureau of Standards
N/C	No Connection; or No Contact
NEMA	National Electrical Manufacturers Association
NFS	Network File System
NFU	Not-Frequently Used
NMI	Non-Maskable Interrupt
NMOS	Negatively doped Metal-Oxide Semiconductor
NOP	No Operation
NRU	Not-Recently Used
NSF	National Science Foundation
NVRAM	Non-Volatile Random Access Memory
OCR	Optical Character Recognition (related to scanners)
ODI	Open Datalink Interface
OEM	Original Equipment Manufacturer
OS	Operating System
OSF	Open Software Foundation
OSI	Open Systems Interconnect
PAL/PLA	Programmable Array Logic (Logic Array)
PB	Push Button
PC	Personal Computer; or Program Counter
PCB	Printed Circuit Board
PCI	Peripheral Component Interconnect
PCM	Pulse Code Modulation
PCMCIA	Personal Computer Memory Card International Association
PE	Processor Element
PFF	Page Fault Frequency
PGA	Pin Grid Array (related to IC packaging)
PIC	Programmable Interrupt Controller
PIO	Programmed Input/Output

PLCC	Plastic Leaded Chip Carrier (related to IC packaging)
PLL	Phase Locked Loop
PM	Preventive Maintenance
PMOS	Positively doped Metal-Oxide Semiconductor
PnP	Plug-and-Play
POST	Power On Self Test
PPP	Point-to-Point Protocol
PQFP	Plastic Quad-Flat Pack (related to IC packaging)
PROM	Programmable Read-Only Memory
PSTN	Public Switched Telephone Network
PTE	Page Table Entry
QAM	Quadrature Amplitude Modulation (related to modems)
QFP	Quad-Flat Pack (related to IC packaging)
QIC	Quarter Inch Cartridge [Committee]
RAID	Redundant Arrays of Inexpensive Disks
RAM	Random Access Memory
RAMDAC	Random Access Memory Digital-to-Analog Converter
RAS	Row Address Strobe (related to dynamic memory)
RCA	Radio Corporation of America
RCC	Routing Control Center
RFC	Request For Comments
RFI	Radio Frequency Interference
RI	Ring Indicator
RISC	Reduced Instruction-Set Computer
RLL	Run Length Limited
RMM	Read Mostly Memory (same as EPROM)
RMS	Root Mean Squared
RMW	Read Modify Write
ROM	Read-Only Memory
RPC	Remote Procedure Call
RPM	Rotations Per Minute
RTC	Real-Time Clock
RTS	Request To Send

SAM	Sequential Access Memory
SASI	Shugart Associates Standard Interface
SCSI	Small Computer Systems Interface
SD	Single Density
SDLC	Synchronous Data Link Control
SIMD	Single-Instruction Multiple-Data
SIMM	Single Inline Memory Module
SIPP	Single Inline Pinned Package (related to IC packaging)
SISD	Single-Instruction Single-Data
SLIP	Serial Line Internet Protocol
SMD	Surface Mount Device
SMT	Surface Mount Technology
SNA	System Network Architecture
SNR	Signal-to-Noise Ratio
SO/SOL	Small Outline
SOIC	Small Outline Integrated Circuit
SPOOL	Simultaneous Peripheral Operation On Line
SPT	Sectors Per Track
SPU	Single Processor Unit
SQE	Signal Quality Error
SRAM	Static Random Access Memory
SS	Single Sided
STDM	Synchronous Time Division Multiplexing
STN	Super Twisted Nematic
STU	Streaming Tape Unit
SVGA	Super Video Graphics Array
TCM	Trellis Code Modulation (related to modems)
TCP/IP	Transmission Control Protocol/Internet Protocol
TDM	Time Division Multiplexing
TI	Texas Instruments
TIA	Telecommunications Industry Association
TPI	Tracks Per Inch
TSR	Terminate and Stay Resident
TTL	Transistor-Transistor Logic
TUV	Technischer Ueberwachungs-Verein

UART	Universal Asynchronous Receiver/Transmitter
UDP	User Datagram Protocol
UMA	Upper Memory Area
UMB	Upper Memory Block
UPS	Uninterruptible Power Supply
USB	Universal Serial Bus
USL	Unix System Labs
UTP	Unshielded Twisted Pair
UUCP	Unix-to-Unix Copy Program
VCR	Video Cassette Recorder
VESA	Video Enhanced Standards Association
VGA	Video Graphics Array
VLB	VESA Local Bus
VLIW	Very Long Instruction Word
VLSI	Very Large Scale Integration
VM	Virtual Memory
VME	Versa Module Eurocard
VRAM	Video Random Access Memory
VTR	Video Tape Recorder
WAN	Wide Area Network
WATS	Wide Area Telephone Service
WD	Western Digital
WORM	Write-Once Read-Many
WS	Wait State
XGA	Extended Graphics Array
XMS	Extended Memory Specification
XOR	Exclusive-Or
XT	Extended Technology
ZIF	Zero Insertion Force

Index

About the Author

Stephen J. Bigelow is the founder and president of Dynamic Learning Systems, a technical writing, research, and publishing company specializing in electronic and PC service topics. A standout figure in the crowded field of computer guidance, he is the author of more than a dozen books for TAB/McGraw-Hill, including the hugely successful *Troubleshooting, Maintaining, and Repairing PCs*, Second Edition, and the *Pocket Reference* Series.

Basic PC Maintenance

Do you want to get the most from your PC and keep it running longer?

If you want to protect your expensive PC investment, than **THIS** is the video you've been waiting for! Whether you're an experienced technician, or just setting up your first PC, this video gives you the step-by-step techniques you need to perform practical routine maintenance on any type of personal computer.

Using only a few inexpensive materials, this video clearly explains how to clean your system and peripherals, check the PC inside and out, clean your drives, and even optimize your hard drive(s) for peak performance. The video is broken down into five easy-to-follow segments:

- Introduction
- External Cleaning
- Keyboard and Mouse Cleaning
- External Checks
- Internal Checks
- Drive Maintenance

Minimum requirements to run MPEG video: *Pentium CPU, Windows 95, 16MB system RAM, 4X CD-ROM or faster, sound board and multimedia speakers, and any standard MPEG player (i.e. XING, ActiveMovie, or MediaPlayer).*

Running Time: 41 minutes (both VHS and MPEG CD versions)

Reseller and Educator inquiries welcome

Order the "Basic PC Maintenance" video TODAY at a SPECIAL DISCOUNT PRICE and FREE SHIPPING!

Please print clearly

Name: _____

Company: _____

Address:_____

City, ST, Zip: _____

Phone: _____

Fax: _____

E-mail: _____

Quantity:	_____ @ $24.95	$_____
Sales Tax:	MA residents add 5%	$_____
Shipping:	FREE WITH THIS ORDER FORM	$ FREE
	TOTAL	$_____

Choose Video Format: ____ MPEG CD ____ VHS

Card #: _____

Exp Date: ____/____ Sig: _____

Mail to: *Dynamic Learning Systems, PO Box 282, Jefferson, MA 01522-0282 USA*
Fax the order to: **508-829-6819**
Phone the order to: **508-829-6744**

The PC Toolbox™

Use this form when ordering *The PC Toolbox*™. You may tear out or photocopy this order form.

YES! I'm tired of fixing computers in the dark! Please accept my order as shown below: (check any one)

_____ Please start my *one year subscription* (6 issues) for $39 (USD)

_____ Please start my *two year subscription* (12 issues) for $69 (USD)

PRINT YOUR MAILING INFORMATION HERE:

Name: Company:

Address:

City, State, Zip:

Country:

Telephone: (   )   Fax: (   )

PLACING YOUR ORDER:

By FAX: Fax this completed order form (24 hrs/day, 7 days/week) to 508-829-6819

By Phone: Phone in your order (Mon-Fri; 9am-4pm EST) to 508-829-6744

By Web: Complete the online subscription form at http://www.dlspubs.com/

___ MasterCard   Card: __ __ __ __ __ __ __ __ __ __ __ __ __ __ __ __

___ VISA   Exp: ___/___   Sig: _____

Or by Mail: Mail this completed form, along with your check, money order, PO, or credit card info to:

Dynamic Learning Systems, P.O. Box 282, Jefferson, MA 01522-0282 USA

Make check payable to Dynamic Learning Systems. Please allow 2-4 weeks for order procescing. Returned checks are subject to a $15 charge. There is a 90 day unconditional money-back guarantee on your subscription.

SOFTWARE AND INFORMATION LICENSE

The software and information on this diskette (collectively referred to as the "Product") are the property of The McGraw-Hill Companies, Inc. ("McGraw-Hill") and are protected by both United States copyright law and international copyright treaty provision. You must treat this Product just like a book, except that you may copy it into a computer to be used and you may make archival copies of the Products for the sole purpose of backing up our software and protecting your investment from loss.

By saying "just like a book," McGraw-Hill means, for example, that the Product may be used by any number of people and may be freely moved from one computer location to another, so long as there is no possibility of the Product (or any part of the Product) being used at one location or on one computer while it is being used at another. Just as a book cannot be read by two different people in two different places at the same time, neither can the Product be used by two different people in two different places at the same time (unless, of course, McGraw-Hill's rights are being violated).

McGraw-Hill reserves the right to alter or modify the contents of the Product at any time.

This agreement is effective until terminated. The Agreement will terminate automatically without notice if you fail to comply with any provisions of this Agreement. In the event of termination by reason of your breach, you will destroy or erase all copies of the Product installed on any computer system or made for backup purposes and shall expunge the Product from your data storage facilities.

LIMITED WARRANTY

McGraw-Hill warrants the physical diskette(s) enclosed herein to be free of defects in materials and workmanship for a period of sixty days from the purchase date. If McGraw-Hill receives written notification within the warranty period of defects in materials or workmanship, and such notification is determined by McGraw-Hill to be correct, McGraw-Hill will replace the defective diskette(s). Send request to:

Customer Service
McGraw-Hill
Gahanna Industrial Park
860 Taylor Station Road
Blacklick, OH 43004-9615

The entire and exclusive liability and remedy for breach of this Limited Warranty shall be limited to replacement of defective diskette(s) and shall not include or extend to any claim for or right to cover any other damages, including but not limited to, loss of profit, data, or use of the software, or special, incidental, or consequential damages or other similar claims, even if McGraw-Hill has been specifically advised as to the possibility of such damages. In no event will McGraw-Hill's liability for any damages to you or any other person ever exceed the lower of suggested list price or actual price paid for the license to use the Product, regardless of any form of the claim.

THE McGRAW-HILL COMPANIES, INC. SPECIFICALLY DISCLAIMS ALL OTHER WARRANTIES, EXPRESSED OR IMPLIED, INCLUDING BUT NOT LIMITED TO, ANY IMPLIED WARRANTY OF MERCHANTABILITY OR FITNESS FOR A PARTICULAR PURPOSE. Specifically, McGraw-Hill makes no representation or warranty that the Product is fit for any particular purpose and any implied warranty of merchantability is limited to the sixty day duration of the Limited Warranty covering the physical diskette(s) only (and not the software or information) and is otherwise expressly and specifically disclaimed.

This Limited Warranty gives you specific legal rights; you may have others which may vary from state to state. Some states do not allow the exclusion of incidental or consequential damages, or the limitation on how long an implied warranty lasts, so some of the above may not apply to you.

This Agreement constitutes the entire agreement between the parties relating to use of the Product. The terms of any purchase order shall have no effect on the terms of this Agreement. Failure of McGraw-Hill to insist at any time on strict compliance with this Agreement shall not constitute a waiver of any rights under this Agreement. This Agreement shall be construed and governed in accordance with the laws of New York. If any provision of this Agreement is held to be contrary to law, that provision will be enforced to the maximum extent permissible and the remaining provisions will remain in force and effect.